LIFE AT *Saint Mary's*

Tempe Neal, a young student, sent her mother a copy of this lithograph when first issued, explaining that "There are most too many gentlemen about."

LIFE
AT *Saint Mary's*

———◆———

By

KATHERINE BATTS SALLEY, Editor
KATHARINE DRANE PERRY, EMILIE SMEDES HOLMES,
ALICE DUGGER GRIMES, NELL BATTLE LEWIS,
JANE TOY COOLIDGE, ANNA BROOKE ALLAN
ELIZABETH WARREN THOMPSON, Art Editor

Chapel Hill

The University of North Carolina Press

1 9 4 2

COPYRIGHT, 1942, BY
THE UNIVERSITY OF NORTH CAROLINA PRESS

TYPOGRAPHY, PRINTING, AND BINDING IN THE U. S. A. BY
KINGSPORT PRESS, INC., KINGSPORT, TENNESSEE

To
Ernest Cruikshank

FOREWORD

MANY delightful and beautiful sketches, essays, and memoirs have been written concerning Saint Mary's—her founders, her students, her teachers. Now on the Eve of her Centennial we believe there could be no better time to put into a more permanent form this comprehensive picture of the first Hundred Years. And so we have written a commentary, sometimes unwittingly, on the life and customs of not only Saint Mary's, but also North Carolina and the South, during this period.

There are omissions, there may be mistakes. But every contributor has labored diligently to portray each picture accurately. Many have been the helpers, important have been those who from time to time have unobtrusively furnished the needed inspiration. To all we are humbly grateful. But especially do we wish to thank the Alumnae Secretaries, Elizabeth Tucker and Sarah Vann, and the President of Saint Mary's, Margaret Jones Cruikshank.

Countless have been those who have aided in the building of Saint Mary's and influenced the lives of her girls. Of those of noble character, fine intellect, or great personal charm—who can say which have given most? Each generation has had its favorites. And because the Class of Nineteen Hundred and Twenty originated the idea of this book, that Class is dedicating it.

But Saint Mary's lives on. There must needs be other leaders, further growth—love, and prayers, and deeds.

KATHERINE BATTS SALLEY

Tarboro, N. C.
August 10, 1941

CONTENTS

CHAPTER	PAGE
Foreword	vii
1. In the Beginning, 1842–1860 By KATHARINE DRANE PERRY	3
2. War Times and After, 1860–1885 By EMILIE SMEDES HOLMES	31
3. Long Dresses—Long Tresses, 1885–1900 By ALICE DUGGER GRIMES	68
4. From "Floradora" to "Tipperary," 1900–1915 By NELL BATTLE LEWIS	100
5. New Lamps for Old, 1915–1930 By JANE TOY COOLIDGE	143
6. "Onward and Upward," 1930–1942 By ANNA BROOKE ALLAN	208
Ernest Cruikshank, A Biographical Sketch By KATHERINE BATTS SALLEY	259
Index	275

LIST OF ILLUSTRATIONS

STAGECOACH ARRIVAL AT SAINT MARY'S SCHOOL	*Frontis*
	facing page
THE REV. ALDERT SMEDES, FOUNDER OF SAINT MARY'S	50
RULES FROM THE BULLETIN OF 1860	51
SAINT MARY'S CHAPEL, BUILT IN 1855	66
YOUNG LADIES OF 1869	66
BISHOP IVES ADMINISTERING THE RITE OF CONFIRMATION	67
ALDERT SMEDES CIRCULAR, 1864	114
ALDERT SMEDES CIRCULAR, 1865	115
THE REV. BENNETT SMEDES	130
BENNETT SMEDES AND FACULTY	131
EMILY WATTS MCVEA	178
JULIET BRISCOE SUTTON	178
"MISS KATIE" MCKIMMON	178
LIZZIE H. LEE	178
THE REV. MCNEELY DUBOSE	179
THE REV. THEODORE DUBOSE BRATTON	179
THE REV. GEORGE WILLIAM LAY, WITH BEARD	194
THE REV. GEORGE WILLIAM LAY, WITHOUT BEARD	194
THE REV. WARREN WADE WAY	195

ERNEST CRUIKSHANK	242
MARGARET JONES CRUIKSHANK	243
THE REV. HENRY FELIX KLOMAN	258
SMEDES HALL	259

LIFE AT *Saint Mary's*

In the Beginning
1842–1860

By Katharine Drane Perry

IN THE fall of 1841 Dr. Aldert Smedes met Bishop Ives, Bishop of the Diocese of North Carolina, in the city of New York, when the following colloquy took place:

"Bishop, what sort of place would Raleigh be for a school for girls?"

"The best in the United States."

"Have you any buildings there?"

"The best in the United States."

"Why don't you open a school there?"

"I am now looking out for a man."

"Bishop, I am your man."

"The very man I want."

As a result of this conversation, early in the year 1842 Dr. Smedes issued a circular announcement of the approaching opening of what was to be Saint Mary's, though without mentioning a name for the school. The same announcement appeared in the papers of that time, and the circular is reprinted below.

"The Rev. Aldert Smedes, of the City of New York, designs to open a School for Young Ladies in the City of Raleigh, N. C., on the 12th day of May next.

"This Institution is to furnish a thorough and elegant Education, equal to the best that can be obtained in the City of New York, or in any Northern School.

"The School Buildings, situated in a beautiful and elevated Oak grove, furnish the most spacious accommodations. The Dormitories are separated into Alcoves, for two Young Ladies each, of a construction to secure privacy and at the same time a free circulation of air.

"Every article of furniture is provided by the School, except bedding (beds will be furnished) and towels.

"TERMS.—For Board (including washing and every incidental expense), with Tuition in English, Latin, &c, $100 per Session, payable in advance.

"The Extra charges will be for French, Music, Drawing, Painting, and Ornamental Needle-work, at the usual prices of the Masters. There will be no other extra charge.

"Pupils will be admitted at any age desired.

"No pupil, except by a written request of the Parent or Guardian to the Rector of the School, will be allowed to have an account at any Store or Shop in the City. A disregard of this prohibition will be followed by an immediate dismission from the school.

"Day-Scholars will be received from such Parents or Guardians as reside in the place.

"The year will be divided into two terms of five months each. The former commencing, after the first term, on the 15th day of May, and terminating on the 15th of October. The latter commencing on the 20th of November and terminating on the 20th of April."

Accordingly, on May 12th, the Monday of Whitsun Week, in the year 1842, Dr. Aldert Smedes without formality and in a very simple way threw open Saint Mary's for the first day of school. There was no Chapel building at the time, and so the opening service was held in the parlor.

IN THE BEGINNING

There the teachers had gathered: Miss Maria Thompson, Miss Long, Madame Clement, and the music teachers, Mr. and Mrs. Brandt. And here the first little band of girls gathered, more than thirteen when the day-scholars were counted, but always handed down to other generations of Saint Mary's girls as the "original thirteen." Annie Haywood, one of the original thirteen, in an article entitled "The First Day of School," written for the *Saint Mary's Muse*, April 1906, says that among the number of girls for the opening of school there were Cora Manly, Margaret Dudley, Kate Badger, Eleanor Williams, Adriana Tucker, Mary Guion, Sarah Saunders, Madeline Saunders, Elizabeth G. Haywood, Jane F. Haywood, Annie Haywood, Sallie Badger, Olivia Daniel, Mary Long Daniel, Lucy Williams, Laura Washington, Harriet Borden, Lizzie Davis, Martha Hinton, and Kate Hanrahan. Mary Anne Kinsey was also among them, perhaps as a day scholar.

As far back as 1832 Bishop Ives was convinced that "our Diocese can never flourish without the means of raising up a Ministry within ourselves." It was decided to have a boys' school, to be called "The Episcopal School." A Committee on the Episcopal School was formed, and a charter was granted by the Legislature of 1833–34 to the Trustees of the Episcopal School. The School Committee, in the 1834 report to the Convention of the Diocese of North Carolina, showed that the Executive Committee purchased a tract of land adjoining the City of Raleigh from Col. William Polk. This tract contained 159½ acres, "is chiefly in woods and is finely situated, about one mile west of the Capitol. Through the liberality of the late proprietor, and the interest which he felt in the success of the school, it was obtained at the comparatively low price of little more than ten dollars an acre." The purchase price, bearing interest from the 3rd of December, 1833, was $1,619.37.

From the 1835 report of the Committee to the Diocesan

Convention, we find that the Executive Committee had erected a "stone building, 56 x 36 feet, two stories high, covered with tin." The stone used in this building, East Rock, and in its companion building, West Rock, was stone which had been quarried for use in building the Capitol of North Carolina. Much of the rock which was necessarily raised from the pit was under the size used in that building, and the citizens who were engaged in building hauled it away and used it. Later on, in 1839, the Commissioners of Public Buildings for the State of North Carolina presented a bill against the Episcopal School for $200.00 for this stone, and the School requested the General Assembly to surrender to the School this demand of the State for "Stone that was useless to North Carolina, and therefore taken and applied to the erection of school houses." In this report to the Diocesan Convention we find that East Rock cost a total of $4,000.00 to build.

The Episcopal School opened for the reception of pupils the 2nd of June, 1834, and soon afterwards it was found that more room would be required, so the Committee on the Episcopal School authorized the Executive Committee to contract for another building of the same dimensions and materials as the one already erected. This was on the 17th of June, 1834, and the building, West Rock, was finished by the 14th of January, 1835. On the 11th of February, 1835, a "Committee on Buildings" was constituted, with power to commence immediately the "Main" Building. "This is a building intended to occupy a central position between the two stone buildings already erected. . . . The Main Building will be 85 feet in length, and 60 feet in width, and consist of four stories, including the basement story. The materials of the walls to be from the foundation to the water table, stone; from the water table to the top of the walls, brick; to be covered with tin; to be divided from bottom to top by two partitions, likewise of stone and brick, including between them a passage through the middle of the building running north and south, of 14 feet width in the clear."

This building was commenced in March 1835 and in the report of the School Committee to the Diocesan Convention of 1835 it was stated that "it is intended and expected (if the means shall be supplied) to complete it by the 1st of January, 1837."

Of the Episcopal School, the Hon. Richard H. Battle, LL.D., said in an address delivered on All Saints, 1902, in the Chapel at Saint Mary's: "It broke down by its own weight, after four years of stormy existence, and its exercises were suspended by resolution of the trustees, in July 1838. . . . A large debt had been incurred for building, equipment, etc., and for its amount Hon. Duncan Cameron bought the property and paid the debt. (Duncan Cameron paid E. B. Freeman, agent of the Episcopal School, $8,886.-66.) . . . Providence seems to have raised up and trained a man, who proved himself able to do, for the cause of the Church and religion in this and other Southern states, through their daughters, what the Bishop and whole Diocese had so signally failed to do through their sons. This man was the Reverend Aldert Smedes, whose ability as a Christian Minister, as well as successful educator, was early recognized."

Born April 20, 1810, in the City of New York, Aldert Smedes was the son of Abraham Kiersted Smedes, a commission merchant of Dutch ancestry; and of Eliza Sebor Isaacs. He entered Columbia College when thirteen years old. Before he graduated, his parents moved to Lexington, Kentucky, and he completed his classical education at Transylvania University in that city. There he studied law and later on he was admitted to the bar. But he realized that the Ministry was his calling, and soon he returned to New York and took a course in Divinity at the General

Theological Seminary. There in 1831, when he was but twenty-one years old, he was ordained Deacon. He became assistant to the Reverend Thomas Lyell, D.D., rector of Christ Church, New York City. Two years later, on July 18, 1833, he married Dr. Lyell's daughter, Sarah Pearce Lyell. Soon afterward he was ordained priest and became rector of St. George's Church, Schenectady, N. Y. There a bronchial affection was developed and soon began seriously to threaten him, and by the advice of his physicians he obtained leave of absence and toured eighteen months in Europe in hope of permanent cure. It failed, however, of that effect, and soon after his return he resigned his rectorship and went back to New York and opened a school for girls. In the winter of 1841–42, meeting Bishop Ives in New York, he decided to come South and occupy the premises of the Episcopal School, which he leased from the Hon. Duncan Cameron. He came, bringing his family and some of his teachers.

In speaking of Dr. Smedes, Dr. Battle said in the same address which he delivered on All Saints Day, 1902:—"of talent to attain the highest distinction in the Church, residence in the commercial metropolis of the Country, and in a new state like Kentucky, his mind broadened for practical affairs and a knowledge of men by the study of law, foreign travel at a time when comparatively few were privileged to enjoy it, with a strikingly handsome face and graceful person, only thirty-three years old and active and energetic, possessed of elegant manners and winning address, with common sense, a quickness of perception and that indescribable quality called tact, which rarely if ever failed him, and some experience as a manager and teacher of a school for girls, and aided and encouraged by a partner 'meet for him,' a most attractive and affable woman, ready to become a sympathizing mother to homesick girls! What better conditions for success could possibly have existed? And success did come and come speedily. For nineteen years before the War between the States, its success never flagged. . . . Dr. Smedes, its sole proprietor and manager, conducted the school on lines mapped out by himself. . . . He sought the aid of competent teachers, and daily taught higher classes in some departments himself. He seemed to learn individual dispositions of the different girls almost as by intuition, and he tactfully treated them accordingly. By a little playful irony, he mildly repressed the forward, while to the backward or diffident he ever had words of encouragement. 'My little girls' was his usual form of address to them. As a result, they almost universally felt for him a filial affection and strove to give him no cause of offense. He could speak plainly and pointedly on occasion, and woe to the wayward girl who violated his ideas of propriety, or wilfully disregarded the rules of the school. They did not soon forget his merited reproof. . . . To the early Saint Maryites, Dr. and Mrs. Smedes were the most winning of couples. Tender and affectionate, without ostentation, and easy, natural and considerate to all about them, they made Saint Mary's a happy home to all of its inmates. . . . Dr. Smedes was a Churchman by conviction. His life inspired nearly every girl intrusted to his tutelage with an admiration for and faith in his Church. . . . His voice was not deep or strong, but its tones were pleasant and attractive in their modulation; and he was an excellent reader, because he always read with understanding. I have heard a man of distinction in the State, and one who was an orator himself, say more than once that Dr. Aldert Smedes read the Bible better than anybody he had ever heard. . . . His sermons were strong, pointed and instructive, and though he generally spoke from manuscript, I have heard him speak *ex tempore* with great power. Take him all in all, Dr. Aldert Smedes was one of the greatest men I have known."

A printed copy of one of Dr. Smedes' sermons, "She Hath Done What She Could," or the Duty and Responsibility of Woman, which sermon was preached in the chapel of Saint Mary's School by the Rector, and printed for the pupils at their request, is at present in the Library of the University of North Carolina.

We are very fortunate to have preserved for us in some of the early copies of the monthly *Saint Mary's Muse* some letters written by early students of the School.* All of them refer lovingly to Dr. Smedes, and it will be well to quote some of them, to show how the girls themselves felt about Dr. Smedes.

Ellen Brownlow, of Greenville, N. C., wrote of "Saint Mary's in the Forties," for the *Muse* of June, 1908, and from this I quote:

"Of course dear Dr. Smedes is the central figure on any canvas of Saint Mary's. How we loved and reverenced him! A young and very handsome man, features almost too regular, but the almost feminine beauty of his mouth and perfect teeth was crowned by a very noble brow instinct with intelligence which gauged the worth and extent of his scholars with a glance, and beneath the breadth of brow shone and sparkled his bright blue eyes with kind appreciation of our efforts to please him."

Fannie Bryan, later Mrs. Isaac M. Aiken, wrote some "Recollections of 1848–'52" for the *Muse* of December, 1906, and she said of Dr. Smedes: "A man truly magnetic in his personality, so genial, his fatherly kindness, his gentle admonitions, his patient teachings, all won the love and admiration of his hundreds of pupils, his life work seeming to be to make his Saint Mary's girls happy while within her

---

* I wish to thank all who have helped me in any way, and especially Mrs. Watkins W. Robards (née Sadie Root, grand-daughter of Dr. Aldert Smedes). I could never have written my chapter without the copies of the *Saint Mary's Muse* and other material she so kindly loaned me. K. D. P.

walls, and to fit them for usefulness in this life and for eternal happiness in the world to come."

Mittie Saunders, later Mrs. M. M. L'Engle, wrote "Thoughts of My School Days" for the *Muse* of December 1906, and in this she says, "First of all, who could think of Saint Mary's and separate it from recollections of our beloved principal and friend, Dr. Aldert Smedes? He was one of the best and noblest of men. Wise, kind, faithful to all duties, the purest of Christians, whose character stood out 'the light upon the hill,' and whose Christian teaching guided and purified and comforted not only the girls he taught and led in those early days, but reached far out through them and their homes to other generations of later faithful Churchmen."

Miss Nannie Lane Devereux attended Saint Mary's from 1855 to 1860, and she wrote in the *Saint Mary's Muse,* of "Saint Mary's in the Later Fifties." Speaking of Dr. Smedes, she says, "Who that ever came in contact with that vivid personality would fail to be impressed by it? His unfailing flow of spirits, his energy, his ubiquitous supervision of every detail of that large establishment, for every department was controlled by him, all made a marvellous union of broad management and minute attention to small things. . . . Dr. Smedes was a delightful and inspiring teacher, with a marvellous gift for impressing the essential points of the lesson and rejecting the less valuable ones. . . . I early began to appreciate the firm and higher side of Dr. Smedes' character, the qualities which made him a power for good and a nursing father to the Church throughout the South. I recall once hearing it said when Dr. Smedes was spoken of as a possible bishop: 'No, never Dr. Smedes; he already has two or three missionary dioceses.' I did not quite understand the remark at the time, but its justice has impressed me more and more as I remember how the girls at Saint

Mary's were drawn from the whole South, from Texas to Virginia."

One story which shows very clearly the kindness of Dr. and Mrs. Smedes is the very unusual story of Stella Shaw. This is her story, as told by Mary Wheat Shober, who entered Saint Mary's in 1850, and it appears in her "Reminiscences of my School Days" in the *Muse* for November, 1910.

"One day in the early days of the School a carriage drove up to the porch of Saint Mary's School from which a lady of evident refinement and a little girl alighted. Introducing herself to Dr. Smedes, she wished to enter her child as a pupil. She was going on a long journey and wanted to leave the child under his care and would remit the tuition as it fell due. Saying farewell, she drove away and was never heard of afterwards. That little girl was Stella Shaw, and from that day she was as a dear daughter to Dr. and Mrs. Smedes, always made to feel she was as welcome and as dear."

Mrs. Lizzie Wilson Montgomery, in "The St. Mary's of Olden Days," tells further of Stella Shaw.

"After a silence of ten or more years the mother came and asked to see her child. She was told she had gone to spend the vacation with a friend in South Carolina. Dr. Smedes tried to prevail on her to wait, as he could have her return in a few days. That she refused to do, so the mother and daughter never met again. Miss Stella taught in the School some years after Dr. Smedes' death, until her health failed. She passed the last years in a hospital in Western Carolina, and for her last sleep she was laid in the corner of the Smedes plot in Oakwood Cemetery, near her friend who never failed to give her a father's care and affectionate interest."

What was the nature of this school, which got off to such an auspicious beginning one hundred years ago? We are fortunate to have an account of the school written by Dr.

Smedes himself for a little magazine entitled *To Our Living and Our Dead,* the official organ of the North Carolina Branch of the Southern Historical Society, whose editor, Colonel S. D. Pool, asked Dr. Smedes to write an account of the school. I quote from this article:

"There is a significance in its name. It is not an Institute, nor a Hall, nor a College. It is simply a school for discipline, for training, for good, honest, hard work. Its title, 'Saint Mary's,' designates it as an institution of the Church, a school of Christ, whose chief desire and care are to instil into the minds of its pupils the wisdom that is from above, and to form in them habits of obedience, industry and piety that will make them blessed and a blessing here and meet for the inheritance of Saints in light hereafter. For this end, deeming the moral and religious education of a child to be as much more important than mere literary culture as the heavens are higher than the earth, . . . pupils will be trained in the godly, righteous and sober ways of the Church. . . . It expects and secures from its pupils zeal in their studies and order in their conduct from motives of duty to their school, to themselves, to their parents and to their God, thus endeavoring to train them in principles and habits in which they are to walk as Christian women in all their future life.

"Next to a sound mind, a sound body is important in the training of a woman. Saint Mary's has been eminently favored in the health of its pupils. To this end, besides the rules and precepts, the instructions and exhortations of the school, its high and salubrious situation, its well ventilated dormitories and its extended grounds of 20 acres of oak grove, largely contribute.

"The course of instruction embraces the studies of young children, as well as those of pupils the most advanced. Special interest is felt in the structure and literature of the English language. The Latin, French, and German are carefully taught. Music, drawing and painting have their full share of attention and pains. In the department of music, four teachers are employed, skilled, patient and successful, trained especially for this business and exclusively occupied in it.

"In arranging the studies of a pupil, care is taken not to exact of her more than she can do thoroughly, while in imparting instruction the object aimed at is to fit the pupil to become herself a teacher.

"Among the distinctive features of Saint Mary's, mention ought to be made of its large and elegant parlor, a room of fine proportions, of ample size to give space and verge for all the pupils, and accessible to them at all hours, when they are not engaged in school duties. It is believed that the facilities which this room affords for innocent recreation, social intercourse and the cultivation of manners, have exerted a powerful influence in refining and polishing the daughters of Saint Mary's."

Miss Rebe Shields, of Scotland Neck and Raleigh, has in her possession a small booklet bound in dark blue paper, entitled *Manual of Saint Mary's School, Raleigh, N. C., 1857*. It contains the rules of the school, and an exhortation to the girls, and was evidently given to each student when she entered the school. The following is quoted from this Manual:

"To the Pupils of Saint Mary's School,

this Manual is offered, as a help to them in the performance of their Duties, in the hope that they will preserve and use it, if not for its intrinsic excellence, at least, as an expression of the sincere love, of

Their Friend and Preceptor,
ALDERT SMEDES.

Saint Mary's School,
   May, 1857.

Rules of Saint Mary's School.

"1. At the calling of the roll, morning and evening, every pupil must be present, unless prevented by sickness.

"2. Every pupil must attend morning and evening prayers, and the daily Services in the Chapel. If prevented by sickness or any other cause, she must inform the Lady who has charge of her Dormitory.

"3. Pupils are required to be punctual at their meals, and must not leave the table without permission.

"4. The practising hours must be devoted exclusively to that duty; pupils must carefully avoid intruding upon one another in these hours.

"5. No works of Fiction are to be read, excepting on Saturday, after the duties of the day are over, and then, only those that are approved of.

"6. On Saturday evening, every pupil must be present at the Musical exercises, unless she has special permission to absent herself.

"7. At least two hours a day must be appropriated by every pupil, to active exercise in the open air. Five times round the grove, twice a day, will be deemed a fulfilment of this requisition.

School Room.

"8. During the study hours, pupils are required to preserve perfect order. Talking, moving of seats, writing letters, and reading books not connected with their studies, are expressly forbidden.

"9. The same order is to be observed during the other hours devoted to the duties of the School, not only in the School room, but wherever the pupil is permitted to pursue her studies.

Visting, Dress, &c.

"10. Pupils are allowed to visit only on the monthly Saturday, and then, only at the house to which they have been specially invited; they are required to be at home by sundown.

"11. No bills are allowed in town unless by consent of the parent or guardian, and then only such purchases as are requisite for a neat, but plain attire, will be sanctioned. Pupils are not permitted to make purchases for themselves.

"12. The uniform for winter is a plain blue dress, with a straw bonnet trimmed with blue. For summer a white or blue dress. Silks, costly jewelry, and expensive laces and embroidery, are inconsistent with this Rule.

Dormitory Rules.

"13. Perfect silence must be observed in the Dormitory from the time of entering it at night, until the Prayer bell rings in the morning. The same order is to be observed on Sunday, after dinner.

"14. No romping, running, dancing, or noise of any description, can be allowed at any time in the Dormitories.

"15. No eatables or lights in the alcoves are permitted.

"16. Every young lady before leaving the dormitory in the morning must have her bed properly made, and every thing in her alcove in perfect order.

"17. On Saturday every young lady is expected to employ at least two hours at her needle, under the care of her teacher.

The Chapel.

"18. Pupils should be orderly in their approach to the chapel, punctual in their attendance, reverential during its services, not hurried, but sedate and thoughtful in leaving it.

MANUAL OF SAINT MARY'S SCHOOL.
The Exhortation.

"My dear Child:

You have left your home, your brothers and sisters, and

parents, at a great sacrifice to them and to yourself, to be here at school. You may be sure such a sacrifice would not be made without some great object.

"Do you realize what this object is? It is your education, which is the drawing out, the developing, the training of all your powers of body, mind and heart, that you may become strong, and intelligent, and good, and wise, and thus be fitted for usefulness and happiness in this life, and for immortal happiness in the life to come.

"Great as this object is, the attainment of it, glorious as it will be, depends wholly on yourself.

"In the pure and invigorating air of these ample grounds, and in the innocent amusements of this large family of which you have become a sister, you will find such exercise and recreation as will secure the health and vigor of your body. These you must remember are gifts of God which it is your duty to preserve and to improve. You cannot do this if you neglect the exercise and the recreation which are not only allowed, but enjoined. You must, then, faithfully comply with our rules on this subject. In the glorious open air, you must 'walk, and leap, and run,' and when the weather will not permit out-of-door exercise, you must avail yourself of the resources of our large house, for that relaxation of mind, and lively action of body, which are so essential to your health and happiness.

"No interest in your studies, no zeal for intellectual superiority, no pressure of sedentary occupation, can excuse your neglect of this duty. It ought to be to you a pleasure. You ought to welcome the summons to your walk or your sports. At all events it is a duty, as imperative as any in the school, and failure in it will be visited with displeasure and censure.

"For the improvement of your mind you will find here a course of study carefully arranged and patiently and faithfully taught. If you pursue it earnestly and perseveringly, you will become an intelligent young woman, an ornament of the domestic and social circle.

"For this end you must be diligent in your studies, observing the perfect quiet and order of the Study Hall, and fixing your whole attention on the lesson before you. No use of pen, or book, or mind is proper in the study hours, which does not immediately bear upon the preparation for your recitation.

"In your classes you must be punctual, regular, and attentive, honestly depending on yourself for your answers, and eagerly drinking in the instructions of your teacher. You must disdain the little tricks by which idleness and ignorance seek to evade the responsibilities of a recitation. Be assured such tricks are seen through by both your teachers and your fellows; and that, like all 'false colors,' they bring you into trouble and contempt. Such devices, indeed, mortify your teachers; they cruelly defeat the purposes and desires which led your parents to place you here; and they are of bad example in the class; but their most injured victim is yourself. It is yourself that you cheat; yourself that you rob, yourself that you expose to present ridicule, and future contempt. Let me beseech you then to be true to your teachers, your parents and yourself, by the best exertions in your power to know and recite your lessons.

"In this way alone can they become interesting to you. The more earnestly you study, the happier you will be,— the faster your time will fly. The idle girl sacrifices even her own present enjoyment, and makes herself weary and miserable. She gives up her advantages and happiness for the present and for the future, and becomes to all sensible people an object of mingled pity and contempt.

"As part of your discipline of body and mind you will be called upon to correct what is amiss, and to study what is graceful in gait, postures, bearing, and manners. The hints which may be necessary on these topics you must receive kindly and endeavor to follow. You know how you are won by a pleasing and graceful deportment in your associates. You know how repulsive a rude, and ungracious manner is, or even one which is wanting in affability and courtesy.

"To a woman a soft voice, and gentleness, and grace of manner are especially becoming. Indeed, without these, she has nothing of her sex, externally, but the dress; and it is much to be feared, that within, there is an equally lamentable deficiency of feminine qualities.

"Remember then, always, what is due to your sex, and take in the best part every reproof and counsel which are designed to prune redundancies, to supply defects, and promote excellence in this very interesting department of a woman's education. You should look upon your school as an affectionate, and, therefore, vigilant and faithful mother, anxious for your improvement, even in the most minute particulars.

"O think not her care too solicitous, her supervision too minute, her eye too vigilant, her hand too severe. Every provision she makes for you, however it may sometimes constrain you and seem to you superfluous caution, has originated in the warmest affection for your person and desire for your welfare; and some of those that seem most irksome, have grown out of the experienced necessities of your position. They have been adopted, because they have been felt to be indispensable for your good.

"It is your part and duty confiding in the love and wisdom of the rules under which you are here to live, in the spirit of childlike obedience to submit yourself implicitly to their control.

"Especially, should you thus second with your best efforts our labors here for the discipline and improvement of your moral character, for the cultivation of those graces of the heart, without which, whosoever liveth is counted dead before God. If you feel no interest in this great subject, you are actually dead in trespasses and sins. Out of this awful state it is time you should be aroused, and urged and encouraged to enter upon the great work of your salvation.

"To aid you in this work you will find here, the daily morning and evening prayer of the family, the daily services of the chapel, the daily study of your Bible and prayer book, the lectures and exhortations of the Chapel during the week, the morning and evening services of the Lord's day, with hymns and catechising at night, the admonition and counsel of your teachers, and their good example joined to that of many of your companions.

"Surrounded by these influences, having the subject of your eternal interests thus daily brought home to you, if you do not wilfully shut your eyes, close your ears, and harden your heart, you must become imbued with a knowledge and, by God's infinite grace, in time, with a love of the truth as it is in Jesus.

"This is an acquisition, the value of which no words can express; in comparison of which the 'whole world' is a bauble! Oh, then, what care, what diligence, what self-denial, what pains ought you to exercise, that you may improve to the utmost the opportunities which you here enjoy of becoming wise unto salvation.

"Be persuaded then to make the best use you can of your privileges. And as your best efforts without the help of Almighty God will be vain, offer to him daily your earnest prayer, that by His Holy Spirit, he will convert your soul, and bring you into the path of righteousness, for the sake of his dear son, Jesus Christ, our Lord."

There follow prayers for different occasions, questions for self examination, scripture quotations to be devoutly pondered, etc.

Ellen Brownlow, who entered Saint Mary's in 1845, described the school in her "Saint Mary's in the Forties" as follows:

"There was then only the large brick building and the two Rock Houses on each side, the latter connected with the Main Building by a trellised brick walk covered with vines and blossoming plants. I dare say the interior of the brick house was very much as now—on the first floor, the long parlor on the right of the broad hall as one entered; the main school room with its desks, blackboards, cases of chemical and philosophical apparatus on the left. The reception room was then almost crowded with musical instruments, the walls nearly covered with works of art."

There were five dormitories (four before the Chapel was built), two in West Rock, one on the upper floor of East Rock, and two on the fourth floor of the Main Building. These dormitories were divided into alcoves which were situated along the sides of the long room, leaving the broad space in the center, in which were ten beds. Mary Wheat Shober, who entered the school in 1850, describes the dormitories in her "Reminiscences of my School Days" in the *Muse* for November, 1910, as follows:

"The cunning little cuddies two girls shared together, consisting of a washstand, a few shelves, a chair, and there you are. Oh, I forgot the most important thing—a looking glass not larger than eight by ten inches! How we did love to decorate and beautify our boudoir! Such curtains for shelves and washstand, with a fancy bright cover for trunk; pictures of loved ones on the wall, nicknacks wherever a place could be found. Our beds so narrow were outside, one on each side of the entrance to the alcove, where a curtain hung to give privacy to the occupants. On very cold nights—for there was no steam heat in those days anywhere—our teacher, Miss French, who had charge of the Dormitory and occupied a larger alcove at the head of the

Dormitory, would allow us to push the two beds together and make one bed, where we two girls could snuggle up together in each other's arms, and sleep the sleep that only the young can ever know and enjoy. . . . There was no running water on every floor, but instead two huge tubs stood at one end of the hall which were filled every morning, and out there we hustled with rather small pitcher to fill for our ablutions."

These pitchers and bowls were of dark red pottery and were made in Wake County. For a hot bath, water was brought from a great cauldron, kept filled in the kitchen, with a constant fire underneath.

The dining room was in the basement under the school room, on the west side of the Main Building, and the Smedes family had all of their meals there, sharing alike with the girls. Pains were taken to provide wholesome and appetizing meals.

Enormous stoves furnished heat for the school room and parlor. Uncle Mose or Uncle Wash coming in to "stoke de fire," all recitation for the time being had to cease.

Among the furnishings of the buildings were many fine oil paintings bought by Reverend Aldert Smedes in Europe. After his death and that of his son, Reverend Bennett Smedes, these were presented to the School by the Smedes family.

In 1845, Dr. Smedes commissioned Mr. William Hart to paint the picture of Bishop Ives administering the rite of confirmation. There seems to be some doubt as to the identity of the girls in the portrait. Ellen Brownlow said, "The girls in the picture were my school-mates, Mittie Saunders, a Senior, Lucy Raegon, Sarah Crawford, and Eugenia Hinton. Lucy Raegon is the one of whose face we have a side view. She was a handsome girl with very dark or black hair. . . . Sarah Crawford is painted with the Bishop's hands on her head."

IN THE BEGINNING

Annie Haywood, later Mrs. Samuel Ruffin of Raleigh, says:

"There have been many guesses as to the identity of the girls in the picture. I recall them all distinctly; Laura Washington, with the Bishop's hands upon her head; Eugenia Hinton of the long curls; Sarah Crawford."

Mittie Saunders, later Mrs. M. M. L'Engle, said:

"And now I would like to touch upon a subject which interests us all—the picture painted by Mr. Hart—later a distinguished artist—portraying Bishop Ives in the confirmation service. Perhaps Mrs. Ruffin, once Annie Haywood, whom I remember well, will be surprised to hear of another aspirant for the honor of being one of the figures portrayed in the class being confirmed by the Bishop. No less a person than myself, once Mittie Saunders of the school days. . . . One dislikes to write of oneself, but the occasion warrants it.

"Dr. Smedes wished to have the portrait of Bishop Ives as a companion picture to that of Bishop Ravenscroft, and it was painted for him by Mr. Hart—rumor stated—to defray the expense of tuition of a near relative of the artist, then at Saint Mary's. Whether she was a half sister or a niece I do not remember, but her name was Claudia Wingate, a shy, delicate girl, and Claudia was my especial friend. Of course the painting of such a picture made quite a stir of interest and chatter, usually *sotta voce*.

"One afternoon while walking with a companion girl just outside of the grove to the west, we were discussing Art and possibly our own skill in drawing, for impulsively I plumped down on my knees and with a stick began drawing circles. While so absorbed, Mr. Hart, on horseback, whom I knew by sight only, suddenly and quietly drew up by my side and asked what we were doing. 'Drawing circles,' we answered. 'Ah,' he repeated, 'drawing circles, the artist's most difficult task; he that can draw a perfect circle may hope to be a good artist.' Not long after this, we, Claudia Wingate and I, received a summons from Dr. Smedes, and were directed by him on a certain afternoon and hour to go to Mr. Hart's studio, which was near the capitol, and that he would expect us. No reason was given, but this in itself promised a rare treat, and we did not fail to keep the appointment. It was there that Mr. Hart told us he was painting the picture for Dr. Smedes; that the central figure was to be a fancy sketch, two other figures Dr. Smedes was to choose, but he had been offered by him to select any girl he desired from among the school-girls, and he had chosen me. Of course the surprise was startling and certainly unexpected, but while I was very much pleased at being 'in the Bishop's picture' and thought it wonderfully kind in Mr. Hart to choose me, I was not half so much flattered then as I should have been, or as much so as I now am at the memory of this choice; but it was a delightful experience, and I certainly felt and expressed gratitude. I was placed in the picture kneeling next on the right of the middle or fancy figure. I do not remember the dress, but I do remember my hair was done up in a funny little knot at the back of my head, which I hope the artist made artistic, for I simply wore it in that way for convenience and to save time, for no day was ever long enough in which to accomplish all that I desired to do. It was not until I left school that I wore my hair curled. Changes may have been made later of which I was not aware, but I have often looked at, admired and thought of the middle figure, as the fancy figure of which Mr. Hart told us."

The handsome, full length, oil portrait of Bishop Ravenscroft was painted by Jacob Eicholtz, a celebrated artist of Philadelphia, who in his day made portraits of many famous Americans, including John Marshall, Chief Justice of the Supreme Court of the United States, and of Nicholas Biddle, President of the Bank of the United States. The portrait of Bishop Ravenscroft, begun in 1829 and finished in 1830, was painted by order of Charles P. Mallett, a devout churchman, who was Senior Warden of St. John's Church, Fayetteville, N. C. It was obtained from Mr. Mallett by Dr. Smedes some years before the War between the States.

Beneath each of these portraits, an old pier table was placed by Dr. Smedes; and these same tables are in the parlor today, having been presented by the Smedes family to the school upon the death of Dr. Bennett Smedes. Also among the furnishings placed in the school by Dr. Aldert Smedes in these early days was the long mirror, which he purchased from Charles P. Mallett.

A distinctive feature of the school life was the blue uniform, dark blue in winter, pale blue or white, with blue ribbon, for summer. A plain straw bonnet with a broad blue ribbon crossed at the top and tied under the chin, completed the uniform.

There were several separate recitation rooms. Dr. Smedes habitually sat in the school room. In the basement was Dr. Mason's room for Seniors and Juniors. Madame Clement had the opposite room for her French classes. The girls of the '40s were close students and diligently attended to their school duties.

The school day started off with morning service in the Chapel at nine o'clock; and at nine at night the girls assembled and were dismissed with prayers. In the afternoon they were required to exercise at least two hours, generally in the grove, although sometimes Dr. Smedes took them directly through the Capitol and a mile beyond, making a four mile walk in all. Dr. Smedes with a teacher headed the procession, and it was a goodly sight to see him walking with his "little daughters," as he spoke of them.

On Sundays the girls were required to listen so attentively to the sermon that they could give a creditable analysis or synopsis of it to Dr. Smedes at Evening Prayers. So after the service, the girls would gather into groups and walk around the grove and talk over the sermon in order to be thoroughly familiar with it.

Twice weekly Dr. Smedes gave "abstracts," clear, illuminating lectures on the Bible Lessons, and the girls were required to write, without notes, their recollections of them. In the course of a few years these abstracts covered all the great points of Church teaching. Each week the girls were required to learn the collect, twenty or more lines of standard poetry, and as many verses of Scripture carefully selected with reference to some doctrine.

Recreations were found almost entirely within the school, but when Dr. Smedes could procure them, singers and performers were invited to give entertainments, and occasionally the girls were taken to town to hear concerts. But for the most part the girls lived at home and found their happiness there.

Outstanding entertainments were the dignified soirées, described by Mittie Saunders of the '40s for the *Muse* of December, 1906. These entertainments were looked forward to and prepared for with great care, curl papers, and braided hair. Visitors from town were invited and many came and looked on from the long divans, listening to the music, often very fine, furnished by harps, pianos and voices. No dancing was allowed or even thought of, but promenaders paced two and two around the long room. Then any girl with an admirer might join the procession. Round and round they went, the fashionable youths wearing the curious boat-like, turned up, pointed shoes which were then "the thing."

Every Fourth of July, the day scholars were invited to spend the day. At noon the big wagon rolled into the grove laden with countless numbers of ice cream freezers, each filled to the brim, a signal that the dinner hour approached.

Dishes of brown roasted fowls and fried chicken, great bowls filled with the Indian dish of succotash, and many other good things were there in abundance. All was harmony and happiness, and at the close of the day, they all assembled around the piano and sang "Yankee Doodle" and "The Old North State."

But ordinarily, the day scholars had their dinner sent from home, and the procession of little negro boys carrying well filled baskets was a daily feature on Hillsboro Street. One girl who objected to the water of the well at school always had a pitcher of ice water sent with her dinner, which of course meant another servant to carry it, and often a third servant was required to bring a watermelon or some other article for dessert!

The opening service of Saint Mary's School was held in the parlor, but very soon afterwards the lower floor of East Rock was fitted up for a chapel. It was simple but beautiful in its appointments, and was fitted up with pews and an upright organ.

In the summer of 1855 the separate chapel building was begun. One of the scholars who was there at the time, Mary Pearson, later Mrs. Davis of Salisbury, N. C., stated in her "Reminiscences of Saint Mary's, 1855-56" for the *Muse* of June, 1908:

". . . all felt delighted when Dr. Smedes said that as soon as possible he was going to arrange to have a new one (chapel), which was to be apart from the other buildings. We all tried to give a little as we could, and in the spring or summer of 1855, it was at last commenced, and from that time until it was finished it was a great source of interest to us all. While we all loved the old one, we were most anxious about the new one."

Miss Adelaide E. Smith, of Scotland Neck, N. C., who attended Saint Mary's in 1856, stated in an article on "The Chapel—Saint Mary's" in the *Muse* for June, 1908, that the Camerons, who owned the property, built the chapel. She stated that Dr. Smedes gave the stone steps at the front door, the protecting hood and the stained glass window above.

In his report to the Diocesan Convention of 1856, Dr. Aldert Smedes said, "To meet its growing demands for room, immediate arrangements will be made; the principal feature of which is the erection of a Chapel of such expressive, tho simple architecture, that it will be a constant witness to the religious character and object of the School, and add much to the interest and efficiency of the services." In his report to the Diocesan Convention in 1857, Dr. Smedes said, "Our new Chapel, a beautiful Gothic structure, will add greatly to the interest of our religious services."

Bishop Atkinson in his report to the Diocesan Convention of 1858 stated:

"April 5th, P.M., I preached in Saint Mary's Chapel, Raleigh, and confirmed sixteen persons belonging to the school. It was the first time in which I had taken part in the worship at the new Chapel, and I was gratified by its beauty, its appropriate arrangements, and its adaptation to its purpose. I need scarcely repeat here my conviction of the exceeding value of the services which has been rendered to the cause of Christian education, and indeed to all the best interests of society, not only in this State, but through a large portion of the South, by this Institution."

Ellen Brownlow, writing of "Saint Mary's in the Forties" (*Saint Mary's Muse,* June, 1908), tells us:

"We had a goodly corps of teachers. Dr. Mason ruled Senior and Junior, and I for one loved and reverenced him with all my strength. He was to me the embodiment of all learning. . . . What teacher comes next? Madame Clement, of course, with her attractive French ways, her strenuous voice and her commanding personality. Madame mostly wore silk dresses and there was always some bright ribbon in evidence. Her toilet table in her room was draped in sheer white muslin, with lace edging over pink lining. Her lounge cushions of bright colors, brackets, vases of flowers, etc. . . . I was there when her daughter Eleanor came. Poor little girl! I was so sorry for her. She had not seen her mother for years. Madame had left her with some aunts, sisters of Monsieur Clement, who had evidently petted Eleanor and loved her very dearly. Now Madame never petted any one and I am sure Eleanor missed it. I saw her in tears one day and she told me she was 'si triste,' that Raleigh was so unlike Paris."

From all accounts, Madame Clement was helpful and energetic, and she proved an able and willing assistant to Dr. and Mrs. Smedes. She came with them from New York when they came to open the school, and remained with them until about 1860. As a teacher of French, her early pupils said that she was unsurpassed. Once one of the girls asked her if she said her prayers in English or in French, and she answered, "Mes enfantes, je ne sais pas!"

Next teacher in authority and personality was the German Music Master, Gustave Blessner, composer and performer on piano and violin. Mrs. Blessner, a lovely English lady, also taught music, and she played the organ for chapel.

Miss Evertson was another of the early teachers who impressed herself upon her pupils. She was tall and slender; cold, quiet, severe, austere, and caustic are adjectives which the girls used in describing her, but they generally agreed that she was strictly just, inspiring respect if not affection. She had a missionary society which met once a week in one of the basement rooms, and she taught the girls to make clothes to send to Dr. Bush for the Indians.

Some of the other teachers who were mentioned in these

accounts of the early days of the school by the students were Miss Thompson, Miss Genners, Miss Green, and Mr. and Mrs. Brune.

And so, under the wise guidance of Dr. Smedes and his able teachers, Saint Mary's grew from year to year. Each year, Dr. Smedes attended the meetings of the Diocesan Convention and gave a brief report. In 1856 he stated, "This School was never in a more satisfactory state, than it is now, in the fifteenth year of its existence. If it has hitherto deserved in any degree, the favor it has enjoyed, its friends may be assured that the future shall see no diminution, but rather a constant increase of its advantages."

At the Annual Meeting in 1857 he reported, "This School continues to be in a very prosperous condition. Our buildings, in consequence of recent additions, afford comfortable accommodations for a hundred and twelve boarding pupils."

And in 1859, his report stated, "This School continues to prosper. There are seventy-eight boarding and thirty day pupils, for whose instruction twelve teachers are constantly employed."

This brings us to the year 1860, with Saint Mary's securely established, and in a very flourishing condition. And now I leave it to the succeeding chapters to carry on the story of Saint Mary's from that time to the present day.

2

War Times and After
1860–1885

By Emilie Smedes Holmes

IN THE decade 1860–1870, Saint Mary's experienced what must surely be accounted the greatest crisis of the first hundred years of her existence. That she not only survived but emerged from it victoriously must be ascribed to the greatness of her founder, whose quality of mind and heart and soul stands revealed in the extremity of the situation.

Here was a man born, reared and educated in the North, of ancestry that had no affiliations with the South; transplanted to southern soil in the fullness of early manhood; a man who so completely identified himself with the South that when her hour of travail came upon her, he stands out with the very best of her native sons to aid in her rebirth and to set her feet upon the path of high adventure that led albeit through sacrifice and suffering of the bitterest kind to the exalted place she now occupies in the nation. Surely the South owes more to her adopted son, Aldert Smedes, than she can ever repay! For Saint Mary's during that decade was not only a seed-bed of culture, character, and religious idealism that played a great part in raising the level of heartbroken young womanhood to a higher plane, but by affording a sanctuary to many of the South's most prominent women of mature years who were compelled to flee from war torn sections, she saved them for the part they played at the close of the war.

Let us take a look at the Smedes family during this decade. Dr. Smedes was now fifty years old, Mrs. Smedes two years younger—both in the prime of life. Mrs. Smedes has been described as being at this time "an able assistant to her husband, especially in the supervision of the younger girls. She was very gentle and sweet by nature so that they came to her for sympathy and advice as to a loving mother." Alas that her life should have been wrecked as it was by the tragic shocks and bereavements that overtook her in the death of three young sons.

But in 1860 there were nine children living a wholesome, happy life within the school; six stalwart young sons ranging in age from Lyell who was twenty-five to George, just ten years old; and three little girls, Bessie, seven; Annie, five; and Sadie, only a year old. The first break in the family circle came, however, the very next year when Lyell died suddenly of pneumonia, within three months after his marriage to Miss Susan Dabney of Vicksburg, Mississippi, who in later years was the author of the widely read volume *The Memorials of a Southern Planter*. Bennett, the second son, was twenty-three at this time, and three years later he was ordained to the ministry in Christ Church, Raleigh, July 24, 1863. He entered Lee's army as chaplain. We do not wonder that the clarion call of the South's desperate need found lodgment also in the breasts of the two lads of nineteen and twenty-one, Edward and Ives. They enlisted in the ranks of the Confederate Army and within a year "Taps" had been sounded for both of them.

Life at the school went bravely on, however, though sorrow and tragedy made indelible impressions on the young hearts so deeply stirred. We are indebted to Sadie Robards for recording reminiscences of that sad period, passed on to her long since by her mother, Annie Smedes (Mrs. Charles Root). Her story was published in the Raleigh *News and Observer* for September 15, 1940.

Through the courtesy of Mrs. Lee Shine, now of Chapel Hill, we are able to give extracts from a number of letters written by her mother, Lou Sullivan, while she was a pupil of Saint Mary's during 1863 and 1864. The letters were sealed with red sealing wax—no envelopes—and afford priceless first glimpses into the daily life of the school at that time. In writing to her mother, Miss Sullivan thus describes her day:

"My whole time is occupied. The rising bell rings before the sun rises. We have just time to dress and make our beds when the bell rings for roll-call and prayers. Immediately afterwards comes breakfast. The next hour is for walking, but Lizzie and I take that hour for oil painting. When that hour is over we return to the schoolroom or to the chapel in pleasant weather, where they go through the ceremony of the Church. Thence we proceed to the business of the day. The School is pretty full. There are over a hundred boarders who have come in already, besides a good many day scholars. There are a good many girls here who are daughters or near relatives of distinguished characters. Among them is a niece of General Burnside. After the last study hour at night the girls, or as many of them as wish, assemble in the Parlor where they have music on the piano and some of them dance until Prayers, which are conducted in the Parlor. Then we retire to our dormitories and are not allowed to speak a word after we pass the door until the prayer-bell rings in the morning. I think I shall become warm-natured if I remain up here. I very rarely go to the fire and don't feel the cold so much. Lizzie, like you all, believes in fresh air and open windows, which

I do not; so we have agreed that she shall have her way one week and I mine the next. We have a good deal of fun to ourselves."

On April 8, 1864, Miss Sullivan writes: "I continue to enjoy very good health; though our fare is coarse it agrees with me. We have molasses for supper three times a week, and Sunday night we had cakes, three apiece. The girls complain considerably. I never have left the table without being satisfied, and common as it is, I always enjoy it. I believe Dr. Smedes provides the table as nicely as he can. Everything is so very scarce and dear around here."

With a burst of enthusiasm in another letter she reports that Dr. Smedes had introduced a new breakfast dish—fried okra—"you have no idea how nice it is when fried brown." Perhaps it was the Saturday breakfasts of smoking hash and hominy that called forth the eulogy of "the most memorable of all days—our sweet, lovely Saturdays."

It may be that on Saturdays Miss Sullivan welcomed the respite from the daily grind of exacting study and enjoyed the morning hours of homely domestic work in alcove and dormitory: the weekly cleaning up, the darning of stockings and mending of the freshly laundered clothes deposited on the foot of each bed by the long procession of smiling Negro washerwomen, who no doubt each expected and received some little perquisite for the trouble in bringing the clothes balanced so skilfully on her head.

Under date of June 1, 1864, she continues: "Dr. Smedes took us down to the legislature. We first went into the Hall of Commons, afterwards into the Senate Chamber, into the Geological Office and the Observatory. We were abundantly repaid for the long, sunny walk. All the members of the legislature of our acquaintance had returned home except Dr. Dickson and Mr. Powell."

In November, 1864, she comments further: "We have had no study hour at night for some time on account of the failure in the supply of gas. Last night in order to pass off the time a magic lantern was exhibited by two of the lady teachers and with very pleasing effect."

As is to be expected, the religious note is often emphasized in Miss Sullivan's letters. That she loved "the antique-looking little chapel where services are held" is attested by the fact that she made a drawing of it.

In connection with their daily walks for exercise, she speaks of "a mineral spring, about three miles from here. Some of the girls go out there every evening accompanied by a teacher—a pleasant change from walking in the grove." (This was probably the lovely spring on her great-grandfather's land which Miss Pattie Mordecai says was variously known as Chinquapin, Cool, or Poplar Spring. It now belongs to the City of Raleigh, and in dry weather many people still flock to it for a cool drink.)

Dr. Smedes was apparently not satisfied with knowing his girls within the walls of the school, but visited their home environments. At least Miss Sullivan refers to a visit he made to Duplin and how he returned "well pleased with 'the land of Goshen' as he termed it."

Miss Sullivan sorrowfully anticipates her departure from Saint Mary's. "Five weeks more and we will be leaving sweet Saint Mary's, as it is frequently called, and I must confess it has become sweet to me. My only regret in coming here is that I did not come sooner. It certainly makes a greater improvement in the girls than any other school of which I have had any knowledge. I assure you I feel amply rewarded for coming."

In 1863 the trip from Warrenton to Raleigh was an adventure, something to be remembered and talked about, as Mrs. Walter Montgomery of Raleigh loves to talk about it today. She was Lizzie Wilson, and among the girls who made this trip with her she recalls Sue and Nannie Cawthorn, Sue Martin, and Juliet and Johanna Somerville. The

Somerville girls were so young that their black Mammy was sent along with them, and of course a retinue of parents were part of the caravan. Such chaperonage was needed, too, for they were traveling on a freight train, and one of the wayside stops was at Henderson, which was said to be such a wicked place that should the angel Gabriel come down to blow his horn it would be stolen from him before he could get it to his mouth. Here, however, a bevy of girls had been assembled from all over Granville County (properly guarded, of course) to board the train for Raleigh. There were six of them—Lucy Henderson, Nannie Turner, Lucy Sneed, Kate Royster, and Eliza and Sue Robards. It must have been a rather wilted group that alighted from the train that hot July afternoon after practically an all-day trip covering sixty miles of travel. The depot was quite a distance south of the present Raleigh Union Station, was surrounded by warehouses, and afforded no waiting room. There were plenty of horse-drawn hacks and an omnibus awaiting them, however, and amid the distracting calling of drivers and waving of whips the travelers took possession of the omnibus and were driven to Saint Mary's. They felt quite "stuck up" when they were placed in West Rock and found among their companions in the dormitory the daughters of General Lee and General Leonidas Polk—Mildred and Lucia. The daughter of Chief Justice Pearson of the Supreme Court was also there, but his exalted position didn't thrill the girls as did that of the generals in the Confederate Army—though Mrs. Montgomery admits that "Laura was a very handsome and lovable girl whose musical talent made her the pride of Professor Hanson."

The heating system (if it can be called such) was, of course, primitive in those days—and remained very much the same for a good many years. The Main Building was heated by two brick kilns located in the basement. They were about three feet long by ten feet high, with pipes running from them through the upper stories. There were registers only in the parlor, the rest of the building being tempered by the pipes. Cord-length sticks of wood were required for these furnaces and it took the entire time of "Uncle Shep" and two horses to keep them fed.

The "old girls" were sometimes granted special privileges and in Mrs. Montgomery's second year she and her set of girls were promoted to the coveted "long room" on the second floor of the Main Building west of the staircase. There was a small room adjoining and in these two rooms were nine girls from Warren and Granville Counties. The wonder is how they all kept well and strong since they slept all winter with the windows tightly closed. The windows opened on a sloping roof and on Saturdays the girls collected there for their weekly shoe polishing.

"We privileged girls," Mrs. Montgomery says, "greatly enjoyed this long room, having no teacher to keep tab on us as to how we kept it and when we retired. We often smuggled up a broiled chicken, hard boiled eggs, and biscuits that we had bought from Uncle Moses, the husband of the cook, Aunt Matilda. Dr. Smedes' youngest son, George, was much in love with one of the girls in our rooms, and one of his love-tokens was a watermelon which he would drop in the middle of her bed. As we had no knife to open it with, we used our white-oak corset split. This inner and then unmentionable article of a girl's attire of that period was made in my home town. One day Dr. Smedes caught George carrying in his love-token—and before the end of the week he had sent him off to St. Paul's School, Concord, New Hampshire."

Needless to say, very homesick, lovelorn letters found their way from George to Saint Mary's. It was evidently not the offering of the love-token itself that brought such dire punishment upon George but his surreptitious invasion of the girl's bedroom for its presentation. His lively imagination expressed itself also in peanuts—a whole barrel of them arrived one day consigned to Sally Hall Smith (Mrs. Fab Busbee), a welcome tribute indeed as we can imagine even today.

Sally's devotion to Saint Mary's and the beloved friends there had triumphed gloriously over her father's decision to send her to Petersburg to school following her first year at Saint Mary's—Petersburg being regarded by him as safer from the Yankees approaching Raleigh from the south. So he duly headed his daughter for Petersburg. But with every mile of the drive the pull of her heartstrings grew stronger, and at Weldon she ordered the horses turned about, and showed up at Saint Mary's. Fortunately her father condoned her independent action, and Dr. Smedes accepted the gold she produced from her trunk and again enrolled her at Saint Mary's.

Mrs. Montgomery recalls one of the bi-monthly musicals when she played "Then You'll Remember Me," and Governor Vance was present. She feels sure he was just as bored as she was tortured.

The most exciting diversion that the girls in the long room practiced—very stealthily, of course—was that of table-turning.

"The deep well in the back yard was a great gathering place for the girls on hot summer nights when they went to get a cool drink before going to bed. And two cisterns provided soft rainwater for washing their hair."

What we call today the comforts of life were non-existent in Mrs. Montgomery's day, but in spite of under-heated halls and dormitories the girls must have kept remarkably well since only one room was set apart as "the sick room." No doubt the rigidly enforced daily "walking hours" kept them in good shape. As five times around the grove were held equivalent of the hour's walk, so also was a walk to

Dix Hill along the top of the fortifications that had been thrown up around the city as protection from the advancing Federal troops. They passed through the west side of the grove from North to South.

It would be wonderful if the names of all the thousands of girls who have attended Saint Mary's School during these one hundred years could be enrolled in this volume. But without their names there is a thrill in the thought that within the walls now more than a century old there has flowed a ceaseless stream of beautiful young life—eager youth, piercing the future with expectant heart and perhaps sensing vaguely that past, present, and future merge at last as Memory plays its part in the role of life. We are blessed as we stand in the presence of beautiful old age and renew our own youth as age recalls the beloved scenes of the distant past. Today we can go even further back than the days of Mrs. Montgomery and Miss Sullivan, and hear Mary Frances Bishop (Mrs. John C. Jacobs of Charlotte) telling of the days before the War. She was born in Roxabel, North Carolina, in January, 1844, and attended Saint Mary's during the year 1860–1861. She recalls the very early rising, and the freezing cold bath and dressing hour, in spite of the fire that was made in the dormitory stove every morning by a slave. (It is said that Dr. Smedes owned only two slaves, and that he purchased these to prevent their being separated from each other.)

The advent of the new decade, the sixties, witnessed the passing of the Saint Mary's uniform, for Mrs. Jacobs says she was not required to wear one. Still there were girls there at the time who wore them, the "old girls" who already had them.

Plays and concerts had their place in Mrs. Jacobs' day, and she especially recalls Eleanor Gregg in a pageant.

As for the buildings, the chapel was there and the two rock houses, connected to the main building by enclosed covered ways. In the basement of the main building were the kitchen and dining room. And here Mrs. Jacobs recalls with what I might call gusto that the corncakes were so delicious that the girls would slip into the kitchen and buy some from the cook; also that Tuesdays and Thursdays were dessert days, and that at noon every day an apple and two crackers were meted out for lunch.

There seems to have been little question of closing the school during the War. Instead, her doors were flung wide open and women of means found refuge under her hospitable roof. Among others Mrs. Jefferson Davis and her children sojourned here for some time. But at the close of the War when Confederate money was worthless, Dr. Smedes was faced with a situation that would have crushed a man of less resourcefulness and initiative. A priceless relic of that day is preserved among the letters written by Miss Sullivan. Two circulars, frayed and stained with age, set forth the measures that Dr. Smedes took to prevent the calamity which the closing of the School would have meant to the South and to the church in the South. And so it came about that in the fall of 1865 Katharine Russell Clements of Wake County (born in 1849; now Mrs. A. J. Ellis of Raleigh) was entered at Saint Mary's by her father "on a bale of cotton." And we may be sure that many another girl was similarly entered—on a barrel of flour, a sack of meal, a side of bacon. Thus the education of young women did not perish from the Southland, but the torch that was lighted in 1842 continued to burn brightly and is still glowing in another crisis that threatens to engulf not the South alone but the World.

Mrs. Ellis has very lively recollections of life at Saint Mary's during the one year that she was a student there. She exclaims: "I am so thankful I can remember as much as I do of that blessed old institution." She quotes the opinion of her father that Dr. Smedes was "the best qualified man to head a girl's school—there never was his superior!" Her own estimate of him is that he was "handsome, graceful, perfect!" Among the faculty she remembers especially Miss Evertson, who, she says, "was loved in spite of being sarcastic," and Madame Guie, presiding over the French table.

Speaking of the dining tables, she says that they were set with oilcloth for everyday use; but on great occasions when they had to "fix up"—as for a visit from the Bishop—white linen cloths were produced. Naturally, Mrs. Ellis' mind turned here to the fare, and it is good to note that in her opinion the combination of food staples received from patrons in exchange for board and the fine garden cultivated by Dr. Smedes resulted in good food for his large family.

Referring to the fashions in dress she says that small hoopskirts and waterfalls were "the thing"; and she has a vivid picture of her fellow-student, Fanny Disosway, lovely in person and dress, and of the unhappy day poor Fanny upset a bowl of soup on one of her choicest costumes.

Mrs. Ellis' reminiscences cluster largely about the young Smedeses. Taking the girls first she says that Bessie (aged twelve), along with herself, "boasted the heaviest braids of hair—the envy of all the girls." Annie she remembers as "sweet and bright." Then she speaks of beautiful Sadie who at the age of seven waxed indignant with the family physician, Dr. Edmund Burke Haywood, for calling her by her name. He should have said *Miss Sadie!* There were plenty of admirers in after years to satisfy this childish appreciation of her importance, for she became one of North Carolina's most popular belles. She married Mr. William Erwin, and their three daughters are Bessie (Mrs. Hamilton Jones of Charlotte), Margaret (Mrs. Jack Glenn of Winston-Salem), and Sarah (Mrs. Hargrove Bellamy of Wilmington).

Bessie, the eldest of the Smedes daughters, married Mr. Moreau Leak of Wadesboro. They had no children.

On September 6, 1876, Annie was married in the Chapel to Mr. Charles Root of Raleigh, the ceremony being performed by her father. Three children were born to this lovely couple: Sadie (now Mrs. W. W. Robards of Sanford), Annie (Mrs. W. W. Vass of Raleigh) and Aldert Smedes Root, beloved today as a baby specialist by all young mothers of Raleigh.

Having disposed of the girls, Mrs. Ellis says of the boys that Abe at the age of twenty was "so shy the girls could never get a look at him, whereas mischievous George loved to tease stiff and stern Miss Evertson—even she couldn't manage him!"

There were three sisters from Scotland Neck at Saint Mary's during the seventies—Lena, Rebe, and Nannie Smith. Lena, the eldest, was there in 1870–71. At that time there were two vacation periods of six weeks each, a summer and a winter holiday. Like many others she was impressed with the value of the soirées and concerts as a means of developing in the girls the arts and graces that would enable them to function happily as leaders in the social life that normally awaited them at home.

High heels were not unheard of in those days, and we may be sure Dr. Smedes did not entirely succeed in ridiculing them out of court, though he would walk behind the girls and comment on "improper shoes for young girls to wear." Miss Smith, however, wonders how he did accomplish all that he did.

"He was his own housekeeper," she continues, "and directly after breakfast would go to the storeroom to give out supplies. As there was no bakery in Raleigh, sometimes it would mean a barrel of flour for the day's breadmaking. Having locked the storeroom, he would hunt up two girls to take out for a drive and on returning would enter the Chapel for the daily opening service."

We have seen how the crisis of the decade 1860–1870 was successfully met by Dr. Smedes. But no man could pass through such personal experiences and such heavy responsibilities as the War had brought upon him without a resultant strain upon his vitality. Although he had tried again and again to purchase the property on which the school was located, his efforts had been unsuccessful; the rent of the place was too profitable an investment for the owner to be willing to relinquish it. And so Dr. Smedes faced a continuing necessity of paying large rental at a time when the South was only just emerging from the ashes of war. No doubt he found comfort in the fact that his son, Bennett, would carry on in the same spirit by which he himself had been animated since the founding of the school, but also he must have realized the weight of the burden that he would let fall upon the shoulders of his son. At the early age of sixty-five Aldert Smedes succumbed to increasing weakness and died, on April 25, 1877.

"The loss of such a man (the Raleigh *Observer* for May 1, 1877, writes) is almost irreparable. He will be greatly, very greatly, missed in the church of which he was a faithful minister and whose bulwarks he has done much to build up. He will be missed in society, of which he was a pillar and an ornament. He will be missed in this community, whose interests he has so materially subserved. And, above all, he will be missed in those halls where he unfolded the treasures of learning to those under his care and taught such valuable lessons of wisdom and goodness.

Peace to his honored ashes!"

When Mr. Bennett Smedes succeeded his father as head of the school in the late spring of 1877, he assumed his responsibilities with courage and zeal. During the summer he conferred personally with the head of a well-known teacher's agency in New York, Mrs. Young-Fulton, and when the fall session opened we find a well-selected faculty who were destined not only to maintain the already high scholastic standards of the school but raise them to higher levels to meet the needs of the emerging South.

Heading the faculty as Lady Principal was Mrs. Catherine deRosset Meares of Wilmington. There could have been no wiser choice for this new and responsible position in the School than this able and distinguished southern lady. Catherine deRosset had first been a student at Saint Mary's in the fall of 1842. She has left letters (in the deRosset and Meares collection in the Library of the University of North Carolina) of this period as well as of the year during which she was a Music Teacher under Dr. Aldert, 1876, and later when she was Lady Principal. The girls soon came to love her for her motherly kindness, yet she was very strict, withal, when occasion demanded. A widow of middle age, rather short and stout, with dark brown eyes and hair, she wore a becoming white muslin cap with a band of black ribbon around it.

She and Miss Czarnomska, the head of the academic department, were effective foils for each other both in appearance and in personality. Miss Czarnomska was tall and slender and of queenly bearing, with steel-grey eyes and jet black hair worn in a French twist, in the coils of which the red rose she affected seemed naturally to belong. She was of Polish and English parentage—a young woman of versatile and brilliant mind, to whom the highest classes in mathematics, literature, and German were given. The girls, generally, dubbed her "The Czar," whether they loved and admired, or feared and admired her.

Mr. Will H. Sanborn, a young man of about twenty-seven from New England, headed the music department. He was not only a musician of the first rank but was also a good business man whose judgment in such matters proved an asset to Mr. Smedes in his first years of administering the School. Already on the faculty were the familiar, loved figures of Mrs. Iredell, Mademoiselle LeGal, and Miss Katie. The latter had entered Saint Mary's as a little girl in 1867, and from pupil had become teacher. Mr. Smedes himself was the science department.

The great event of the fall of 1877 was the marriage of Mr. Bennett Smedes to Henrietta Rhea Harvey. Back in 1872, Mr. John E. C. Smedes (a younger brother of Dr. Aldert) accepted the position of Principal of Saint Augustine's School for Colored People and brought his family to Raleigh. Among them was the future Mrs. Bennett Smedes. Of course no one was aware of this fact, not even Mr. Bennett and least of all "Miss Etta." But there she was, the oldest member of the family of Mr. and Mrs. John Smedes —member by adoption, that is. She was a native of Louisiana, on her mother's side a cousin of Mrs. John Smedes and on her father's side a grand-daughter of Governor Harvey of New Hampshire. The younger members of the John Smedes family were Eliza, twelve; Charlie, ten; Bancker, eight; Emilie, six; and Henrietta, three. As no building was yet provided for their occupancy at Saint Augustine's, Dr. Aldert had invited them to stay at Saint Mary's and this they did for two years, while Mr. John daily mounted his horse, Prince, and rode to his work at Saint Augustine's.

It isn't surprising that the acquaintance thus begun between Bennett Smedes and Henrietta Harvey should have ripened into a courtship culminating in marriage five years later. She was twenty-two years old when they met, a Titian beauty with red-brown eyes and a heavy suit of auburn hair—thinking not of marriage but of teaching the little cousins to whom she was as it were an older sister. But she was destined to be the companion of Mr. Smedes throughout the entire period of his rectorship of the school.

As the date set for the wedding approached, Mr. Smedes kept the girls on the anxious bench by announcing frequently his intention of being married during the ten-minute noon recess, so they would lose no time from their studies. However, nine o'clock on the morning of November 20, 1877, found the girls present in a body at Christ Church, with the assurance of ice-cream and a holiday ahead of them. The ceremony was performed by the rector of Christ Church, Reverend Matthias M. Marshall, assisted by Bishop Lyman. The bride was given away by Mr. John Smedes.

Mrs. Smedes was of a retiring nature and it was the timid girls like herself who each year soon learned to find refuge from their homesickness in the happy family over which she presided in the Rector's apartments. But she was not only "the friend of the lonesome" as she soon came to be called. She had a gift for feeding folks, and the faculty and the girls generally were her guests in small groups from time to time—and such chicken-salad suppers as she would set before them! Now and then in the hunting season it would be partridges, for Mr. Smedes was a notable hunter. The death of Ligon, one of his faithful hunting dogs, is noted in the *Muse,* November, 1882.

As in the 1860's and again in the '70's, so in the '80's we find a family of small children growing up under the shade of the great oak trees, and of course the girls delighted in making pets of them. There were Bessie and Margaret and their cousin Sadie Root (living across the street) of about the same age as themselves, and a few years later the twins, Mary and Helen, whom Aunt 'Liza Cook loved to take out in their double perambulator. "Us strikes a light," she would say proudly, "when us goes down town." And she was quite right about it, for the shining faces of these brown-eyed, yellow-haired twin babies kindled a responsive light in the faces of all who crossed their path.

Bessie, the eldest child, loved music, and Henrietta Smedes recalls that sometimes during her twilight practise-hour in the parlor the doors would open quietly and she would see a tiny figure slip in and curl herself up in the big sofa to listen to the classical music. But one September when the girls returned for the opening of school, little Bessie was missing from among their pets. God had taken her to himself.

The day scholars were in on pretty nearly everything in the days when Miss Lizzie Lee was one of them. She entered the school in '73 and her special companions on the daily walks to and from school were Lavine and Ellie Haywood and Eliza McKee. Girls didn't grow up at so early an age then as they do now, and there were few exciting distractions in the home, so the day pupils welcomed eagerly the association with the boarders and the good times they all had together. As some classes were held after dinner the parlor was turned over to the day scholars for dancing during the dinner hour—and how they did love it! On rainy days, however, Mr. Bennett would invite them into a basement room and call on the cook to serve them something hot. The day scholars opened their homes to the boarders and considerable freedom was allowed the girls in spending the day with friends in town.

In the school room Miss Lee recalls slates and pencils and mental arithmetic—no blackboards; also Mr. Bennett's experiments in his chemistry class—for instance, making her long golden curls stand out straight from her head.

"At this time Miss Katie was a member of the academic faculty, teaching French translation and arithmetic, and an excellent teacher she was," says Miss Lee, "always sweet, too, with lovely dark eyes and wavy hair." Her hair grew white with the passage of years, but it never lost its soft wave, nor her eyes their sparkle. One can imagine how they snapped when as a little girl of thirteen she climbed the high fence surrounding the grove, perched herself on the gatepost and made faces at the Yankees as they marched past. And one can also imagine her satisfaction when the punishment meted out to her (bread and water) was not for making faces at the Yankees but for being so unladylike as to climb up and sit on the gatepost.

Miss Katie was possessed by two supreme loyalties—the Confederacy and the Church. One wonders if this early experience did not serve to deepen that inborn devotion to the Confederate cause that everyone who ever knew her recognized as one of the influences that dominated her to the very end. What fun it was for her pupils when on February 12 every year she would ask them whose birthday it was, and without waiting for a reply would say, "Lincoln's. There—I've told you. Now forget it!" *Noblesse oblige* even when it costs, and there was nothing except Miss Katie's conscience that could get the best of her feelings—but that always did.

It was in 1873 that Emmie and Ella Tew from Charleston, South Carolina, and Eliza Mills from Clinton, Lousiana, entered Saint Mary's as pupils. Emmie and Ella were daughters of Colonel Tew who had lost his life in the Confederate Army. As the protegés of a Confederate Society they were sent to Saint Mary's, but the funds of the society gave out after a year or two, and Dr. Aldert and later Mr. Bennett kept the girls at Saint Mary's until they had each completed her course in the School. A devoted friendship was formed between these two girls and Eliza Mills which has lasted for nearly three-quarters of a century.

Eliza was a friend of the John Smedes family in Louisiana and was not long in following them to Raleigh, bringing her high-backed Saratoga trunk filled (as she writes us today) with "sturdy everyday garments and dainty Sunday finery." She was escorted by her young uncle, Mr. David Pipes, who after having supper at the School had to take his departure when Dr. Aldert laughingly told him that there was no room in his dove-cote for such as he. Until the day of his death in 1939 Mr. Pipes would tell with infinite zest and many embellishments how cruelly he suffered in being "turned out" of that place where at supper he had seen such a bewildering lot of beautiful girls.

Two outstanding girls of the late seventies came, one from the remote mountain fastness of Macon County and the other from the then almost equally remote town of Elizabeth City in the East. Letters to her mother from Fanny Siler of Franklin have been preserved by her son and daughter, Reverend Rufus Morgan and Mrs. Ester Freas. They touch upon many aspects of school life, giving glimpses of fellow students, of teachers, of the religious life, of fashions, fun, and recreation. I quote here and there from several of these letters:

"There are seventy-eight girls here—enough to make considerable noise I assure you. It is very fashionable to wear 'horseshoe breastpins' and hang horseshoes over the door for good luck. Somebody hung one over the kitchen door, and the girls asked Uncle Pim if he put it there. 'No, chile, de luck's wid de Lawd, and de ol' horseshoe ain gwine change it any.' . . . I don't think the girls dress extravagantly here. Of course it is much more than *we* are accustomed to, but from the homes most of them have and the character of the school, I think they are plain in their dressing. Some of them wear muslin or plain white during examinations until the last night when some wear bunting, or some such dress. Of course, some dress more—but I don't care! Sometimes some circumstance calls it up, but I am certainly far from being miserable over it."

She asks her mother to send her "a bonnet" for walking hours in the grove. "So much trouble to go to the fourth floor for a hat twice a day." (The slat bonnets, crocheted fascinators, and shawls were hung in the back hall of the main floor).... "Hallowe'en, and Mr. Smedes gave up the parlor to us and told us to enjoy ourselves. We danced to Mrs. Meares' delightful music, told fortunes, bobbed for apples. (I didn't care enough about my future husband to dip my face in the pan.)" A year or so later she was married. Rebe Smith, her beloved friend from Scotland Neck, was present at the marriage; Fanny had long wished that Rebe from the coastal plain could discover exactly what mountains were like.

"Mr. Smedes gives us only two days Christmas vacation —the girls minds are distracted, he says, by long vacations and he will try to make the season profitable and pleasant at the School. They are going to have something like an opera during the Christmas holidays. The piece is Cinderella. The girls are to have different costumes. They are Persian and are striking to say the least. The 'boys' will have red, blue, and yellow trousers, a short bright skirt reaching to the knees, red waists, and bright jackets with turbans that would delight a Cherokee Indian. All the old dresses in school have been hauled out. Gabrielle deRosset is to appear in one scene in a plaid silk wrapper of Mrs. Meares'. Someone asked her if it came out of the Ark. She said, 'No,' but she believed it was made for Mrs. Abraham. 'Fraulein' is to be Cinderella, and after her fairy godmother touches her, will be dressed in a beautiful blue silk covered with tarleton. Mrs. Meares asked me if I couldn't sing well enough to take part in it, but I declined. All the other girls except those dressed in mourning are in it. Sallie Pippen's voice is the best alto in the operetta. Four or five of the girls are going home for Christmas."

Fanny's references to the beloved Bishop Atkinson's calls at the School, on pupils and teachers alike, and the hospitality frequently extended to them by Bishop Lyman in his

THE REVEREND ALDERT SMEDES, FOUNDER OF SAINT MARY'S

Leading "his girls" from 1842 to 1877 in gentle but disciplined ways, Dr. Smedes was "the best qualified man to head a girls' school—there never was his superior."

Rules of St. Mary's School.

1. At the calling of the roll, morning and evening, every pupil must be present, unless prevented by sickness.

2. Every pupil must attend morning and evening prayers, and the daily services in the Chapel. If prevented by sickness, or any other cause, she must inform the lady who has charge of her Dormitory.

3. Pupils are required to be punctual at their meals, and must not leave the table without permission.

4. The practicing hours must be devoted exclusively to that duty; pupils must carefully avoid intruding upon one another in these hours.

5. No works of Fiction are to be read, excepting on Saturday, after the *duties* of the day are over, and then, only those that are approved of.

6. On Saturday evening every pupil must be present at the musical exercises, unless she has special permission to absent herself.

7. At least two hours a day must be appropriated by every pupil, to active exercise in the open air. Five times round the grove, twice a day, will be deemed a fulfilment of this requisition.

SCHOOL ROOM.

8. During the study hours, pupils are required to preserve perfect order. Talking, moving of seats, writing letters, and reading books not connected with their studies, are expressly forbidden.

9. The same order is to be observed during the other hours devoted to the duties of the School, not only in the School room, but wherever the pupil is permitted to pursue her studies.

VISITING, DRESS, &c.

10. Pupils are allowed to visit only on the monthly Saturday, and then, only at the house to which they have been specially invited; they are required to be at home by sundown.

RULES FROM THE *BULLETIN* OF 1860

"It is your part and duty confiding in the love and wisdom of the rules under which you are here to live, in the spirit of childlike obedience to submit yourself implicitly to their control." From the *School Manual*.

stately home in Raleigh, where he delighted to show them personally the beautiful treasures of his art gallery, make delightful reading, but space does not permit of further quoting from these interesting letters.

It was Blanche Griffin (now Mrs. Oscar Temple) who came from the East in 1878, via the Dismal Swamp Canal and Norfolk! But Blanche found herself well rewarded for the long trek—as her mother had before her. Years afterwards she sent her daughters all the way from Denver, Colorado, to get the training and find the joy that Saint Mary's had given to her. She comes east every year or two, and when she and Sally Manning Venable get together in Chapel Hill their conversation just naturally turns to their school days and the lifelong friends they made there—among them Fanny Huger of Charleston, Carrie Ihrie of Pittsboro, and Alice Pettigrew of Cresswell whom they picture as wearing her high-buttoned shoes indiscriminately on either foot.

Blanche must have been a rewarding pupil, for her writings adorn the pages of *The Muse,* especially in translations of German stories, and there was scarcely ever a Saturday evening or a Commencement program on which she did not appear in music, recitation, or a German play. Judging by these programs one might think that Saint Mary's was a Language and Music School, for French, German, and even Latin recitations and plays appear as frequently as do those in English, and music was emphasized then as now.

Saint Mary's was well in the van in the matter of ensemble playing, which is now coming so prominently into vogue in the musical world. There was hardly even a program that did not include an overture to one of the great operas, arranged for two pianos and four players, or a concerto for two pianos and two players. The fine team work thus called for was greatly enjoyed.

There was no glee club in those days, but the whole

school had the benefit of practising for chapel services. Since these were often fully choral, a Saint Mary's girl of those days must have felt quite at home in later years wherever she might attend service. The psalter was chanted antiphonally, and Sue Cuningham (now Mrs. Lewis Walker of Milton, N. C.) recalls that since the whole psalter for the day was sung, there was naturally grumbling among the girls, who had, of course, to stand throughout. Sometimes her own back would nearly break, she says. Indeed, now and then a back would give way entirely, and there would be a ripple of excitement among the girls to discover whether it was Annie deRosset or Chip Roberts or Lizzie Battle who had fainted and was being revived and helped into the fresh air.

Today it is interesting to recall that hats were not worn at either the daily or the Sunday services except in the case of the Holy Communion service on the first Sunday in the month. In preparation for that service Mr. Smedes used to have a brief but solemn service that we all loved to attend. He often invited Dr. Marshall of Christ Church or Mr. Rich of the Good Shepherd to make the address. The former moved us deeply by the beauty of his countenance and his rich voice, and the latter by his earnest eloquence. In order that the girls might have an intelligent interest in diocesan affairs, Mr. Smedes would have us attend a session of the Convocation when it met in Raleigh, and sometimes several of the clergy would visit the School and hold a service for us in the Chapel—which always meant an oyster supper to follow.

Of course we had a missionary society, in which both students and faculty were organized for work. We took orders for sewing and fancy work. We had mite chests, too, which we filled largely by fines for delinquencies in table manners. Besides our gifts in support of home, domestic, and foreign missions we gave generously to St. John's Hospital

WAR TIMES AND AFTER

(as "Rex" was then called) and to the fund for the poor of Raleigh. But Saint Mary's was also well represented in the offering of lives for service in missionary work. A very striking example is that of Cecilia Dabney Foster of Louisburg, N. C. She was a pupil at Saint Mary's in 1851 and was baptized in the Chapel at that time. After marrying and then being left a widow she joined the Sisterhood of the Good Shepherd, and eventually returning to North Carolina as "Sister Cecilia," organized the first work of this kind in the parish of Saint James' Church, Wilmington, where she served for twenty years. Less spectacular, perhaps, but equally fruitful was the work of Pattie Hicks (Mrs. Buford) among the Negroes living in her neighborhood in the mountains of Virginia. The foreign field also had an appeal for Saint Mary's girls, and we find Julia Gregg of Texas teaching in Africa, and Nellie Cole of Nashotah, Wisconsin, going to Japan. These of course are only examples of the laborers who go forth from Saint Mary's to labor in the Master's field which is the world.

It was a great day for Saint Mary's when in 1876 she issued her first school publication. Since it came into being under the auspices of the Music Department, and its joint editors signed themselves "Euterpe" and "Calliope," it was inevitable that it should be named *Saint Mary's Muse*. Its cover was in Saint Mary's blue. There is no hint as to the identity of these two Muses, which isn't surprising since Ella Tew Lindsay of the class of '79 now reveals the fact that "Euterpe" was none other than Mr. Sanborn! Well, he was a "magerful" man who always was whatever he chose to be. The graceful writing of Calliope came from the delightful mind of Mrs. Meares. The publication must have been a valuable asset in keeping constantly before the public the advantages offered by the school, and also in affording a medium of advertising for the merchants of Raleigh.

Following shortly upon the publication of *The Muse* came the organization in June, 1879, of the Alumnae Association. The officers elected at the initial meeting were Mrs. William Boylan of Raleigh, president, Mrs. Catherine deR. Meares, vice-president, and Miss Katie McKimmon, secretary and treasurer. A constitution was drawn up by Mrs. R. S. Tucker, Mrs. W. R. Cox, and Mrs. George Snow, all of Raleigh, and an annual membership fee of one dollar was decided upon, the fund to be devoted to the founding of one or more scholarships for needy daughters of alumnae or others whose claim might be judged to be equally strong. Mr. Smedes authorized the statement that two hundred and fifty dollars a year would provide a full scholarship covering board and tuition. The fund was to be raised and maintained as a tribute to Dr. Aldert Smedes, and a year later it was announced that the first scholarship had been duly awarded to a "young lady who will do honor to Saint Mary's." A committee was also appointed charged with the responsibility of advising former students of the organization of the Association and promoting the formation of local chapters. The organizers of the Alumnae Association were of course all of them loyal alumnae of the school. Not all of them, however, had the enviable distinction that belonged to Mrs. Tucker—Florence Eugenia Perkins, of Pactolus, Pitt County. Her six daughters, six granddaughters, and one great-granddaughter have swelled the ranks of the school from generation to generation, from kindergarten to "finishing," and are still represented on the list of active members of the Alumnae Association.

One of my most vivid memories is of the first class to be formally graduated. It was the Class of 1879. They wore white organdy dresses on Commencement Day, simply made, but with a *train*. Adopted by the class of 1879, this graceful feature of the graduation dress held sway until 1881, after which fate, or fashion, decreed its abolition.

There were only five graduates, but they were worthy forerunners of the large classes of today. Lucy P. Battle was the valedictorian, Ella G. Tew had the salutatory, which she delivered in French, and the other members were Eliza Smedes, Kate Cheshire, and Josie Myers. Of course all of these were outstanding in their classes, or they would not have been found at the chancel rail on Commencement Day receiving the coveted diplomas from Mr. Smedes. In 1929 the class reassembled in the grove in celebration of its fiftieth anniversary, and summoned Miss Czarnomska, then in her eightieth year, to meet with them. At the Alumnae luncheon that day these old ladies made a great hit. Each one had something to say, and the girls listened openmouthed to the spicy talks that gave them a new conception of what the fiftieth anniversary of one's graduation may be like.

Another vivid memory centers about Fraulein Blume, the voice teacher who was added to the faculty in the fall of '79. Mr. Sanborn found her in the Royal Conservatory of Leipzig, and she proved to be a wonderful find. Young as she was (only eighteen), she had sung in the world-renowned Gewandhaus Concerts. Her glorious voice, her broken English, her friendly charm—all combined to make her the central figure about whom we clustered with romantic enthusiasm. When Christmas came she introduced us to a Christmas tree devised in true German fashion. When the parlor doors were flung open on Christmas night, and we marched in singing a carol, we beheld a holly tree reaching from floor to ceiling ablaze with lights and hung with gifts for everybody. A thing of light and beauty and loving kindness! The tree so planted in the heart of Saint Mary's took root and still lives to bring merriment to the girls of today.

Naturally everybody wanted to take lessons from Fraulein, whether or not she was blessed with a voice; but there were some lovely voices among the girls—not one, however, quite so lovely as Fanny Sharp's. When at Commencement she appeared upon the stage and with irresistible charm sang "Jamie, Dear," the heart of every one of the "Jamies" banked in crowds against the walls and in the windows of the parlor must have been set a-pounding while they applauded and brought her back for an encore. None of them, however, was blessed with a poetic father except Bancker Smedes, who no doubt felt sure that he had won out over them all when her autograph album carried in his handwriting the following verse:

> "Tell, Heavenly Muse, (Euterpe is thy name
>   Among the Nine, and music is thy care)
> Tell me the sweetest note that ever came
>   From heaven to distant earth!" So ran my prayer.
> The goddess thus replied: "Earthward this harp
>   Incarnate sweetness sent erewhile—F. Sharp"

But after all Bancker lost out, and it was Mr. Thomas Roberts Jernigan of Harrellsville, N. C., who captured Fanny as his bride and whisked her away to Japan and China where he represented our Government as consul during President Cleveland's administration.

Autograph albums were the joy and the fad of the day, and if our lives have not been as "happy and free as the dancing waves on the deep blue sea," or if they have not been blessed with "just enough clouds to make a glorious sunset," it certainly could not have been for the lack of such well-wishing on the part of schoolmates when the sad June day of partings rolled around.

The delightful Ravenel twins of Charleston, Alice and Jennie, belong to this period. The faculty welcomed them with rather an uneasy feeling; but if they deserved the reputation for unruliness that preceded them, Saint Mary's worked a miracle in them from the moment they entered her doors. They were models of docility and good behavior towards the faculty, and fairy godmothers to friends among their schoolmates who were less blessed than they with worldly goods. Among their coterie of friends were Maggie Jones of Tuscaloosa, Ala., Sally Young of Henderson, N. C., the rather poverty-stricken "two Emmies" (McVea and Smedes) and Florence Slater—and how joyfully we did welcome them back to the School for their almost annual visits! Jennie's album, like Fanny Sharp's, bore a poetic inscription which ran like this:

> *Jane, or Jennie, matters little*
> *Not a single jot or tittle*
> *Which her name is, how you spell it.*
> *Name the rose amiss—now smell it;*
> *'Tis the sweetest still of flowers!*
> *So in fair Saint Mary's bowers*
> *Know the happy swains who meet her*
> *Change of name can't make her sweeter;*
> *Still they each would fain implore her,*
> *Change it. So would her adorer!*
> *(Charles Watts Smedes)*

But she didn't. They lived for many years and were always "the Ravs" to us—loyal and devoted "old Saint Mary's girls."

There is also Alice Winston (Mrs. F. S. Spruill of Rocky Mount) who claims the distinction of being the youngest girl ever to come to Saint Mary's as a boarder. She came at the age of eight. Perhaps it was to save her from being spoiled by her big brothers that her mother sent her all the way from Windsor to Saint Mary's. The distinguished Winston brothers from Bertie County did not monopolize the family honors, for Alice achieved the distinction of membership on the Board of Trustees of Saint Mary's and also of being president of the Diocesan Branch of the Woman's Auxiliary.

There was that delightful group from New Bern, Lillian Roberts whose dance music no one could resist, and Lalla, her cousin, whose stammer only added spice to her witty remarks; and Jennie and Nannie Hughes, whose gorgeous reddish gold braids of hair proclaimed their presence even when Jennie wasn't singing so joyously about "the little summer shower that had lasted quite an hour"; and with them their constant companion from Wilmington, pretty blond Kate Lord who chose to study Latin because of the teacher whose loveliness of person and character thrilled her.

Kate must have been a discriminating young woman, because long years afterwards this teacher, Eliza Smedes, was thus described by one who knew her intimately: "She was both sweet and strong—characteristics not often found together; broadminded, understanding, and an independent thinker, gifted, cultured, delightful. Her mental and spiritual attainments were so well balanced that a rare soul was the inevitable result."

The mention of Eliza Smedes instantly calls to mind her two life-long friends, Ella Tew and Gabrielle deRosset. They were on the faculty together for a brief time after their graduation. We who were in Miss Tew's dormitory have carried with us through life the memory of her delightful readings during the Sunday afternoon "quiet hour." When the reading came to the death of our favorite hero Guy (of *The Heir of Redclyffe*) we stifled our sobs but we could not eliminate the traces of our tears before the bell rang and we found our grief-stricken way to the chapel for service.

As for Gabrielle deGondin deRosset, she was proud of her name and the ancestry that it betokened, and she lived

WAR TIMES AND AFTER

up to them. She was proud, too, to recall that at the age of six she had sat upon the knees of Lord Lytton and Thackeray in their homes in England. She was a tiny person, but the Colonial Dames of North Carolina espied her and elected her president of their society, from which position she served them with éclat and delighted them with her sparkling wit.

During the early years of Mr. Smedes' administration three notable changes were made in the physical equipment of the school. A new organ was bought in the summer of '79, and for its accommodation a transept was built which added greatly to the architectural beauty of the Chapel. The transept was designed by the Reverend Johannes A. Oertel, to whose artistic genius the Church in North Carolina is indebted for a number of religious paintings.

On returning to school in September, '81, the girls found hidden far away among the trees a real infirmatory with a real nurse in charge, Miss Jennie Coffin. Miss Jennie was not a trained nurse, but, far better, she was a born nurse, who combined with her natural ability a fund of humor that made the girls welcome rather than dread a sojourn away off yonder in the infirmary. For minor ailments we enjoyed the ministrations of Sister Eliza, the gentle deaconess from Long Island. She was an aunt of Miss Czarnomska, who came to spend the winter with her. With beef tea and wine, pills and nostrums, she coddled the girls and kept them well—and spoiled.

Finally the long cherished aspirations for an art building began to be realized in '83, when the foundations for it were laid. The building was completed the following year, but alas for the high hopes of Miss Hyde and her students in '84! One short year later the building was burned to the ground; but being well insured, it was quickly replaced.

I recall the year when china painting was all the rage,

and the delicate cups and saucers were sent North to be baked. I recall, too, some of the girls whose beautiful work was acclaimed by the throngs who crowded the studios on "Art Evenings." For instance, in decorative art, there were Lula Tucker, Maud Cuningham, Mary Osborne, and Sallie Carter; while Easdale Shaw excelled in water colors, and Mary Lyde Hicks in oils. Mary Lyde (Mrs. Marshall Williams of Faison, N. C.) is well known today as a portrait painter.

There were many minor changes during these same years, though all of them were great in the estimation of enthusiastic girls. Double alcoves gave way to single ones ("a girl's very own") and wood stoves to Baltimore heaters; new walks made access easy to chapel, infirmary, and kitchen. There was new flooring (oh joy, for dancing feet!) and the music room was carpeted and decorated, and miniature copies of Thorwaldsen and other Danish sculptures were found on the tables. Electric bells jingled cheerily in every class and practice room at fixed hours, and the telephone connected us with the outside world. The "long room" was converted into the coziest of libraries where many a distracted composition writer would fly for quiet thought and study.

Classroom work was supplemented by delightful evenings spent in the cozy atmosphere of a teacher's sitting room. Here the seniors gathered every Friday evening to enjoy the reading of poems, plays, and sometimes novels, while they occupied their fingers with handiwork of some kind. Rickrack trimming was the fad of the day; enough was made in a month to reach around the equator, it seemed. But if one came empty-handed, she would be provided with strips of newspaper from which to fashion "lamplighters," a very useful article since each gas jet throughout the buildings had to be lighted individually. We probably soon forgot our experiences with Dante and his Inferno and would find it hard to explain Browning's poetry, but we will never forget the joy and inspiration of those happy evenings spent together. Sometimes Miss Czarnomska or Mrs. Iredell would hand the book to one of us to read, and the sound of Mittie Dowd's mellifluous voice was always a joy.

The faculty was quite as indispensable in our play as in our work, for the girls of those days were not the independent creatures that they are today. Our Hallowe'en games (charades and dumb crambo) and our Thanksgiving phantom party were often led by the teachers. Miss Dora Hyde was a thrilling gypsy fortune-teller and dear Mlle. LeGal in comic costume was something to remember.

The Commencement of '81 stands out in my memory with special clearness. We felt as though our world was tumbling about our ears for not only was our dear Mrs. Meares leaving us but also Mr. Sanborn and his able assistants, Fraulein Blume, Miss Eliza Smedes and Miss Gabrielle deRosset, with whose enthusiastic co-operation he had been able to raise the Music Department to a high standard of excellence. The fine work of these teachers culminated in the best of Commencement programs. *The Muse* notes that Mr. Sanborn must have felt more than gratified at the results of his work, and so must the following pupils who received from him Certificates of Distinction in music: Kate Sutton, Sally Young, Emilie Smedes, Mamie Settle, Maggie Jones, and Fannie Hardin.

Our prima donna, Fanny Sharp, was awarded a "superb book of Tennyson's poems set to music by the most eminent modern composers."

There were only two graduates in this year of 1881. The salutatorian was Minnie Albertson. Mamie Settle was the valedictorian; her recitation of Tennyson's *Dream of Fair*

Women would seem to have been prophetic of the effective role that she later played as Director of Elocution and Athletics at the North Carolina College for Women.

A bit of mystery surrounded the departure of Mr. Sanborn and Miss Blume. No one seemed to know what the plans of either of them were for the next year—they simply weren't coming back. Miss Smedes was setting sail for Germany, to study, and she had promised to act as foreign correspondent for *The Muse.* When she took passage on the Steamship Meckar of the North German Lloyd Line, whom should she encounter as travelling companions but *Mr. and Mrs.* Sanborn! The cat was out of the bag at last.

In June of 1880 Miss Czarnomska had accepted a position at Packer Institute, her Alma Mater; but on the resignation of Mrs. Meares she accepted Mr. Smedes invitation to return to Saint Mary's in the capacity of Lady Principal. Dr. Kursteiner became head of the Music Department, Miss Nanette Stone, the vocal teacher, and Miss Dora Hyde succeeded Miss Norwood in the Art Department.

Contact was close between school and town. A Philharmonic Society was started by Dr. Kursteiner. Saint Mary's girls attended a concert given by Peace Institute in Tucker Hall, and confirmation services at Saint Augustine's as well as at Christ Church and the Good Shepherd. Receptions were given in Fair Week—dancing, promenading, small talk; callers all day Friday until the bell rang at six o'clock when weary Ellen at the front door would sigh, "Study hour at last, ain't I glad." Of course the "Bingham boys" played a leading part on such gala days as these. They complimented Saint Mary's by giving a special drill in front of the school, and Saint Mary's returned the compliment with a reception to them.

We had every opportunity of becoming really learned for there were lecture courses galore, and perhaps some of the information that sifted through our brains found lodg-

WAR TIMES AND AFTER

ment. At all events we enjoyed the contacts with the distinguished lecturers. One of our favorites was the State Geologist, Professor William C. Kerr, who must have enlightened us considerably about the geology of North Carolina for he gave us a course of six lectures, though it may be we got most out of the walks with him to the graphite mine.

I am approaching the end of my period, and it seems rather like holy ground that I am treading upon, for my story is woven about the Class of 1884, of which I am the sole surviving member. There were seven of us, and the acquaintance begun among us four years before had rapidly ripened into devoted friendships. We had worked and studied and read together; we had played and prayed together; we were united by a common devotion to Saint Mary's and Mr. Smedes and our teachers. And in recalling these friendships, Florence Slater is always included, for although she had graduated two years earlier, she was one of us from the beginning.

Easter was always the supreme day of the year for us, with every thought centered upon the Chapel and its glorious services. No one was allowed to go home, and I don't believe any of us ever wanted to, for the whole school was trained to sing the full choral service. Saturday was busy with preparations: the gathering of wild flowers from "the penitentiary woods," the collecting of blossoming shrubs from the gardens of friendly neighbors, the dressing of the Chapel—and the trying on of our Easter hats as belated bandboxes arrived from Miss Reese's Shop. Just at dusk came the solemn service of preparation in the Chapel when we sang "Shadows Falling" while we looked forward to the same music early the next morning when it would be "Sunlight Streaming" on a world made glorious by the Resurrection. A beautiful breakfast awaited us—flowers, of course, and at every place a card from the Rector and a handpainted egg from the Lady Principal.

In May the great violinist, Remenji, gave a concert in Tucker Hall. Of course, Saint Mary's turned out in full force to hear him and the next morning sent flowers to him at the hotel. Whereupon he sent a note saying that "her ladyship, the violin," would shortly be up to thank us in person. Upon his arrival he talked to us in the parlor and then, leading the way into the schoolroom, took his beautiful little instrument from its case, and played and played to us. After which we seniors gathered close about him in Miss Czarnomska's cosy sitting room where we served glasses of orange juice, and the school's two oldest babies, Bessie and Margaret, came shyly in, hand in hand, to see the great maestro.

Of course there never was before nor has been since a Commencement like that of 1884. And didn't the twenty-six-year-old magnolia tree burst into blossom that year for the first time in its life—just in our honor, was Miss Czarnomska's verdict. She also said that she had long waited for the girls who could fill the leading parts in the moving drama *King Rene's Daughter* and at last her hopes were fulfilled in Carrie Mathewson, Alice Hagood, and Emilie McVea.

We were on tenterhooks until the class pins were in hand. Quite appropriately the design was a ladder, since our motto was *Gradatim,* meaning (I interpret for the benefit of the non-classical students of today) *step by step.* In our state of exaltation because we had successfully passed all of our examinations, I think we felt as though we had already attained the laurel wreath that surmounted the gold ladder.

Belle Graves, the youngest member of the class, was valedictorian. Her brilliant examination paper on Spherical Trigonometry and Mathematical Astronomy carried her triumphantly over her competitors. Lovely Annie Phillips was our salutatorian. But each member of the class was said to be first in something: Lizzie Battle and Belle Graves in mathematics; Alice Hagood in elocution and singing; Emmie Smedes in French and Emmie McVea in composition and *belles lettres;* Mittie Dowd in metaphysics and music and Annie Phillips in painting and music. (I myself would say that Mittie was first in *charm* and Annie in *sweetness.*) However, in spite of our "firsts," we were not all destined to be career women. Three of us found our niche within the walls of the home.

Belle Graves became a leader in educational and religious work, and was the Principal of the Church School at Valle Crucis. As for Elizabeth Dancy Battle, Emilie Watts McVea and Martha Dowd, they simply could not escape the destiny to which they were surely foreordained, that of inspired teachers and leaders in wider fields of the educational world.

Concerning two of this group, while they were yet working together on the faculty of Saint Mary's to which Mr. Smedes had called them, I quote the impressions of one of their devoted students:

"Miss Battle," she writes, "was Lady Principal when I went to Saint Mary's. She was twenty-six years old, very handsome and distinguished, with a terrible ease in sarcasm—and to older eyes very delicate. She looked like a blooded racer, a little too fine-drawn, pulling to get away. She was subject to severe headaches, and her Latin class would sometimes be called to recite in her bedroom in East Rock house. I can see her now, propped up on her couch, evidently in great suffering, and forcing her brilliant mind to listen to our blunderings and to correct and guide them into something approaching her own fastidious scholarship. Young as she was she ruled that large school justly and admirably, and never commanded less than profound respect. She was also greatly loved.

"Miss McVea was an equally vigorous teacher, but everybody adored her. She was so big and jolly with her scorn of sham or conventionality, her tremendous vitality, her enthusiasm in friendship, her intense ambition for each one of her students to get out—out of herself and into a bigger world where she would grow for the sake of others. She used to wear big, heavy shoes like a boy's and a badly made gray flannel dress like an ill-fitting wrapper—but wherever she moved things came alive! She hated any personal attention. Once we got up a little manuscript news sheet in Miss Katie's dormitory, and tried our hand at limericks on all the teachers, but Miss McVea's name was unrhymable and she firmly refused to tell what "W" stood for. However, some canny soul sent a day student scouting in Raleigh, and our edition came out with:

> *There's a lady who's just within call,*
> *Who the editors much did appal:*
> *She declared to her name*
> *No poem should give fame—*
> *But "Watts" in a name, after all?*

She had to admit she didn't mind that. I saw her twenty years later, when she was President of Sweet Briar College. I marveled then how we girls could ever have thought her 'ugly.' Why she was not only wise and strong—she was beautiful!"

The gentle and beloved Miss Dowd stayed on at Saint Mary's and became the head of the Music Department. There are windows now in the Chapel sacred to the memory of Lizzie and Mittie, and in the Library Emilie McVea speaks to the girls through many volumes that are sacred to her memory, as is indicated by the bookplate bearing her name.

Florence Slater was the last of these brilliant Saint Mary's girls of the early eighties to pass away. She died on

From a sketch made by Lou Sullivan about 1864.

SAINT MARY'S CHAPEL, BUILT IN 1855

The artist's perspective may not be true, but all Saint Mary's girls understand why she, as she said, loved "the antique looking little chapel."

YOUNG LADIES OF 1869

Time out was taken on the steps of Main Building, from "English, Latin, French, Music, Drawing, Painting, Ornamental Needlework."

From the painting done in 1846 by William Hart

BISHOP IVES ADMINISTERING THE RITE OF CONFIRMATION

"There seems to be some doubt as to the identity of the girls in the portrait."

January 22, 1941, and left to Saint Mary's a legacy to be used for the upbuilding of the Science Department. She may well be accorded the highest place as a scientist among Saint Mary's girls of the first one hundred years of the life of the School.

But on that June day in 1884 the future was all unknown. Commencement was the biggest thing in our lives.

Finally we found ourselves together in the Chapel for the last time, and thrilling—can you believe it—to the strains of the "Hallelujah Chorus." In his brief charge to the graduating class Mr. Smedes took as his theme "Here have we no continuing city," leading up to his final word: "God grant that in His heavenly courts your voices and ours may one day join in the eternal Hallelujah!" We passed out of the doors of the Chapel singing "Jerusalem, high tower thy glorious walls" and bearing in our hands the sign-manual of the school that we were equipped at least in some measure to become worthwhile members of society.

3

Long Dresses—Long Tresses
1885-1900

By Alice Dugger Grimes

IN 1885 THE Main Building in Saint Mary's grove was of three stories and basement, with a rather small front porch. In the basement were three classrooms, a large dining room, a smaller one for the Smedes' children, a large store room, a butler's pantry, and a long hall. The dining room was large and well ventilated. One of the tables was reserved for those studying French, the conversation throughout the meal being in that language.

The first floor of the Main Building contained a broad hall leading to the spacious parlor on the right, to the equally spacious schoolroom on the left, and to a smaller hall in the rear which led into the sitting room.

There were no rugs of any kind on the parlor floor; a rather large table with a red cover, around which the teachers sat, centered each corner of the room, and upholstered settees for the girls lined the walls. There were also a handsome horsehair davenport with a very large mirror hanging above it, a glass paneled case containing books and curios, and two beautiful console tables. Over one of these tables hung the portrait of Bishop Ravenscroft; over the other was the portrait of Bishop Ives. Two concert grand pianos added their splotches of ebony to the beauty of the room, a room whose walls were almost covered with fine oil paintings collected from many sources by the Smedes' family. Over the mantel to the north hung a portrait of Dr. Aldert Smedes; over the one to the south hung a portrait of Mrs. Aldert Smedes, with her quaint lace headdress.

The schoolroom contained modern desks for two. Upon the eastern wall was a long blackboard on which was written every Friday the Bible lesson for the following week, quotations to be memorized and recited. Mrs. Iredell taught the class at this time.

The rear hall was given over to the girls' everyday wraps, hung on rows of hooks. These required wraps were shawls, so ugly and so disliked by the girls, and overshoes, never where they were left.

A flight of stairs from the main hall led to the second floor. The eastern half of this floor contained the living quarters of Mr. and Mrs. Smedes, their children, and Miss Annie Harvey, sister of Mrs. Smedes. It had been the Rector's Apartment since the founding of Saint Mary's. At this time it consisted of the living room and Mr. Smedes' study, three large bedrooms and a smaller one. This study of Mr. Smedes' was also his office—the walls lined with books, his desk in the center of the room—and the only telephone of the school was here.

The hall next to the Smedes' apartment at the head of the stairs was a broad nook with cases filled with books. This was the school library which contained at that time only a few thousand volumes, but Mr. Smedes' large private library was at the disposal of the girls for reference work at all times. In this hall every Saturday morning Mrs. Iredell gave out the books, stamps, and school supplies for the week.

The western side of this floor contained the two large rooms of the Lady Principal, Miss Czarnomska, the two rooms of Mrs. Iredell, and the "sick room" as it was called. Mrs. Iredell's rooms adjoined those of Miss Czarnomska on the west. The larger room was lovely with its old mahogany furniture and choice bric-à-brac. Mrs. Iredell sitting in this room, surrounded by its lovely furnishings and portraits, was the embodiment of every virtue of the true southern lady, and her influence was thoroughly typical of the kind expected along every line at Saint Mary's of that day, a quiet lady being paramount to a "blue stocking" or a career seeker. Admiring Mrs. Iredell exceedingly, I did so long to be like her! Her influence for the attainment of higher things was felt without exception by every girl at Saint Mary's during her long regime.

Up another flight of stairs and we were on the third floor, the floor containing the two junior dormitories, both excellently ventilated and lighted by many large windows.

These dormitories were divided by partitions six feet high into single alcoves, giving each girl complete privacy. In each one was a bowl, pitcher, and tin foot-tub, our bathing outfit; and on Wednesday and Saturday nights hot water was brought in huge tubs to the rear hall on this floor for the semi-weekly hot bath to be taken in our alcoves.

The single beds were primitive, built stationary against the alcoves, without springs and with the mattress lying upon the slats; but the sleep of healthy youth came to each of us quickly, the rising bell at six in the morning being the daily *bête noir*.

The teacher's alcove was much larger than those for the girls; her bed and other furnishings, a little less primitive, were within the alcove.

Each one of us took pride in decorating her alcove and

enjoyed tremendously the little, tight bouquets of homey flowers our washer-women brought to us on Saturday mornings along with our laundry. This laundry was done by approved colored women in Oberlin, a nearby settlement. So friendly were we on these Saturday mornings, so merry as we darned stockings or sewed on buttons, with our long tresses often frowsing around our shoulders after a shampoo!

The girls gathered in the parlor in Main Building every morning at seven o'clock for roll call by the Lady Principal and prayers by Mr. Smedes. Breakfast was around seven-fifteen, and light luncheon was informally served from the storeroom at eleven. I'll wager every Saint Mary's girl of that period remembers the three crackers and the one apple, though sometimes that apple changed into a piece of cheese, a generous lump of brown sugar or a slice of broiled roast beef. But not often!

The fare, though not elaborate, was good. Mr. Smedes never bought anything for the table except the best quality. There was good service, too, and good cooks were always in the kitchen. The kitchen was typically southern, being away from the house, connected by a covered way. Yet the biscuits were always hot and the Saturday morning battercakes, too, really melted the butter. Right now I can hear Alfreda Eppes of City Point, Virginia, seated at the senior table, make her oft-repeated and giggled-at remark, as the plate of batter-cakes was passed to her, "Oh, these have been near the fire." (Alfreda, by the way, married an English Officer of very high rank, and went to live in India.)

Grace was said by Mr. Smedes at the beginning of each meal, all standing, and at dinner before and after the meal.

The first studying of the day began in the schoolroom immediately after breakfast. "Miss Katie" always presided over this period. After a brisk walk in the grove we answered a bell at nine for the opening hour of the school. There was a short service in the chapel, which every student was required to attend. Three days a week there followed the Bible class, held in the schoolroom, and on the other two we went to the parlor for Dr. Kursteiner's chorus class. There were periods of forty-five minutes each for recitation, study, music, and art, continuing until three o'clock, with an interim for the eleven o'clock lunch.

One morning when the bell rang for this eleven o'clock snack, the storeroom was unlocked and the housekeeper pleasantly presided amid the crackers and apples; but no girls. Minutes passed; no girls. Finally the housekeeper's watch told her it was door-locking time—still no girls—what could have happened? The next day the storeroom door was opened as usual. A mere handful strolled in before closing time. A larger number came the next day, and before the week ended all was normal in the storeroom. The leader of the "strike" was said to have been a handsome, high-spirited girl from Texas.

Dinner, at three, was awaited most eagerly, for the first mail of the day was then distributed. It was quite an honor to be asked to distribute these letters, and for many months Mollie Sargeant had this honor. A Texan, she had come with her father to North Carolina to be entered at Saint Mary's for a three-year duration, and there was to be no home-going in the meantime.

Soup was not a popular dish with the girls, as it was served every day. They dubbed it "the substance of things hoped for, the evidence of things not seen." Tuesday night was gingerbread night, Thursday was dessert day, and Sunday night supper meant a large cake for each table and lovely canned fruit. With the warm days of the early fall and late spring came ice cream for Sunday dinner, and there were strawberries for lunch many days during May, and just as much ice cream as one wished on Commencement day.

In the afternoon there were many kinds of recreation, tennis being the prime favorite. At six began the evening study hour. Supper was at seven.

The happiest gathering that took place in the big basement dining room was the feast given every year to the girls by Mrs. Smedes at the end of the winter examinations. Chicken salad—just as much as you wanted—beaten biscuits, pickles, olives, fruits of all kinds, and hot chocolate. Mrs. Smedes as hostess was deluged with genuine thanks. How pretty each girl looked, dressed in her very best and so thoroughly, smilingly happy!

"Aunt Ellen," the dish-washer, with her very young daughter, seemed always to be standing in the butler's pantry wiping dishes as we passed the open door. The little daughter could sometimes be persuaded to sing, if you could call it singing, the classic:

> *Uh, ranktum, tanktum,*
> *Uh, going to the fair*
> *Uh, see Paulina*
> *Uh, curl her hair,*

accompanied by a unique shuffling of feet, always bringing laughter from the girls who were so honored.

Into the parlor the girls would go after the schedule of the day. There would be prayers by Mr. Smedes and the distribution of the evening mail. And then, light of heart and light of feet, the girls would begin to dance under the compelling strains of Miss Clench's music. Miss Clench was one of the most efficient music teachers ever to have been at Saint Mary's. She was a graduate of the Stuttgart

Conservatory of Music, Canadian born, and an English woman through and through. Many of the girls too would play for the dancing. Lillian Homesly of Shelby was a prime favorite. So was Miss Dowd.

On Saturday evenings musicals were often held in the parlor. On these nights the girls dressed themselves in their best bib and tucker and the parlor became a gala scene.

Commencement exercises were always held in the parlor. A raised platform was built and made attractive with flowers, vines, and other decorations.

Of the people who lived in Main Building, the Smedes family require first mention—Mr. and Mrs. Smedes, arm in arm, he in his Prince Albert, as the frock coat was called in those days, and she in her black silk dress and black silk coat, walking through the grove on their afternoon strolls to town. Then there were three small girls, Margaret, Mary and Helen, and also Miss Annie, their aunt. The twins had chickens, cats, dogs, goats, and old "Charlie Horse"; they had everything, with Carrie, the little darkie, to look after them and their live-stock.

Mr. Smedes was especially solicitous concerning the girls' health. Often, after they had gone from the dining room, he made the rounds of the tables to see what and how they were eating and questioned Miss Annie, the housekeeper, concerning their likes and dislikes.

He also showed many pleasing attentions to the girls. At that time mail was not delivered at Saint Mary's, so every day Mr. Smedes drove quite a distance to the Post Office to get the mail. On pretty days he would invite some girl to enjoy the ride with him, and often at dinner he would announce, especially if the day were fine, that a carriage and pair of horses would be at the disposal of a mentioned girl for a long drive around town, she to choose her companion.

Mrs. Smedes lived a very retired life at Saint Mary's, but she knew the poor and needy far beyond its acres. Many a layette came from her capable fingers, as well as food and medicine, for the expected baby in homes of dire poverty. She was deeply loyal, and pretence was abhorent to her. She was a solace to the homesick girls; they seemed to gravitate to her. Knowing her well, I loved her dearly.

Miss Czarnomska, the daughter of a Polish count, was very handsome and of dominant characteristics, highly educated, outstanding in any assemblage. Many of the girls stood in awe of her, but any girl with an open mind learned from her things not written in books—just her presence inspired a desire to improve along every line. She left Saint Mary's to accept a chair at Smith College, later going abroad to study further at Göttingen University.

The "sick room" was presided over by Miss Anne Saunders, a typical southern lady, strictly unreconstructed, a sister of Col. William H. Saunders, then Secretary of the State of North Carolina. She always wore black, and her costumes were those of a former era, even to her bonnets. The sick room was for girls with minor ailments; if really sick they were sent to the infirmary, a small cottage to the rear, with a trained nurse, if that were the physician's orders. Dr. Peter Hines of Raleigh was then the school physician. He was an imposing looking man with a most kindly face and kindly manner. The health of the girls was remarkably good and I remember no outbreak of illness of any severity during my stay of several years.

The teacher who presided over the west junior dormitory when I first knew the dormitory was Miss Steinbrenner. She read to us nightly. Perhaps that was one reason we all liked her. Lovely Kate Steadman of Wilmington, with her abundant dark curls; equally lovely Lizzie Badham of Edenton; sprightly, dark-eyed Clara Springer of Wilmington; Evelyn Goodyear from Boston, a daughter of the

Goodyear rubber family, were a few of the girls during the late eighties in this dormitory. Later, when I occupied the teacher's alcove, there was in this dormitory young Marcellite Thorne of Texas and New York. Her mother, the sister of Fanny Davenport, one of the most famous actresses of the American stage, had been an actress also and her father belonged to a socially prominent New York family. Both her mother and father were dead, and her grandmother Frost, to be near Marcellite during the winter months, would come, with her maid, from New York to the old Yarborough House in Raleigh for a short stay. Many were the courtesies she extended to Marcellite's young friends. Chief of these chums was Mabel Green, a decided blonde, who was not only an excellent student and pianist of ability, but also one of the sweetest, gentlest, most lovable girls ever to have been at Saint Mary's.

Christine Sanders of Charleston, S. C., was both interesting and romantic, not only to this dormitory, but to the whole school, as she had a real, sure enough boy friend. He was to come during Commencement week and they were to be married in the Chapel. Mary Johnson, also of Charleston, would tell us, during the Saturday morning talkfest, as her father had told to her, of the time he, a Northern soldier in Sherman's army, was one of those encamped in Saint Mary's grove.

Miss Alice Pearson, of Salisbury, a near relative of Chief Justice Pearson, was the teacher in charge of the dormitory to the east at this time. She was sweet and gentle, and neatness itself.

Going down the wide steps of the front porch over the brick walkway to the west we entered the West Rock. This building contained the two senior dormitories, Senior A on the first floor and Senior B on the second floor.

Miss Dowd of the music faculty was the teacher in charge of Senior B dormitory as I remember it, while Miss

Kate McKimmon ("Miss Katie" as everyone called her) was for many, many years in charge of Senior A dormitory. Generations of Saint Mary's girls have known and loved Miss Mittie and Miss Katie.

I remember that one Good Friday there was a gathering of girls to inspect the lovely Easter finery of some of Senior B's girls, Claude Holt (Mrs. Oates of Charlotte) in particular, for she always had lovely dresses, hats, and accessories—and later to listen to the lecture from Mrs. Iredell on the sinfulness of such a procedure on Good Friday.

Across from the West Rock was the East Rock, the oldest building in the grove. Here one heard the confusing strains of many pianos. A knock on the door to the right and Dr. Kursteiner, the Director of Music, greeted you; usually there was a girl at the piano for her lesson and Mrs. Kursteiner, middle aged and handsome, rocking and knitting. Dr. August Kursteiner was born in Basle, Switzerland. At the time I knew him he was about forty. He was highly educated, and besides being Director of Music was the organist of the Chapel (with Miss Florence Slater as his assistant) and director of the chorus classes and all ensemble work of the school.

Following Dr. Kursteiner as director was Herr Havernick, a German. He was an excellent teacher but unfamiliar with the church services. This often caused confusion in the chapel. After a short time of conscientious endeavor he resigned as director. Mr. Albert A. Mack of the Stuttgart Conservatory of Music succeeded Herr Havernick. He was a delightful man of engaging mien, untiring endeavor, and unending patience, so of course the girls liked him extravagantly. And I'm not telling tales out of school when I include the teachers in that word "extravagantly." His wife taught German. Both were exceedingly popular at Saint Mary's for many years.

Across the hall from the Director's suite were the rooms

of Miss Nannette Stone and Miss Clench, both of the music faculty. Miss Stone taught voice. She came of an artistic family, Dr. William Mason, an outstanding figure in the world of American music, and John Mason, one of the most celebrated actors of the American stage, being her kinsmen.

Down the hall was a small room occupied at one time by Addie Riddick of Fayetteville. Addie, one of the loveliest of Saint Mary's daughters, spent many years at Saint Mary's, first as a student and later as a chaperon. I am going to tell a bit of a secret about her. During the nineties, when the finances of Saint Mary's were at a very low ebb, Addie, knowing of this, offered her services to Mr. Smedes without financial remuneration. Mr. Smedes accepted her offer, and no finer influence was ever felt at Saint Mary's. As Mrs. J. Alves Huske she has lived in Fayetteville, the mother of two attractive daughters, Addie Burr and May Katherine, both Saint Mary's girls.

At the end of the hall were two adjoining rooms occupied by Miss Battle, who became Lady Principal after Miss Czarnomska left. She conducted her Bible class every Sunday evening in her sitting room and on week days the girls came there to consult with her. Her teaching was done in another building.

The upper floor of East Rock was divided into practice rooms. Some of the pianos were of the square type, while the newer ones were uprights. Every year Mr. Smedes would give an especial talk to the assembled school concerning the care of musical instruments, pianos in particular. He so regretted the spirit of vandalism seen in their disfiguration.

Music had always been a strong point of Saint Mary's cultural life, and the concert given on Wednesday night of each Commencement week was worthy of professional consideration. Piano, organ and voice were stressed; the violin came a little later. Among the girls of those days with lovely voices were: Annie deRosset, soprano, easily the leading voice during her stay at Saint Mary's; Nellie Waddell (Mrs. Brenizer), with a fine voice and fine stage presence; Lily Hamilton of Hillsboro; Lillian Homesley (Mrs. Lillian Bott of Charlotte), who had a sweet, appealing voice and was also a delightful pianist; Mary Snow (Mrs. Charles Baskerville of New York City, whose son is the internationally known artist and portrait painter with whom she now lives), an extremely dainty girl, with a deal of sentiment; and May Wells, a lovely, brown-eyed Georgia girl with a full, pleasant voice, and an attractive stage appearance.

When gatherings of importance—the Legislature, the Episcopal Convention, etc.—met in Raleigh, a concert was usually given at Saint Mary's in compliment to them. For one of these occasions May Wells was chosen as a soloist. Her mother sent her a beautiful dress, with all accessories, for the event. The girls had flocked around her full of praise for wearer and for costume before she presented herself for higher inspection. "May, you look lovely and your dress is exquisite, but you are breaking the rules in wearing it, and you will have to change into a simpler one," smote upon her ears. In a dark red woolen dress she sang her solo with little expression and without a smile! But the girls, knowing of her disappointment, saw to it that she received intense and prolonged applause.

There is generally in every girls' school more talent instrumentally than vocally, and there were some Saint Mary's girls whose musical ability, instrumentally, was vastly beyond that of the usual school girl. I wish I could remember them all. Among them were: Fanny Caldwell of Salisbury, whom Dr. Kursteiner considered exceptionally gifted; Laura Johns (Mrs. Abbott) of Mount Airy, a brilliant pianist, whose best renditions were compositions of Grieg; Selma Katzenstein (who now lives in Philadelphia and is quite prominent in musical circles), of Warrenton, clever in her studies as well as a gifted musician; Lula Holden (Mrs. Frank Ward of Raleigh), who not only played beautifully but received blue ribbons on china paintings; Lucy Alice Jones, sister of Mr. William H. Jones, who later was the very efficient head of the Music Department of Saint Mary's for nearly twenty years, and Dora D. Jones (of Berlin and New York), a musician of international recognition, who was a pianist, an organist, and a vocalist, doing outstanding work in all three. As Mrs. Hancock she was for many years organist and choirmaster of Christ Church, Charlottesville, Virginia, where she is now living. There were also: Celeste Talley Cunningham of South Carolina; Annie and Nellie Gregg; Mary Stuart Wall, believed to have had the noble Stuart blood coursing through her veins; and Nannie Branch Craige of Salisbury, a handsome brunette, who had a lovely stage presence.

In the middle nineties the Department of Music added the study of the violin, very popular from the beginning. The practice rooms were in the basement of the Main Building; both the violin and orchestral classes were under Miss R. V. Ward, a graduate of the New England Conservatory of Music, Boston. The orchestra consisted of: violins—Florence Boylan, Pauline Cameron, Sarah Cheshire, Ethel Norris, Belle Pescud, Helen Smedes, Wyndham Trapier, Edna Watson, Miss Ward, James Thomas, W. H. King; cymbals—Annie Cheshire; drum—Annie Root; triangle—May Smedes. The orchestra occasionally played in the Chapel, augmenting the choir delightfully.

A short distance east of the East Rock was the Art Building, two storied and of Gothic design. The southern half of the first floor was occupied by the primary department, of which Miss Katie was in charge, and the preparatory department, over which Miss Alice Pearson presided. The northern half of the first floor was the gymnasium, a large room where Miss Florence Slater, student of Avon D. Burnham of Boston, then "America's finest gymnast," held full sway. The walls were lined with dumb bells, Indian clubs, and other gymnastic equipment, and a raised platform held the piano.

The greater part of the second floor of this building was occupied by the art studio, an unusually handsome gallery for a school of this size. Miss Cooke was the art teacher of the mid-eighties. And how Annie Johnson of Littleton did adore her! Miss Wells, from New York, was the next teacher in charge of the studio. She was as short and plump as Miss Cooke was tall and thin. She had received excellent advantages, traveled abroad considerably, and was regarded as an excellent teacher with unusual artistic discrimination.

Miss Clara Fenner, a Baltimore girl, the next head of the Art Department, was jolly and full of fun, though a splendid disciplinarian. In love with her work, she spent many summers abroad browsing among European art galleries, often taking some of the girls with her.

To the west side of the Art Gallery was a large room used by Mr. Smedes as a classroom and laboratory. My two classes under Mr. Smedes were "Paley's *Evidences of Christianity*" and "Butler's *Analogy*." In class one day, I did not know the answer to a question; Mr. Smedes held up his spectacles, and said to me: "If these glasses could speak what would they say?" As I remained tongue-tied he answered for me, "Eusebius" (Eu-se-bi-us). Later I taught two classes in this room myself.

The Art Gallery was open to the public during Commencement week. The walls were covered with the students' work. Outstanding among these students were: Carlotte Dancy, Lottie as we knew her, of Tarboro, with her lovely water colors; Kate Denson (Mrs. Beverly Raney of Raleigh) and Lizzie Bridgers, with their oil paintings; Mittie Ellis (Mrs. Henley of Raleigh) with her drawings and later her oils; Ellen Morrell of Savannah, outstanding in drawing; and Mamie Pulaski Cowper of Raleigh, who worked delightfully in water colors and oils, with china painting as her hobby. A little later Pattie Lewis and Sadie Root (Mrs. Watkins Robards of Sanford) of Raleigh attained distinction in oils. Pattie was also a fine pianist and made unusually high marks in all her studies. There were Susan Marshall and Georgia Wilkins with their water colors, and Tempe Hill with her pen and ink sketches. In the later nineties the outstanding girls of the studio who exhibited original designs, which were then being stressed, were Annie Hinsdale, Caroline Means, Georgia Wilkins, and Frances McRae (Mrs. John Lamb of Baltimore) of Chapel Hill, who also did excellent work in water colors and oils.

Perhaps the two girls of the nineties who have gained most distinction in the artistic world were Laura Carter and Anna Dunlop, much better known to us in those days as "Jimmie." The former established a successful studio in Philadelphia, and the latter studied in New York and Paris, becoming a member of the New York Art League, and attaining considerable distinction in Paris.

There were always several young girls at Saint Mary's and Jimmie Dunlop, a tomboy if there ever was one, who was quite young, soon began teaching them all sorts of boyish ways and pranks. How they loved to play with the twins and the goats! But the limit was reached one day when Jimmie was found, surrounded by excited, gaping girls, skinning a snake.

Among the younger girls at Saint Mary's at this time were Mary Fowle, daughter of Governor Fowle of North Carolina, Freida Jackson of Texas, who with her mother and older sister spent the school months at Saint Mary's, and Madelon Battle, daughter of Dr. Westray Battle of Asheville. Madelon married an English Officer and lived in India. Later, during the World War, she was a nurse in an English hospital. There the wounded soldiers loved her so dearly that they gave her the name of Gloria, and as "Nurse Gloria" she became known throughout England and America.

When I taught in the Art Building, both of my classes were composed of smaller children; in the younger class there were two boys. Saint Mary's was open to young boys at that time and had been for many previous years.

If we left the Art Building and went through the covered ways or through the grove, the Chapel came into view to the northwest of West Rock. It was of wood, Gothic in design, and smaller than at the present time. The organ and robing room for Mr. Smedes were to the left of the chancel. There were no choir stalls. The girls marched in, double file, led by the choir, all singing, and seated themselves in the first rows of pews on either side of the aisle. The triple window now in the western transcept was over the altar. (There has been a new altar placed in the Chapel since then.) There were just a few memorials: a brass cross to the memory of Eleanor Haywood; the stained glass window in memory of Elizabeth Dancy Battle in the rear of the Chapel over the seat which she always occupied; a brass reading desk given by the Raleigh Alumnae on All Saints' day in 1890 in memory of Dr. Aldert Smedes, and the brass rail given as a thank offering for deliverance from death in the tragic switch-back accident of 1893.

Miss Katie had charge of the Chapel, assisted by the girls who volunteered their time and talents. It was her best loved duty; every flower, every cloth, was laid as an offering to her Heavenly Father.

During the years of the '80's and '90's there were only

a few marriage ceremonies held in the Chapel. The afternoon of November 11, 1886, was the wedding day of Eliza Smedes and Dr. Augustus Washington Knox of Raleigh. Eliza, a former graduate and teacher, was the daughter of Mr. John Smedes and niece of Dr. Aldert Smedes. She wore a bridal costume of heavy white silk with accompanying veil, and Saint Mary's Chapel has seen very few brides so appealing.

One lovely morning, the 11th of June, 1890, the marriage of Christine Sanders to Edward Rembert of Cheraw, S. C., was solemnized. She was such a dainty bride, and so pretty in her frock of gray with pink roses in her hat. Her attendants were Miss Florence Slater and Miss Alice Dugger. She was the first girl at Saint Mary's to go directly from the schoolroom to the altar.

Another beautiful June morning, June 13, 1894, was my own wedding day. Mr. Walter H. Grimes of Raleigh and I were married by Mr. Smedes on that date. Dainty little Mary and Helen, dressed in beruffled muslin frocks, were the attendants and the altar was lavishly decorated with flowers sent by Mrs. Charles Root from her own garden.

October 18, 1892, was the wedding day of Sarah Lyell Smedes and Mr. William A. Erwin of Durham. Miss Sadie, as all of us knew her, the daughter of Dr. Aldert Smedes, was one of the most beautiful women ever claimed by North Carolina. The attendants were Miss Katherine Carter of New York, a cousin, and Mr. Robert Holt of Burlington. Mr. Erwin was ever a staunch friend of Saint Mary's, giving most generously both time and money for its advancement.

The average southern girl of this time had little aspiration for a diploma. Courses for graduation were arranged at Saint Mary's, but the majority of the girls preferred less study and easier subjects. The necessity for an education was not stressed then as it is today. The longing for higher education being in its insipiency easily accounts for the small graduation classes of this time. And, too, requirements even then were high. We had full graduates and partial graduates in those days.

During this period a distinguished man brought his young daughter to Saint Mary's. Placing her in the care of one of the teachers, a relative, he said: "There are just three things I wish my daughter to learn—music, dancing, and how to dress."

From a delightful letter recently written by Jessie Degan of Charleston, S. C., class of 1894, I quote:

"What did we study? Latin, Mathematics, English Literature, History, and French or German made the regular program for the last two years, with Paley's *Evidences of Christianity,* junior year, and "Butler" senior year, both under Mr. Smedes.

"At Wellesley College I 'passed off' Jevons' *Logic,* which Mr. Smedes had taught me, with practically no review—and got credit for it as a College subject, with a mark in the 90's. We used Dowden's *Commentary on Shakespeare,* and that course was equally thorough. My course in Solid Geometry and Trigonometry under Miss Annie Moore was also worth a year's credit at Wellesley. I read Horace with Miss Battle, and we were encouraged to put our translations into appropriate English verse form. Miss McVea taught the English History—J. R. Green's *Short History*—ten pages a day, five days a week, solid packing of facts in unforgettably beautiful English, with a stiff examination in May—a diet most prep school girls couldn't take nowadays. She also taught the senior course in Botta's *Handbook of Universal Literature*—again, strong meat for babes. There was a good deal of memorizing of dates, and one had a good drill in the elements of pronunciation of a dozen languages, for we had to pronounce authors' names and titles correctly. Translations of the finest poems and essays were read to us and we had to write on them. It was one of the most valuable courses I ever had. The term "Junior College" had not been invented, but two years of work beyond High School scope were required for graduation and to make at all a creditable showing demanded our best every day. I never had more scholarly, exhaustive teaching than at Saint Mary's during the two years I was there, from the fall of 1892 to Commencement 1894."

The four girls who comprised the class of 1885 were girls of more than average ability. Anna Hartwell Lewis, the valedictorian, was a genuine student and wrote well. The salutatorian was Sophia Dabney Thurmond, who ran Anna a close second. Julia Horner (Mrs. Henry Cooper of Oxford, N. C.) held her banners high, and the partial graduate of the class, Carrie Lee Matheson, was outstanding in music and elocution. Outstanding girls also were the Amyette sisters, Mamie and Maude (Mrs. Stephen Bragaw of Washington, N. C.).

Jane W. Bingham (Mrs. Walter D. Toy of Chapel Hill) was the only graduate in 1886, gaining first distinction in Music, French, and Elocution. A lovely musician, her plump fingers fairly flew over the keys, and her determination showed in the depths of her chords. She returned to Saint Mary's the following year as a member of the Music faculty. Much later she, together with Mrs. Bickett, was elected to the Board of Trustees of Saint Mary's School. Annie Luke Blackmer, also of Salisbury, was another prominent girl of this year, winning first distinction in French and Elocution, but she left Saint Mary's before graduation. Nosing around, I have found that she is an aunt of Sidney Blackmer, the actor.

The valedictorian of the class of 1887 was Henrietta Rhea Smedes. She is the author of a number of published poems, has given many years as organist of the Chapel of the Cross, Chapel Hill, and is now librarian of the Rural Social Economics Department at the University of North Carolina. Elizabeth Wilson McLean of Cheraw, S. C., salutatorian of this class, and Henrietta Smedes were great friends and both were perfect patterns of punctuality, behavior, and scholarship. The other members of the class were Kate Irene Gregory (Mrs. Roberts of Scotland Neck) and Frederica P. Mayhew, who married Rev. Troy Beatty, later Coadjutor Bishop of Tennessee.

The class of 1888 was made up of two full graduates, Jessie Gregory of Halifax and Caroline Frances Allston of South Carolina, and two partial graduates, Malvina Graves and Mabel Hale, granddaughter of the Secretary of the Navy, George E. Badger. All four girls were extremely pretty. Mabel Hale returned to teach Latin at Saint Mary's and later made for herself an enviable niche in the educational world of the North. She was widely known for her aggressive stand on Woman's Suffrage.

In the class of 1889 there were four partial graduates: Louise Finley (now Librarian of the University of the South, Sewanee); Laura Johns (most interesting to us because she was the cousin of a princess—Princess Troubetzkoy); Elizabeth Badham; and Beatrice Holmes (Mrs. Robert Allston of Asheville), who was English by birth. Of the two full graduates of this class, Fannie Yarborough was valedictorian.

Fannie Neal Yarborough was one of the most popular girls ever to have been at Saint Mary's. Gentle, but forthright, the love of those around her became a part of her without effort. She was the first May Queen at Saint Mary's and was unanimously chosen; there was not one single jealous girl. Later she studied at Harvard and the University of Chicago. After her marriage to Thomas Walter Bickett who became North Carolina's World War Governor, she went to Europe in 1918 to be of service among the soldiers, as a representative of the Y.M.C.A. in France.

I shall say only a few words concerning the salutatorian of the class of 1889, for in writing of her I am writing of myself, Alice Marshall Dugger, Warrenton, North Carolina. My father, Captain John E. Dugger, a pioneer educator, died during my second year at Saint Mary's. I could not have returned for my graduation year but for the generosity of Mr. Smedes. That year's education he gave me—a gift, not a loan. Later, when I returned to Saint Mary's as a teacher, he refused to take any payment from me.

The class of 1890 was unusually fine. There were: Annie Moore, of Wilmington, the valedictorian, considered the outstanding girl mentally of the entire school, who later taught at Saint Mary's; Mary Phillips (Mrs. Hal Wood of Edenton), salutatorian; Elizabeth H. Bridgers; Charlotte Dancy (all three from Tarboro); Daisy Louise Horner (Mrs. Robert Strong); Betty Clarke Gregory (Mrs. E. O. Smith, Newport News, Va.) of Halifax; Alice Henderson, of Sublett's Tavern, very much the Virginian; and Lucy Gertrude Hester, of Raleigh, quiet and retiring, who, after studying and living in the North many years, returned in 1917 to be the Lady Principal of Saint Mary's during that year, 1917–1918. Selma Katzenstein, with the highest marks of the partial graduates; Mary Pringle Frost; Carrie Gilliam Hall; and Martha Helen Haywood, of Raleigh, complete the list.

Charlotte Franklin Bush, one of the three fine Bush sisters of Pittsboro, all Saint Mary's girls, was the valedictorian of the class of 1891, with Grace McHardy Jones of Asheville, a very close runner up, the salutatorian. Emily Hazzard Barnwell (Mrs. Ravenel of Charleston), Lily Strong Hicks (Mrs. Bancker Smedes, Boonton, N. J.), and Dixie Cooke Murray (Mrs. Weldon Smith) were also full graduates. Virginia Ellison Thomas was a very handsome girl who found her way to Saint Mary's from Mobile, Ala., because her mother, one of the Ellison sisters, had been a Saint Mary's girl. She and Laura Wirt Wesson, one of the outstanding beauties of the school, received the highest marks of the partial graduates. There were also: Susan Pringle Frost, Charleston, S. C.; Henrietta Smedes McVea, sister of Miss Emmie McVea, who was witty and bright in conversation and a frequent contributor to *The Muse;* and Marion A. Mallett from Fayetteville.

The six members of the class of 1892 were graduates of the full course, and every member made a general average above 90. Jennie Hinton Pescud (Mrs. W. A. Withers, of Raleigh) was valedictorian, while Janet Wilson Dugger was the salutatorian. The other members were: Charlotte Allston (Mrs. Maurice Moore, of Charleston); Elise Carwile; Frances Tunstall (Mrs. Clem Dowd of Charlotte); May Hill Davis (Mrs. J. V. Higham of Raleigh).

The graduates of the class of 1893 were all fine girls. The valedictorian, Daisy B. Waite, a very ambitious, thorough student, after obtaining degrees from Cornell and Columbia Universities and studying at Harvard University, was first head of the English Department at the East Carolina Teachers' College (Greenville, N. C.) and then head of the English Department of the Woman's College, Greenville, S. C. Now she lives in Raleigh, busy in research work. Annie Gregg, Luling, Texas, was the salutatorian; Bessie L. Whitaker, very successful in teaching the adult dumb to speak, now lives in Ann Arbor, Michigan; Nannie Branch Jones (Mrs. Thomas Ashe of Raleigh) was staunch and true in every endeavor; Blanch Blake (Mrs. Blanch Blake Manor of Raleigh) is widely known through her column, "Chatter," in the Sunday edition of the *News and Observer*. The other three members of the class were: Estelle Brodie, of Wilson (partial graduate); Loula McK. Woodell; and Lillie Masten, of Winston-Salem, a niece of Miss Slater and a lovely dancer, who, before her untimely death, married DeBrutz Cutler of Wilmington. Loula also died young, and the litany desk has been placed in the Chapel as a memorial to her.

The six graduates of the class of 1894 were: Mary A. Wilmerding (Mrs. F. W. Ambler, of Summerville, S. C.), granddaughter of the Bishop of Texas, valedictorian; Jessie Degan (Long Standing, Byfield, Mass.), of Charleston, in every way an outstanding girl, salutatorian; Julia Daggett, of Wilmington; Laura B. Newsom (Mrs. Maurice O'Neill of Henderson); Marie D. Lee (Mrs. H. H. Covington) of Sumter, S. C.; and Mary Page, of Raleigh. Jessie Degan, who graduated from Wellesley in 1898 and was for some time head of the May School in Boston, has written an account of the switchback accident for us:

"Mr. Smedes' picnic for all of us on Tuesday, April 4, 1893, at the near-by State Fair grounds was to have been a great event. As the summit of joy for the little ones, he had engaged the switchback railroad and along with it the men who were accustomed to operating it. There were two parallel tracks starting from a high platform at each end, where the car switched from one track to return to the other.

"I had had no desire to ride on the switchback, but a group of small day scholars begged us, Mabel Green, Annie Gregg, and me, to ride on the switchback with them. Good-naturedly we got in, I on the back seat with a very small girl hugging each arm, Mabel and Annie ahead of me, each with a partner, and off we started.

"We were coasting down a long slope when I looked ahead and saw the other car coming towards us on *our* track! Either the mechanism or the man's hand had slipped on the opposite platform. There was no time to speak, no hope of escape, and death approaching.

"The next I knew I was 'coming to' out of unconsciousness, hearing cries and moans all around me, and finding myself on the edge of a mass of wreckage—bent iron, splintered wood. I sat up. I was alive after all. I could move. I was only bruised and shaken and aching. I got up and began to uncover girls in the wreckage. I found Mabel Green, who murmured, 'I think my leg is broken.' I bent down and felt it and though I had never touched a broken leg, that was unmistakable.

"Other girls and teachers were running to us from every direction. There being no telephone at the Fair grounds at that season of the year, Mr. Smedes urged me, if possible, to go to town as I looked fairly capable physically of doing so, and to send help from town as quickly as possible. He had already sent several people to the A. and M. College for help.

"Nearby lived some of our laundresses. I stopped at the first cabin and asked them to send someone as fast as they could to the nearest telephone and ask for doctors. Finally I reached the car line, and as I rode into town, doctors' buggies began to fly past me towards the Fair grounds.

"Just as I got off the car in front of Saint Mary's, a line of A. and M. boys, carrying stretchers and mattresses, filed through the gate. All figures were covered with sheets and of course I didn't know whether they were alive or dead.

"Next morning Miss Battle was at the wheel. She had been out of Raleigh for the Easter Holiday. She immediately had every girl in the school examined by a doctor. To protests of 'I wasn't there,' 'I wasn't on the cars,' etc., she answered 'You're all in such a state you don't know where you were. I'll take no risks.' So I, protesting that I was all right, only sleepy and sore, went up, and was found with a badly split collar bone, which kept me in the infirmary for some weeks. My out-of-joint-finger was set right and my aching leg treated. I had a dent in the right leg below the knee, which even now can be felt. I was thankful enough, only rebellious at having to stay in bed so long for such a seemingly trifling break.

"As to the others who were hurt, there was Annie Root with both legs broken, Helen Smedes with both legs broken, and Florence Boylan with a broken nose which was said to have been eventually the cause of her death. Fair Payne was badly hurt, too, as was Mary Smedes. Every rider was bruised or tremendously shaken up. Over a lapse of more than forty years other names have become vague, but I do remember that Miss Clench, holding little Margaret Boylan high over her head, was hurt, but that Margaret escaped all injury."

The valedictorian of the class of 1895 was Eleanor Vass of Raleigh. A handsome blonde, she stood out, not only in her classes, but in all activities of the school. The salutatorian was Farinda W. Payne (Mrs. Cam MacRae of Asheville), called Fair. Other members were: Elizabeth Ashe (Mrs. George Flint), of Raleigh, prominent in all school activities; Loula H. Briggs (Mrs. John Brewer of Wake Forest), of Raleigh, receiving first distinction in vocal music; Marie A. Walker (Mrs. Hamilton Jones of Tryon); Margaret V. Hill (Mrs. W. E. Schroeder of Portsmouth); and Evelyn Holmes (Mrs. J. R. Brumley) of Bowmens' Bluff. An outstanding girl of this class was Miriam Lanier of Tarboro. When she came to Saint Mary's her mother came with her. They had never been separated, so Mr. Smedes had a room prepared for them. This filial affection was a salutory influence throughout the school.

The girls graduating in 1896 were: Margaret M. Jones, valedictorian; Nannie Skinner, one of the five handsome Skinner sisters of Raleigh who attended Saint Mary's, salutatorian; Mary Pride Jones (Mrs. Castleman of Raleigh), one of the prettiest girls of this period; Bertha Stein of Raleigh; Susan Marshall of Raleigh, outstanding in Latin and painting; and Lucy Cobb of Raleigh, author of folklore tales, poems, and plays.

In 1896 occurred one of the most important events in the history of Saint Mary's, the transfer of Saint Mary's School from private ownership to diocesan ownership. The following account of this transfer is taken from the same speech mentioned in the first chapter of this book, the memorial address delivered in Saint Mary's Chapel on All Saints' Day in 1902 by Dr. Battle:

"Financial depression had come increasingly on the country and it proved especially hard on the patrons of Saint Mary's and those who would have naturally become its patrons. Expenses were increased while receipts diminished.

"In 1896 Dr. Smedes, whose health had suffered from anxious care of the school, requested the Diocesan Convention to take charge of Saint Mary's and relieve him of a burden he found too heavy for one man with no greater means than his own to bear.

"The convention acceded to his request, and trustees were selected to organize a corporation and get a charter from the General Assembly of the State and, taking charge of the institution, purchase for the church, so much of this property as might be required for the needs of the school.

"A charter was granted by the Legislature March 2, 1897, incorporating trustees from the Dioceses of North and East Carolina and the jurisdiction of Asheville, and this was amended by an act passed January 16, 1899, by confirming the power to elect additional trustees for the Diocese of South Carolina.

"At the convention of the Diocese of South Carolina in May, 1899, Saint Mary's was adopted as its Diocesan school. So now it is the school of the church in the states of both North and South Carolina.

"These buildings and twenty-five acres of land, including the grove, garden, etc., were bought for the corporation and a deed taken from the descendants of Judge Cameron who had bought the property so long before. The purchase money was $50,000.

"The trustees promptly elected Dr. Smedes rector, gave him Miss McVea as an assistant in the practical management of the school, and the teachers he designated—thus showing entire confidence in his judgment, his zeal, and his ability to conduct the school."

The class of 1897 was composed of five girls, four of whom were from Raleigh. Nannie Grist Clark, of Tarboro, a girl of strong purpose and fine intellect, was the valedictorian; Lily Elizabeth Koonce was the salutatorian. The others were: Mary Merrill Hanff (Mrs. John Paylor), the daughter of a Saint Mary's girl of the long ago, Ardella Merrill; Theodora Marshall (Mrs. Duncan Cameron, Coronado Beach, Cal.), one of the beauties of the school; and Isabella Willis Pescud (Mrs. Walker Williams), granddaughter of one of the original Saint Mary's girls, Jane Hinton, who entered the school the second day of its opening, and daughter of a Saint Mary's girl. Belle, as she was generally known, loved her violin and was a member of the original Saint Mary's orchestra.

The Business School, which began as a part of the ordinary school course in 1897, succeeded so admirably that it soon became a regular business department. The course included Stenography, Typewriting, Bookkeeping, Arithmetic, Penmanship, Spelling, and Grammar. The School was under the supervision of a most competent instructor, Miss Lizzie Lee. An assistant, Miss Juliet Sutton, was soon added.

The first certificates in Stenography and Typewriting were awarded at the Commencement of 1898; the girls, all from Raleigh, receiving them were: Isabel B. Busbee, Susan Marshall, Margaret H. Smedes, Iva F. Upchurch,

Mary Tonnoffski, Bessie Hines White, and Jane Hinton Pescud.

The girls of the class of 1898 were: Kate McKimmon Hawley (Mrs. M. R. Bacon of Fayetteville), niece and namesake of "Miss Katie," valedictorian; Sadie Smedes Root, granddaughter of Dr. Aldert Smedes, salutatorian; Ethel Worrell; Olive Armstrong (Mrs. G. D. Crow of Wilmington); Jessamine May Higgs (Mrs. Henry C. Walter, East Orange, N. J.), barely seventeen when she graduated; Margaret Harvey Smedes (Mrs. John I. Rose, Greenville, S. C.), daughter of Mr. Bennett Smedes, first distinction in music; and Frances Cameron. Frances married an army officer, Charles Burnett, and while in Japan translated several poems into the Japanese language. These she sent to the Empress of Japan who received them graciously. Many courtesies to Frances followed. She and General Burnett now live in Washington, D. C.

The Kindergarten was established in 1898. It was headed by Miss Louisa Busbee who was assisted by Miss Anna Jones. A large, well-equipped room in the Art Building was provided for it.

During the unusually severe weather of snow and sleet of the February of 1899, Dr. Smedes contracted a cold which rapidly developed into pneumonia and within a few days, on February 22, he died. After the memorial services which were held in the Chapel at Saint Mary's the next afternoon, his body in the white robes of his sacred calling rested before the altar until Friday morning. A purple pall with its white cross covered the casket, a cluster of palm branches resting at the foot. At eleven o'clock on the morning of the twenty-fourth of February the funeral services were held at Christ Church. The officiating clergymen were Bishop Cheshire, Reverend M. M. Marshall, Reverend I. McK. Pittinger, Reverend Julian E. Ingle, of Henderson, and Reverend Thomas Bell of Wilson. Having been Chaplain in the Confederate Army and a member of the L. O'B. Branch Camp Confederate Veterans, the camp was represented by four members, each wearing his Confederate uniform. More than two hundred from Saint Mary's, boarding pupils, day pupils, and teachers, were of the cortege. The teachers and pupils of Peace Institute attended the services in a body and sent handsome floral designs. A tremendous outpouring of all classes, races, and creeds were at Christ Church and at the graveside in Oakwood Cemetery, attesting their esteem and sympathy. Beloved of all who knew him and respected by all with whom he came in contact, the years have shown how well he did his work.

After the death of Mr. Smedes, Saint Mary's was carried on jointly, with much success, by Miss McVea, the Lady Principal, and Miss Martha Dowd. Of course for a while sadness brooded over the school, but everything was done to reestablish its former brightness. Mrs. Smedes, Margaret, and the twins (Mary and Helen) continued at Saint Mary's throughout the remainder of the school year.

Lucy B. Clifton was the president of the Class of 1899, standing third scholastically in this class of twelve. They established Class Day as an annual event at Saint Mary's and gave the first Class Day exercises. Christiana Busbee, the valedictorian, returned to teach at Saint Mary's, but later attended the University of North Carolina and Cornell University, taught at Mount Holyoke, and is now teaching in the Jamaica, Long Island, High School. The salutatorian, Minna Curtis Bynum (Mrs. Archibald Henderson of Chapel Hill), also the class poet and editor-in-chief of *The Muse,* was perhaps the most versatile girl of this entire period. She was brilliant in her classwork and gifted in voice, piano, art, and languages. Other members of the class were: Lucy Kate Cannady (Mrs. Harry Williams of Oxford), assistant editor of *The Muse;* Kate Connor Wilson; Nina Watson Green (Mrs. LeRoy Theim of

Raleigh), very musical; Margaret Trapier (Mrs. Allan Rogers of Raleigh); Lily E. Dodd (who later received degrees from the University of Tennessee and Columbia University); Josephine Ashe Osborne, of Charlotte, Miss Katie's right-hand-man in both chapel and dormitory, business manager of *The Muse* and class historian; Annie Dugghi (Mrs. J. D. Maag of Raleigh); Alice Smallbones (Mrs. G. M. Brunson of Charlotte), class prophet and assistant editor of *The Muse*.

Theodore DuBose Bratton, D.D. began his work as the head of Saint Mary's School at the beginning of the school year 1899–1900. He was born at Roseland, the family plantation near Winnsboro, S. C., November 11, 1862. His father was John Bratton, a Brigadier General of the Confederate Army, his mother Elizabeth Porcher DuBose Bratton. Receiving his early education from an aunt, he entered the grammar school of the University of the South, Sewanee, Tenn. After beginning study in the University proper, he had to return home to manage the plantation while his father directed the Democratic campaigns for South Carolina offices of 1880. Returning to Sewanee to continue his activities, he entered the School of Theology —Saint Luke's Theological Hall—graduating in 1887. In 1888 he married Lucy Beverly Randolph of Virginia. He was ordained Deacon by the Right Reverend W. B. A. Howe, Bishop of South Carolina. His first work was as an Episcopal missionary in the counties of York, Lancaster, and Chester, S. C. After his ordination as Priest came his rectorship of the Church of the Advent, Spartanburg, S. C. He served this parish many years, during which time he was professor of history at Converse College.

The class to greet the Twentieth Century numbered these twelve attractive girls: Rebeccah Routhe Bridgers (Reba as everyone called her), editor-in-chief of *The Muse,* vice-president Athletic Association; Mary H. Andrews

(Mrs. William Person), associate editor of *The Muse;* Ellen Bowen, class prophet; Mildred L. Cuningham, treasurer of the class; Alice Leonora Love (Mrs. H. P. S. Keller of Raleigh); Annie S. Love, class poet; Caroline Means, assistant editor of *The Muse,* member of Varsity, outstanding in art work; Anna Louise Pittinger (Mrs. Leigh Skinner of Decatur, Ga.); Annie Pearl Pratt (Mrs. J. J. Van Noppen of Madison), class secretary; Mary MacAlister Renn (Mrs. Paul Taylor, Bronxville, N. Y.), vice-president of the class; Mary C. Thompson (Mrs. J. G. deRoulhac Hamilton of Chapel Hill), president of the class and salutatorian; and Nannie Belvin, valedictorian and president of Sidney Lanier Literary Society, to whose memory there is now in the Chapel a lovely stained-glass window.

In the nineties athletics were coming to the fore. Hitherto our exercises had been of the mildest variety, indoor gymnastics, dancing, walks in the grove, with occasional chaperoned strolls in the nearby woods, and tennis. By 1900 there was an Athletic Association with its officers, executive committee and advisory committee. Miss McVea's niece, Miss Imogen Stone, although a teacher of English, taught the girls the new game of basketball. She had become fond of it at Cornell and started a Club with its officers and colors. The Mu basketball team had as its color bright blue, while the Sigma team had white. Each had its yell. Those playing tennis now boasted a club with officers, colors, and a yell. There was a Cycling Club with officers, the Walking Club with its President and members, and the Kodak Club with its officers, colors, motto, emblem, and clever yell:

> *I used to say*
> *Potrack, Potrack,*
> *But now I say*
> *Ko-dak, Ko-dak.*

As for baseball, there were two nines—Sunny South (colors, red and green) and Dixie (colors, red and light blue).

For years there had been steam heat and gas with Wellsbach burners. Now came the white iron beds with springs, and bath tubs and toilets were installed.

Membership in the Junior Auxiliary was part of the church interest expected of each resident girl, and the girls never held back. There were four chapters, each having a teacher as directress with girls as officers—President, Vice-President, Treasurer and Collector, and Secretary. The names of the four chapters were St. Monica, St. Margaret, St. Cecilia, and St. Elizabeth.

The months of attendance upon the chapel services rarely failed to leave their impress and so I am using the following, sent me by a girl of this period, as a fitting close for this chapter:

"Chapel service was as natural a part of our daily life as food or hard work, and we took it so. During Lent we also had Evensong each day and so came to know some of the most beautiful but less familiar psalms. We were well trained in chanting, using prayer books with the pointing printed. Even now there are some psalms I never read without hearing, in my mind, the music to which we sang them at Saint Mary's. These daily services seldom took over ten minutes, they were restful, we loved the music, and unconsciously, through the daily repetition, we came to know the beautiful liturgy so that it became a part of us. I think that is the best way. Anyway, however much we may have loved the rest of the school life, that is the part that abides with Saint Mary's girls."

4

From "Floradora" to "Tipperary"
1900–1915

By Nell Battle Lewis

WITH ITS customary decorum and conservatism, Saint Mary's had entered the twentieth century, which during its first half was to bring two world wars, the enfranchisement of American women and a revolution in their dress, the perfection of the automobile, the airplane, the radio, and the motion picture, the apotheosis of the gadget, and a highly accelerated tempo of life. Only thirty-five years lay between the opening of this new century and Appomattox, and by not even a full generation was Reconstruction in the past. The young ladies of Saint Mary's in the early 1900's—and young ladies is, indeed, the proper term for them—still memorialized in their school annual the Confederate flag as "the grandest flag that ever waved" and paid tribute to the Negro mammies, former slaves, who had reared most of them and who with such admirable faithfulness and devotion after their emancipation had attached themselves to "their white-folks."

Specializing in the education of daughters of the Southern Quality, Saint Mary's was permeated by the conventional atmosphere surrounding the southern woman of the best class, in which she was regarded as primarily the charming, modest, religious home-maker. This was excellent for the development of character, but otherwise in education it left something to be desired. It was a viewpoint, long prevalent in the South, which had produced in this region a breed of women who probably were unsurpassed in charm, grace, personal purity, and moral rectitude by those of any other society in the world, but who in the advance of women in education, economic independence, and political interest lagged behind most of their sisters in the rest of the United States.

That comparative backwardness, however, was of no real concern at Saint Mary's at the beginning of this century. The young ladies there in their billowing skirts and high-collared, tight-sleeved waists or in evening gowns of modest decolletage wished, properly enough, to be womanly above all else. From afar rumors had reached them of certain unsexed females who wanted the ballot and of still others who had attended those institutions of higher learning which aped the colleges for men, such as those established by Matthew Vassar on the Hudson River and by Sophia Smith in the valley of the Connecticut; but like their mothers, fathers, and brothers, most Saint Mary's girls of that period regarded these peculiar females with pitying scorn and something of horror as displeasing and pathetic anomalies of the gentler sex. In the minds of the majority it was hardly less reprehensible to wish to secure higher education than to be "fast" enough to smoke a cigarette.

> *You may break, you may shatter*
> *The vase as you will,*
> *But the scent of the roses*
> *Will cling round it still.*

The vase before the shrine of southern womanhood into which the chivalric knighthood of the region had placed its votive floral offerings had been badly cracked in the collapse of southern feudalism after the War between the States, but its remnants were still redolent with the fragrance of the old idealization of The Southern Lady as the rose-crowned queen of chivalry, a perfume loved by southern women young and old. What could the northern spinster, Susan B. Anthony, and her suffragists offer to compare with that?

As the Saint Mary's girl of the early 1900's day-dreamed while she read her best beau's latest gift, a handsome edition of James Whitcomb Riley's *An Old Sweetheart of Mine*, illustrated by Howard Chandler Christy, or mused modestly upon the basic biological relationship romantically pictured by that popular artist and his contemporary, Charles Dana Gibson, she never lost sight of her chief function. Happily unbetrayed by the specious blandishments of Feminism, she saw herself in the future in true perspective as wife and mother and distrusted any educational pabulum which did not nourish her to that end. At Saint Mary's she found the diet eminently satisfactory.

From 1900 to 1915 the most conspicuous developments at Saint Mary's were the material enlargement and improvement of the school in 1909 by the addition of the East and West Wings, Clement Hall, and the big porch of Smedes Hall, made possible largely by a $30,000 legacy left the school by Miss Eleanor Clement, former student and teacher at Saint Mary's; and the elevation of the academic standing of the institution through the efforts of its fifth Rector, the Reverend George William Lay. Both scholastically and materially Saint Mary's went forward during Mr. Lay's administration.

Coming from the strict atmosphere of a New England church school for boys, St. Paul's in Concord, New Hampshire, where he had been one of the masters for almost twenty years, Mr. Lay took charge of Saint Mary's in the

Fall of 1907. Energetic, brusquely honest, invariably just, and sincerely interested in education, Mr. Lay was a priest who also was a school-master of long experience. He arrived in Raleigh to find Saint Mary's drowsy, demure, and rather down-at-the-heel. Whereupon he immediately proceeded to give it a good shaking-up. When he had finished eleven years later, there were some sore toes upon which he had trod, but Saint Mary's was a much better school. Although Mr. Lay had his critics, some severe, he had also many firm friends who were aware of his contribution to Saint Mary's and grateful for it.

He was the third of the Rectors who from 1900 to 1915 headed the school. Saint Mary's had entered the 1900's under the guidance of the Reverend Theodore DuBose Bratton, a man of marked ability, noble character, and great personal charm, who had come to the institution in 1899 and who left it in 1903 to become Bishop of Mississippi. Both he and his wife, the "School Mother," were much beloved; and during his administration the enrollment increased, the Rectory and the North Dormitory (Senior Hall) were built, and the curriculum was reorganized as that of a college, with Freshman, Sophomore, Junior, and Senior classes.

Dr. Bratton was succeeded as Rector by his cousin, the Reverend McNeely DuBose, who served Saint Mary's devotedly for four years, resigning in 1907 to return to the ministerial field which he preferred and to which he thought his abilities better suited, becoming Rector of Grace Church at Morganton, N. C., and director of the neighboring missions.

As one reviews the life of Saint Mary's from 1900 to 1915, one thinks of a continuing stream, flowing and widening through the years, a stream of blithe and promising girlhood. Its central current is ever the same: youth and hope. Its bed is the ideal of Christian character which from the first Saint Mary's has consistently maintained. Only the surface of the stream changes, through the vagaries of fashion or the events of the time or the gradual modification of mores. Now one, now another name rides briefly the crest of its waves, to be swiftly succeeded by others. Some of the annual surface changes of this stream are described in what follows.

"A New Century, a New Class, a New Book, but a loving greeting as of old to all our Friends," proclaimed the annual *Muse* of 1901.

The members of the faculty and officers of Saint Mary's whom Dr. Bratton headed during this session were: Misses Alice E. Jones, Latin; Adele E. Roux, French; Edith D. Marsden, German and Science; Imogen Stone, English; Eleanor W. Thomas, Mathematics; Elleneen E. Checkley, History and Preparatory Department; Virginia A. Blanchard, Art and Physical Culture; Mr. John W. Jeudwine, Director of the Department of Music; Misses Martha A. Dowd, Piano; Genevieve A. Schutt, Piano; Lucy Alice Jones, Voice; Gertrude M. Potwin, Violin; Lizzie H. Lee, Principal of the Commercial School; Juliet B. Sutton, Assistant; Kate McKimmon, Principal of the Primary Department; Louise T. Busbee, Director of the Kindergarten; Mrs. T. D. Bratton, School Mother; Miss Anne Saunders, Matron of the Infirmary; and Mrs. M. N. Quinby, Housekeeper.

The Director of Music, Mr. John Wynn Jeudwine, had been a barrister of Lincoln's Inn, London, who in order to regain his health had given up his practice and gone to western North Carolina, where he farmed and kept country store for a number of years. He married a widow from Charleston, S. C., Mrs. Leila Lesesne Smith. His musical training and ability were known to Miss Dowd, of the music faculty of Saint Mary's, and it was probably through her influence that he came to the school. Both he, a cultured Englishman, and Mrs. Jeudwine, a Charleston old-timer, "added color and distinction to the Saint Mary's family of those years," in the words of one of their friends. Mrs. Jeudwine's at-homes are recalled as occasions of much charm. After leaving Saint Mary's in 1902, the Jeudwines went back to England, and Mr. Jeudwine wrote a number of historical books.

It was in response to a question by Miss Checkley, the history teacher at this time, that one of Saint Mary's prize boners, which bids fair to be immortal, was uttered. In one of her classes Miss Checkley asked the extent of the Dark Ages, whereupon the answer of an inspired student was, "From the fall of Rome to the Straits of Gibralter."

The nuclei of the two literary societies, Epsilon Alpha Pi, named in honor of the southern writer, Edgar Allan Poe, and Sigma Lambda, named for the Georgia poet, Sidney Lanier, had been formed during the preceding spring by Miss Imogen Stone, who had divided the English classes into two sections; and these societies were functioning successfully during the session of 1900–'01. Miss Stone, described by one of her former students as "a very vital person and the best teacher I ever had," was a power at Saint Mary's in her day, not only in the classroom but in the general life of the school. Even after forty years, she is vividly recalled by the girls whom she taught, and their admiration of her is undiminished.

Her mother, Imogen McVea, sister of the Lady Principal, had been a Saint Mary's girl immediately following the Civil War. Miss Stone's three years of teaching at Saint Mary's came in an interim in her studies at Cornell, where she later got her B.A. and M.A. Afterward she taught for thirty-five years at Sophie Newcombe College in New Orleans. At present she is living in Clinton, La.

During this session the first of four organizations of a sort new at Saint Mary's appeared: Alpha Kappa Psi, the first of the sororities, was founded, as *The Muse* says, "under the kindly fostering auspices of the beloved Rector." A later Rector, Mr. Lay, felt rather less kindly and fostering toward these exclusive sisterhoods, and at his request they made a final exit in September, 1912. But for a decade they flourished, to the more or less smug satisfaction of their members and for the heartaches and occasional tears of some of those who were excluded. The number was limited to four; and after Alpha Kappa Psi, there came in 1902: Gamma Beta Sigma (later a chapter of Alpha Sigma Alpha), Upsilon Delta (later Phi Mu) and Phi Delta (later Kappa Delta).

South Carolina was always strongly represented in Alpha Kappa Psi; Gamma Beta Sigma went in for old North Carolina Quality of the more conservative sort; Kappa Delta, whose members were sporty, stylish, and frequently rich as well as blue-blooded, usually had, in addition to its predominant North Carolina membership, a scattering of the élite from Georgia; Phi Mu's Tarheel sisters seemed to attract some of the few girls from the North. Each of the sororities had its *Sorores in Facultate:* Miss Thomas, Miss Checkley, Mrs. Jeudwine, and Miss Bowen were members of Alpha Kappa Psi; Miss Lee and Miss Vedder, of Gamma Beta Sigma; Miss Hull, Miss Cribbs, Miss Rosalie Russell, and Miss Buxton were Kappa Deltas; and Miss McKimmon and Miss Dowd belonged to Phi Mu. The sororities skimmed the social cream of the school. For the girls in these charmed circles they were fun; for the girls outside they were not. They did Saint Mary's no particular good —and no serious harm—and Mr. Lay had good grounds in democratic theory when he requested that they surrender their charters.

The two german clubs, Tau Delta and L'Etoile, were important organizations of the period. A dance at Saint Mary's to which boys were invited was quite unthinkable

FROM "FLORADORA" TO "TIPPERARY" 107

in 1900–1901, although the healthy association of adolescent girls and boys was just as necessary to their future happiness then as it is now. It took a sensible married woman with daughters of her own to introduce that harmless form of normal diversion into a school whose atmosphere had previously been too exclusively feminine. Mrs. Ernest Cruikshank, as President of Saint Mary's, inaugurated the dances to which boys could come. In the german clubs of 1900–1901 the girls who could "lead" dressed in skirts and shirt-waists, standing collars and ties, and acted as beaux. Several formal dances were given by the clubs during the year, when in german figures, waltzes and two-steps the members got good practice for engagements at Chapel Hill and other men's colleges.

The University of North Carolina, by the way, at that time numbered only 507 students, as recorded in its advertisement in the annual *Muse;* and the A. and M., now the State College of Agriculture and Engineering, had only 301. Tuition at the latter was $20.00 a year.

"History is the essence of innumerable biographies," wrote the historian of the Class of 1901; so on this tip, the names of the student leaders at Saint Mary's each year are included in this sketch. Eliza Harwood Drane was one of the most prominent girls of 1900–'01. Voted the "most studious," she was president of the thirteen Seniors and of the Choral Society and was secretary of the Dramatic Club. Other leading lights of the year were: Rosa May Gordon, president of Sigma Lambda; Isabel Davis Roundtree, editor-in-chief of the annual *Muse* and president of L'Etoile German Club; Julia Harris, president of E.A.P.; Mary Philips, president of the Athletic Association; Ellen Bowen, president of the Altar Guild; Beulah Armstrong and Hallie Park, presidents of the Tau Delta German Club; Arabel Nash, president of the Tennis Club.

"Cute" is a word much used by school-girls today, but

one is rather surprised to find that it has been in the schoolgirl vocabulary for so long. In 1900–'01 Marie Phinizy was voted the "cutest" girl at Saint Mary's.

Through Saint Mary's in 1900–'01 were still echoing the songs of the Spanish-American War, such as "Just Break the News to Mother" and "Just as the Sun Went Down." Another hit was "Just Because She Made Them Goo-Goo Eyes." The telephone was the greatest invention of the day, and the fact was reflected in the popular song, "Hello, Central, Give Me Heaven," in which a bereaved child was supposed to be trying to communicate with her deceased mamma. But the song on the lips of all Saint Mary's girls who were really up-to-date came from the comic operetta, *Floradora,* and began, "Tell me, pretty maiden, are there any more at home like you?" Two of the most popular novels of the year which Saint Mary's girls were reading were Winston Churchill's *The Crisis* and George Barr McCutcheon's *Graustark.*

Miss Eleanor Walter Thomas began teaching English at Saint Mary's in 1901, having taught mathematics there the year before, and continued to do so as long as she was in the school. Miss Susan W. Moses, later the wife of Edward Kidder Graham, President of the University of North Carolina, taught French, German, and Greek. Miss Clara Fenner, who until her death in 1926 was to be identified with Saint Mary's and very influential in its affairs, and whose good humor and *esprit* were happy elements in its atmosphere, came to teach art. Miss Lola E. Walton succeeded Miss Anne Saunders as Matron of the Infirmary, and Miss Saunders became the Rector's assistant.

There were only four Seniors in the class of 1902, so there were offices for all the members of the class; in fact, two offices for some. Marie Bacot Brunson was the Senior president and also president of the E.A.P. and editor-in-chief of the annual *Muse.* Louise Manning Venable headed

Sigma Lambda; Mattie Moffatt, the Altar Guild; Jennie Marshall Gibson, Tau Delta; Margaret Gray Stedman, L'Etoile; and Olsie Clark, the Dramatic Club.

The first of the annual inter-society debates was held this year. On the question as to whether poetry has done more for man than prose the Sigma Lambda debaters, Kate deRosset Meares, Mary Henderson, and Lucy Taylor Redwood, who upheld the negative, triumphed over Jennie Trapier, Anna Gifford, and Mary Spruill Weeks, of E.A.P. As long as they were held, these annual debates were a source of the wildest excitement and most intense rivalry among the students. Following them, bosom friends who chanced to belong to different societies might be estranged in stony silence for days. The desire to live no longer should the rival society triumph was frequently expressed by the loyal.

How the athletic clubs functioned in that period is one of the major mysteries. Modesty decreed that members of the basket-ball teams should wear full skirts below the knee over bulging bloomers, long-sleeved blouses and stockings. Tennis players had to do the best they could in shirt-waists and long, full skirts. What would modest Saint Mary's lady-like athletes of 1901–'02 have thought of their bare-legged daughters in shorts on the front tennis courts in full view of Hillsboro Street? "Hussies," one fears, would have been the word.

Dancing at Saint Mary's in 1901–'02 was to the music of "Under the Bamboo Tree," "Please Go 'Way and Let Me Sleep," and "In the Good Old Summer Time," among other popular pieces. Of course, too, for sentimental moments there was always "The Rosary." If any Saint Mary's girls of that year read in the newspapers of the society woman at Saratoga, N. Y., who shocked the resort by riding astride, the probability is that they strongly disapproved.

A new Director of Music came to Saint Mary's in 1902–

'03, or rather, an old friend returned, for Mr. W. H. Sanborn had been in the school in the '80's. His wife taught piano. Miss Charlotte Kendall Hull was the new violin teacher. She became a fast friend of Miss Chelian Pixley, who had come to Saint Mary's the year before to teach piano, and these two together were one of the most familiar —and one of the prettiest—sights around the school. They both were lovely, and the combination was extremely sightly. While she was at Saint Mary's, Miss Hull organized and directed the Saint Mary's orchestra, which included not only musicians at the school but also some from Raleigh.

Other new faculty members in 1902–'03 were Miss Christiana Busbee, who taught Greek and assisted Miss Marie M. Gerber in teaching French and German, and Miss Louise Pittinger, who was an assistant in English.

Usually the negative side won in the inter-society debates, but so eloquent and so logical were Mary Henderson and Kate Meares that, even defending the affirmative for Sigma Lambda, they overcame the E.A.P. debaters, Anna Gifford and Helen Davies. The query was: "Resolved: that man has done more for the world than woman." It was a sweet tribute to southern chivalry by some of its chief beneficiaries that at Saint Mary's in 1903 it was decided that he certainly has.

Kate deRosset Meares was the "big shot" of the year, president of the fifteen Seniors and six "associate Seniors" who also got their individual pictures in *The Muse* along with the regular members, editor-in-chief of *The Muse*, and president of Sigma Lambda. Augusta Porcher Jones headed E.A.P. Octavia Winder Hughes was president of Tau Delta, and Margaret Stedman was again the head of L'Etoile. Florence Thomas directed the Altar Guild. Mary Henderson, inter-society debater for the second time, was prominent in other activities.

Dr. Bratton was consecrated Bishop of Mississippi in the Summer of 1903, and Saint Mary's opened in September of that year with a new Rector, the Reverend McNeely DuBose, a cousin of Bishop Bratton, and his choice as his successor. Like Bishop Bratton, Mr. DuBose was a South Carolinian—Charleston was his birthplace—and a graduate of the University of the South at Sewanee, where he received his B.S. and B.D. He was Rector of Trinity Church at Asheville, N. C., just before coming to Saint Mary's. Neither by training nor by experience was Mr. DuBose a schoolman or an administrator. He was a priest whose preferences and abilities lay chiefly along pastoral lines. However, he faithfully and satisfactorily discharged his duties as Rector of Saint Mary's for the four years during which he held that office. His attitude toward his charges is suggested by the fact that it was his custom to address them as "Daughter," a paternal attitude apparently consistent with the spirit of the school where the aim, as announced in the catalogue, is "to make the daily life of the students that of a Christian household."

In addition to the new Rector, there came to Saint Mary's in the Fall of 1903 a tall and very thin young man who had as much influence on the life of the school as any Rector in its history. His name was Ernest Cruikshank, and he was to teach Latin and Science. For three years he did so, but in 1906 he gave up teaching Science to become Secretary of Saint Mary's and, for one year, Librarian. In 1909 he became Business Manager of the school, an office which he held until he left in 1921.

Mr. Cruikshank, a man of fine mind and peculiar charm, soon became absorbed in the school and almost indispensable to it. Saint Mary's "entered into his soul," and his influence quickly became a vital part of its spirit. He gave himself to Saint Mary's without stint in his continually multiplying duties; he lived and breathed for it; and his contribution to it, more intangible than material, was very great. He was an extremely interesting person, and the girls—always quicker to respond to personality than to pedagogy—reacted with enthusiasm to his sincere interest in them and their activities. He was universally liked, and by a number of the students—usually the most discriminating—he was beloved and admired. As long as he stayed at Saint Mary's, he was the main cog in the machinery of its administration and a powerful factor in the student life. Details of his life are found elsewhere in this book.

Another man, an old-style gentleman, who was for years to be closely identified with Saint Mary's and a valuable factor there, joined the faculty this year: Mr. William Enos Stone, who taught English and Philosophy. Probably most Saint Mary's girls who knew Mr. Stone remember him as the shepherd of feminine flocks on Sunday afternoon walks across "Cameron field" (now Cameron Park) and through the pine woods on the west, a diversion much more popular in pre-auto days than now.

Mr. Stone was born in Boston, Mass., in 1859. He studied in Geneva and Vevay, Switzerland, and Munich, Bavaria, before entering Harvard University, from which institution he was graduated. Before coming to Saint Mary's he had taught at the Academy at Edenton, N. C., and at the Porter Military School in Charleston, S. C.

The war between Russia and Japan, in which the sympathies of most Americans were with Japan, was in progress this year and was reflected in the subject of the inter-society debate: "Resolved: that the victory of Japan would be more advantageous to the world than that of Russia." Sympathizers with Japan were disappointed, however, when the negative E.A.P.'s Cornelia Coleman and Elmer George, defeated Sigma Lambda's Anna Clark and Marjorie Houghson.

During this session the old wooden Infirmary burned, and the present brick building was erected.

Campus leaders of the year were: Cornelia Coleman, Senior president; Ann Kimberly Gifford, president of E.A.P., and editor-in-chief of *The Muse;* Isabel Ashby Brumley, president of Sigma Lambda; Mary Bolling Sturgeon, president of Tau Delta; Margaret Gray Stedman, president of L'Etoile and the Basket Ball Association; Mildred Tilton, head of the Dramatic Club, voted by the students "most accomplished"; Carrie Helen Moore, president of the Altar Guild; Lucy Taylor Redwood, head of the Tennis Club; and Sarah Jones, "most attractive."

Feminine dress during 1903–'04 came very close to an all-time-low, scarcely equalled in hideousness by the long-waisted, pillow-slip dresses and coal-scuttle hats of 1928. In 1904, a fashion note from Paris stated that "gowns even for young girls are complicated with ruchings, pleats, shirrings, and all manner of handiwork." The more wasp-like the waist, the more stylish the figure. Belts were pulled down far in front and fastened in a point with a big pin. Above them, waists bloused in a manner most matronly. "Renaissance" sleeves, an ampler variation of the old "leg-o'-mutton," were enormous. Skirts were very long and full, plumped out with thick layers of starched petticoats. Pompadoured hair was piled heavenward in a tall tower on top of the head, whereon the magazine, *Judge,* commented:

> *She's taken a fancy to fix her hair*
> *In a sort of strange "sky-scraper" affair.*

But the bloom of the 'teens can triumph over many disadvantages; even with such heavy handicaps many Saint Mary's girls of 1903–'04 were pretty, believe it or not. Of them all, Leize Holmes Weaver was voted the "prettiest";

and Lucy Taylor Redwood, the "handsomest." And even voluminous, be-ruffled skirts and serial petticoats did not interfere much with the lively steps to which Saint Mary's danced to

> *Oh, Bedelia-elia-elia,*
> *I've made up my mind to steal yer ealyer-ealyer,*
> *Bedelia dear!*

Advertising was becoming a force in American life, and one of the booming railroads, which to date were man's most wonderful—if grimy—inventions for transportation, was appealing to dainty young ladies with numerous jingles anent a spotless heroine, such as:

> *Phoebe Snow,*
> *About to go*
> *Upon a trip to Buffalo;*
> *Her dress stays white*
> *From morn till night*
> *Upon the road of anthracite.*

Saint Mary's girls, like everyone else, were to be the beneficiaries of two events of great importance which took place in December 1903, when Wilbur and Orville Wright flew at Kitty Hawk, N. C., and M. and Mme. Curie discovered radium.

Miss Kate C. Shipp, later head of Fassifern School, came to Saint Mary's in September 1904 to teach English and Literature in the temporary absence of Miss Thomas.

The school song beginning,

> *Saint Mary's, wherever thy daughters may be,*
> *They love thy high praises to sing,*

CIRCULAR.

St. Mary's, Raleigh,
March 14, 1864.

Dear Sir:—I have just received a letter from a friend in Savannah, of which the following is an extract:

"As the late act of Congress may find you with a large amount of unappropriated funds on hand, to fund which may embarrass you, I propose that you fund for each patron *in his name* the unappropriated balances, which would answer his purposes for taxes; and that he, as soon as the new issue can be obtained, reimburse you in it to the same amount."

I most cordially thank my friend for his suggestion, which, though not more than just, I cannot, under the circumstances, but feel to be considerate and generous.

The charges for the present Term at St. Mary's were fixed early in December. They are much lower than those of many, I believe, of any school of similar grade in the Confederacy. The curtailment effected by the late law in my income must necessarily embarrass me, and compel me to fall back upon the provision made in my circular against a deficiency of income.

Six thousand pounds of meat engaged for me, were taken by the enemy on the way to Tarborough. Three thousand pounds were lost to me through the failure of a letter to reach me in due season. Other disappointments have occurred, and reduced me to the necessity of living, in these times, with a family of nearly one hundred and fifty persons, from hand to mouth. I cannot, therefore, fund, excepting for the purpose of paying my own taxes. I need the money in my hands for our daily bread. To most of my friends the bonds of the new issue will be equivalent to the money of the new issue. They can, without loss to themselves, and probably, in view of their liability to the *saving clause* in my circular, with positive gain, follow the example of my kind and thoughtful correspondent, whose letter has suggested this communication.

Such is the patriotism of our girls that they not only are content, but even grow fat, upon the plainest fare; and I have no doubt, if allowed to follow the course suggested, that I shall get through the Term without the necessity of resorting to my reserved rights. If you are disposed to authorize me to fund for you one half of your payment in advance, with the understanding that I am to be reimbursed to the same amount in the new issue, you will oblige me by sending a line to that effect immediately, to your

Obedient servant,
ALBERT SMEDES.

The crisis of the War brought "these measures that Dr. Smedes took to prevent the calamity which the closing of the School would have meant to the South and to the church in the South."

ST. MARY'S SCHOOL,

RALEIGH, N. C.

RIGHT REV. THOS. ATKINSON, D. D., VISITOR.
REV. ALDERT SMEDES, D. D. RECTOR.

The next term will commence FEBRUARY 1st, 1865.

Satisfied that it will be impracticable to purchase provisions for a large family, I am compelled either to close my School or to require payment for the board of pupils in provisions.

FIFTY DOLLARS, payable in provisions at the prices of 1860, will be the charge for board; $8 a barrel will be allowed for flour; $6 for corn; 16¾ cents a pound for bacon or lard; for beef, poultry, sugar, coffee, molasses or sorghum, &c., allowance in like proportion will be made.

For many persons, bacon and lard being the least bulky, will be the most convenient medium of exchange; they will be the most acceptable to me.

TERMS FOR TUITION, PAYABLE IN ADVANCE,

IN CURRENCY:

English, $125; French, $50; Music, with use of Piano, $150; Private Singing Lessons, $150; Drawing and Painting in Water Colors, $50; Latin, $40; Pens, Ink and use of Library, $10; Fuel, $50; Washing, at the charge of the Laundress—probably $100.

For light, we rely on the gas-works, whose operations and charges depending on the supply and the cost of rosin, are uncertain. An assessment of the actual cost of lights will, therefore, be made on each pupil at the close of the term.

Pupils are required to bring with them sheets for a single bed, pillow-cases and towels. They must also bring a cup or mug of any material, a plate, knife, fork and spoon. Their clothing should be marked with the owner's name in full. The regulation in reference to uniform is, for the present, suspended. Pupils are advised and requested to bring with them such of the following books as they may have in their possession. If not needed by themselves, they can, probably, be advantageously disposed of to others; they should bring, also, slates, pencils, pen-holders and the music which their elder sisters have accumulated.

BOOKS.—Fasquelle's French Course, and Napoleon; Ollendorf's French Grammar, Jewett; Pinney and Bandoise' French Grammar; Pinney's French Reader; Bolmar's Verb Book; Bolmar's French Fables; Charles XII; Telemaque; Conrs de Literature, par M. Chapsal; L'Allemagne, par Madame de Stael; Rowan's French Reader; Bullion's English Grammar; National 5th Reader; any good Geography, including Maps; Smith's Astronomy; Emerson's Arithmetic; Davies' Elementary Algebra, and Geometry; Scholar's Companion; Quackenboss' History of the U. S.; Weber's Outlines of U. H.; Quackenboss' Rhetoric; Blair's Rhetoric, edited by Mills; Paley's Evidences of Christianity; Parker's Nat. Philosophy; Porter's Chemistry; Town's Analysis; How's Shaksperian Reader; Whateley's Logic; Guizot's History of Civilization; Cousin's Psychology; Butler's Analogy; Bingham's Latin Grammar; Viri Romæ; Virgil; Horace; Thompson's Season's; Young's Night Thoughts; Prayer Book; Bible.

Any former pupil, or any friend of St. Mary's, who may see this list of Books, will confer a favor by forwarding such of them as can be spared, for our use during the ensuing terms.

Applications for admission should be made immediately.

Parents will please state the kind of provisions it will be most convenient to them to furnish.

RALEIGH, Jan'y 2d, 1865.

Provisions to be delivered in Raleigh, freight paid.

came into being in 1905 through the creative efforts of Herbert E. Hodgson, elder brother of the popular authoress, Frances Hodgson Burnett, and Miss Margaret M. Jones, of the school faculty. Mr. Hodgson began his visits to Saint Mary's in the 1880's and was a familiar and welcome figure around the school for more than thirty years. A native of Manchester, England, he had come to this country with his family in 1863. He was an organ builder of Norfolk, Va., and a musical composer of considerable ability. At intervals he visited Saint Mary's to look out for the school organ and to see that the pianos in the rows of practice rooms that ran from the east covered-way to the Art Building were in tune. His elder daughter, Frances, had been a student at Saint Mary's in the '90's, and he always had a lively interest in the girls there and their doings. With a Gilbert-and-Sullivan bent, he was a very talented improviser on the piano and was much given to light verse, which he wrote under the pen name of "Chaw Sir" and which often appeared in the monthly and annual *Muse*. He was the author of numerous class songs for Saint Mary's. The thrilling A. and M. cadet of the period, to whose military uniform Saint Mary's girls reacted with normal feminine susceptibility, was celebrated by Mr. Hodgson thus:

> *Though his head were solid mutton,*
> *That beautiful brass button*
>   *Would excuse the slight deficiency above;*
> *It's not his handsome face,*
> *His smartness or his grace,*
>   *But those buttons, those brass buttons, that we love.*

The annual *Muse* of 1914 was dedicated to Mr. Hodgson, in appreciation of his interest in the school and in testimony to the affection in which he was held there.

Chiefly through the efforts of Mr. Cruikshank, who

henceforth supervised its publication, the monthly *Muse* was revived during the session of 1904–'05, after several years of quiescence. Anna Barrow Clark, who also edited the annual *Muse,* was editor-in-chief.

The story of *The Muse* was begun in a preceding chapter. In 1879 Mr. Will H. Sanborn, then Director of Music, decided to have a little eight-page pamphlet published monthly to further the development of his department and to be issued "in the interest of art, literature and education and of Saint Mary's school." It contained brief notes and comments on various topics of current interest in the musical and literary worlds and some items about the school.

Mr. Sanborn turned the supervision of it over to Mrs. Meares, the Lady Principal, and under her direction it was edited by Euterpe and the Pierian Club. Miss Czarnomska took up *The Muse's* supervision when she succeeded Mrs. Meares as Lady Principal, and it was issued quarterly in 1880, 1881, and 1882. Only two numbers appeared in 1883, after which publication was suspended. In 1896 Miss McVea, then Lady Principal, was the moving spirit in the revival of *The Muse;* but during that year only two numbers, May and October, appeared. In 1898 another effort at revival resulted in a single copy, the "Holly Berry Muse."

Led by Minna Bynum (later Barbara Henderson) the class of 1899 in its final year turned from magazine to year book and published *The Smedes Memorial Muse,* which had as many pages as the usual college annual, but was more of a magazine, with paper cover, few photographs, many essays and the like. This was the connecting link between the magazine-newspaper at Saint Mary's and the year-book, which became an annual feature with that of 1900, and which for some years after its beginning was a good deal like a magazine, rather heavy with reading matter. One of the earliest of the annual *Muses,* for instance, contained essays on "Horace as Poet, Moralist, and Satirist" and on the three southern poets, Timrod, Hayne, and Lanier.

In 1904–'05 Charles Brantley Aycock, North Carolina's "educational Governor," was still conducting his campaign for universal education in this state, and in spots the issue was still heated. As a result of the inter-society debate, it was decided at Saint Mary's that "the indiscriminate education of all classes is productive neither of discontent nor of evil to the individual and society." Sigma Lambda's Anna Clark and Ellen Gibson defeated E.A.P.'s Elmer George and Rena Clark.

At this time the Chapel was only what is now the nave. In 1905 it was rebuilt and enlarged through the efforts of the alumnae. The transepts were added, and the three windows above the altar were moved to the end of the west transept, and a large triangular window in memory of Sarah Lyell Smedes, wife of Dr. Aldert Smedes, was substituted. The altar of carved wood was given by Saint Mary's girls in memory of the first two Rectors. Mrs. Annie Ruffin Cameron, of Hillsboro, gave a handsome pulpit in memory of her little grandson, Paul Carrington Cameron. Memorial windows now in the Chapel are those to: Anne Saunders, Mary Johnson Iredell, Elizabeth Dancy Battle, Nannie Belvin, Martha Austin Dowd, Gertrude Sullivan, Stella Virginia Shaw and Jean Graham Ellis Rossell.

Leading girls of 1904–'05 were: Margaret Rosalie DuBose, president of the Senior Class; Rena Hoyt Clark, president of E.A.P.; Sadie Jenkins, president of the Altar Guild; Mary Ellis Rossell, president of Sigma Lambda; Senah Critz, president of L'Etoile; Jennie Atkinson Murchison, president of Tau Delta; Anna Barrow Clark, editor-in-chief of the monthly and annual *Muse;* Mary Robinson, president of the Corinthian Athletic Club; and Jean Carson, president of the Olympic Athletic Club. (The Mu and Sigma Associations had temporarily changed their names, for some reason.)

At this period Saint Mary's girls could be very dangerous, for they wore extremely large hats which were affixed to their coiffures by spear-like hat-pins extending far beyond the brim. Such hat-pins with big ornamental silver heads were favorite and much-cherished gifts from beaux of the day. Hat-pins of this sort were also considered virtue's chief weapon of defense.

It is practically certain that, discreetly concealed in the rooms of Saint Mary's girls of 1904–'05, were several smuggled copies of Thomas Dixon's *The Clansman,* which was considered very improper reading for maidenhood at that time. For that was long before what a later wag described as "sex o'clock," and the boards of Broadway theatres were so pure that *Mrs. Warren's Profession* by George Bernard Shaw could not be produced thereon. Much more acceptable to popular taste was Maude Adams in *The Little Minister* and *Peter Pan* by the ingenuous Barrie. Indeed, the Age of Innocence!

> *Dearie, my dearie,*
> *Nothing's worth while but dreams of you,*
> *For you can make every dream come true,*
> *Dearie, my dearie-e-e!*

warbled many a sentimental soprano at Saint Mary's in the good year 1905, and at her manless school dances the Saint Mary's girl of that year two-stepped to "Wait Till the Sun Shines, Nelly!" and "In the Shade of the Old Apple Tree." That she considered holding her suitor's hand as virtually the next step to the altar is indicated by another song she liked:

FROM "FLORADORA" TO "TIPPERARY"
You can't give your heart to somebody else,
And still hold hands with me!

With a famous row of blond curls surmounting her stylish pompadour, Miss Yanita Cribbs came upon the scene at Saint Mary's in September 1905, to teach elocution and physical culture, to supervise the dormitory across from that of Miss Sutton, and to lend éclat to the Kappa Deltas.

The dormitories, of which at that time there were three, are worthy of passing note. Miss Katie, Miss Sutton, and Miss Cribbs were in charge of them. Miss Katie's was in West Rock, and the other two were on the third floor of the Main Building. In general, they were for the younger girls, who slept in two long rows of beds opposite each other with a passage-way between. The dormitory extended the whole width of the building. Miss Sutton's, for instance, was as big as the parlor two stories below it; Miss Cribbs', as big as Study Hall. The girls kept their belongings in small, dark alcoves behind their beds, where they dressed and undressed. Though privacy was at a minimum in the dormitories, there was more of what you might call family feeling in them than in the rest of the school, which probably softened the shock of being transplanted from the home soil for some of the tenderer plants.

Roosevelt the First was President of the United States in 1904–'05, and one of the excitements of the fall for the girls at Saint Mary's was when they rushed in a body to the summer-house to watch him pass on his way to the "Great State Fair," and "saluted him with Harvard 'rahs.'" According to *The Muse,* "he seemed much pleased with his reception and bowed most graciously." One girl commented, "And how he did smile!" as she recalled Teddy's toothy grin.

Miss Anne Saunders, who had been a Saint Mary's girl

and for thirteen years one of the officers of the school, died in May 1906; and with her there disappeared one of the old landmarks of the institution.

The Sigma Lambdas, Frances E. Wolf and Lillian Farmer, holding the position that "the enormous growth of the modern novel" was not "a disadvantage to education," triumphed over Jane Iredell Green and Margaret Mackay of E.A.P. in the inter-society debate.

For the first time, there was awarded at Commencement 1905 the Niles Medal for general excellence in studies and deportment, the highest honor in the school, which was instituted by the Reverend Charles M. Niles, then Rector of Trinity Church in Columbia, S. C. The first recipient of this medal was Lillian Hauser Farmer of the class of 1907.

Prominent girls of 1905–'06 were: Francis E. Woolf, president of the Senior class; Sarah Gertrude Sullivan, president of E.A.P.; Virginia Bailey, president of Sigma Lambda; Ruth Foster, editor-in-chief of the annual and monthly *Muse;* Margaret Eldredge, president of the Athletic Association; Mary T. Lassiter, president of the Altar Guild; Josephine Boylan, president of the Dramatic Club; Leonore Seay, president of the Sketch Club; Jane Iredell Green, inter-society debater and prominent in various organizations.

The tremendous hats of the period were often decorated with birds, which gave rise to a popular song in the refrain of which a hat-bird was supposed to speak disparagingly and ungrammatically of an unsuspecting suitor:

> "Well, he don't know Nelly like I do,"
> Said the saucy little bird on Nelly's hat.

Other favorites of Saint Mary's girls of that year were: "Waltz Me Around Again, Willie," "Why Did I Pick a Lemon in the Garden of Love?," "Cheyenne, Cheyenne,

Hop on My Pony," "Everybody Works but Father" and "Love Me and the World Is Mine!"

The San Francisco earthquake was the year's greatest catastrophe in the United States, but undoubtedly the news read most avidly at Saint Mary's—when the girls could get hold of it—related to the trial of Harry K. Thaw for the murder of Stanford White in a notorious triangular complication.

In the fall of 1906 there was enrolled at Saint Mary's the daughter of a Princeton professor who later was to become President of the United States. Eleanor ("Nell") Randolph Wilson entered the school this session, stayed for two years, and was awarded an English Certificate at Commencement 1908. Her mother and Mrs. DuBose had been girlhood friends; Mrs. DuBose had been one of Mrs. Wilson's bridesmaids. Professor Woodrow Wilson wanted his daughter to study Greek at Saint Mary's, so when she elected it, she created an impression of intellectuality which she maintained throughout her stay and caused her to be voted the "most intellectual" girl at Saint Mary's in 1908. She was not, however, what could be called a "greasy grind," but took part in various school activities. She was a member of Alpha Kappa Psi, an inter-society debater for Sigma Lambda in 1908, an editor of both monthly and annual *Muse*. She was also a member of the Sketch Club and the Dramatic Club and started the Riding Club, most of whose members had got around to the advanced position held by the Saratoga lady in 1901 and were riding astride—not in breeches, of course, but in divided skirts.

Most southern girls cared nothing for higher education in 1906–'07, but at least there was discussion of its value in some southern schools. The subject of the inter-society debate this year was: "Resolved: that the higher education of women makes happier homes." It could hardly be expected that the affirmative would win, and it didn't. Serena

Cobia Bailey and Helen Strange, the Sigma Lambdas, who claimed that home was happier without higher education, defeated Lillian Farmer and Louise Hill, the E.A.P.'s.

This was the first year of the Muse Club, which was responsible for publication of the monthly and annual. Usually the editor-in-chief of the monthly *Muse* was, ex officio, president of the Muse Club, but not always. The organizer and guiding spirit of the club was Mr. Cruikshank, and at the end of the first year the members gave him a gold watch-fob in appreciation of his help.

The Auditorium was built during this session, the gift of Mrs. Mary Eliza Pittman, of Tarboro, in memory of her daughter, Eliza Battle Pittman, formerly a student at Saint Mary's.

A third literary society, Alpha Rho, was organized for the Preps.

Faculty changes in 1906–'07 were: Miss Eliza A. Pool, to teach French and to be the Rector's Assistant; Miss Ada B. Smith, Mathematics; Miss Sarah H. Spurlock, German and Science; Miss Mary E. Spann and Miss Margaret DuBose, Preparatory Department; Mr. Almon W. Vincent, Director of Music; and Mrs. Marie Agnes Vincent, Voice. Miss Spurlock died in February 1907, and funeral services were held in the Chapel at Saint Mary's before her body was carried to her home in Tennessee.

Leading girls of the year were: Beatrice Hollman Cohen, Senior president; Sue Brent Prince, president of Sigma Lambda; Serena Cobia Bailey, president of the Muse Club, editor-in-chief of the monthly *Muse,* "prettiest," "most energetic"; Lillian Hauser Farmer, president of E.A.P., editor-in-chief of the annual *Muse,* "cutest"; Marguerite Le Cron, president of the Altar Guild; Rosa Heath, president of the Sketch Club and "handsomest." The Niles Medal was won by Paula Elizabeth Hazard, of the class of 1910.

The most daring attire that Saint Mary's wore that year was the "peek-a-boo" waist, which was covered with openwork embroidery. The most daring book they read—surreptitiously, of course—was Elinor Glynn's *Three Weeks*. The popular music they liked best was: "Red Wing," "I'm Afraid To Go Home in the Dark," "My Wife's Gone to the Country, Hurray! Hurray!," "Honey Boy," and the music from the comic operettas, *The Merry Widow* and *The Red Mill*. A few of the more fortunate of them saw a gorgeous big new show that was in its first year in New York, the Ziegfeld *Follies*. The most important thing that happened in their world during 1906–'07 was that Guglielmo Marconi talked over his wireless machine from Nova Scotia to Ireland.

Along about this time in the history of Saint Mary's part of the color of the school, both literal and figurative, was "Ducky," one of the maids, a small darkey who doted on the girls and invariably addressed them in terms of endearment such as "Dahlin" and "Sugah." Ducky was a favorite with them, and as she delighted to recite pieces—although she pretended to be overcome with embarrassment—they often asked her to entertain them in this way. When she finished, she would cover her face with her hands in mock shyness which fooled no one, because everybody knew that she was having the time of her life.

Mr. DuBose resigned as Rector in July 1907, "not because of any lack of interest in Saint Mary's," as *The Muse* said, "but because the details of the work as President of the school keep him from giving that attention to ministerial functions which to him comes first." The Reverend George William Lay came to take his place.

Mr. Lay was born in 1860 at Huntsville, Alabama, where his father, the Reverend Henry C. Lay, later Bishop of Easton, Maryland, was then Rector. Mr. Lay's mother was a niece of Bishop Atkinson of North Carolina. He was educated at St. Paul's School in Concord, N. H., and was graduated from Yale in the class of 1882. He received his B.D. from the General Theological Seminary in New York in 1886 and was ordained to the priesthood that same year. After his ordination he was assistant at churches in Erie, Pa. and Newburgh, New York; and from 1888 until he came to Saint Mary's, he was a teacher in St. Paul's School in Concord, N. H. In 1894 he married Anna Booth Balch, of Baltimore, Maryland, daughter of Rear-Admiral George Beall Balch of the United States Navy.

With Mr. Lay's advent at Saint Mary's, the Rectory overflowed with little Lays, seven of them; and an eighth, Thomas Atkinson, named for his kinsman, the North Carolina bishop, was to be born there in 1910 and die there in 1915. Before he had been christened Thomas Atkinson in the Chapel, he had been denominated "Octavius" by the student body, as the eighth of the Rector's brood. The quiet charm of the mother of this numerous juvenile Laity endeared her both to Saint Mary's and to Raleigh.

When the Lays arrived in the Summer of 1907 from the up-and-coming North, Saint Mary's, like an impecunious patrician, seemed a little shabby and behind-the-times. The dining-room then was in the basement of Smedes Hall. It was unscreened, as was the rest of the school. Little Negro boys waved fans to shoo away the flies. One of them was Ducky's son, Uriah, named after that "mighty man of valor," Uriah the Hittite. Dark Uriah of the Saint Mary's dining-room displayed his valor against winged and buzzing invaders. Cows wandered over the scraggly turf of the grove. The school kept horses and hogs—not always fragrant—in the stables and pens in the rear.

Mr. Lay took a keen look around, and then things began to happen. First, the wandering cows were sold. Later the hogs went, too. The grove was plowed up and planted in fertilizing peas and clover, to be sown a few years afterward in grass. Screens were forthcoming, and the labors of Uriah were eased. The curriculum got attention. A course in home economics was instituted and the preparatory work was put under a regular director. The whole academic side was jacked up. A regime of discipline was inaugurated, to the surprise and displeasure of some parents who could not understand why exceptions could not be made in the case of their daughters. Saint Mary's School was in the hands of an experienced schoolman, able and firm. Its most progressive regime to date had begun.

Mr. Lay had his mellower moments, too. One fall after three weeks of rainy weather, when many homesick tears had accompanied those of Nature, the sun shone again on a school day. Whereupon, out of a clear sky, Mr. Lay decreed a holiday, cheered by which the school morale shot up like a rocket.

One innovation by Mr. Lay was to have several A. and M. boys sing in the Chapel choir at vespers on Sundays. At St. Paul's he had been used to boys' voices, and he thought they would improve the choir at Saint Mary's. The A. and M. boys, who were carefully shepherded by the Rector himself, seemed to enjoy participating in the Chapel service, and undoubtedly improved the music. This custom continued for several years.

Mrs. Leonora W. Shieb, a handsome widow from Louisiana, was Mr. Lay's first Lady Principal. Mlle E. de Joubert La Loge came this year to teach French, and Miss Scharlie E. Russell was made Director of the Preparatory Department, with Miss Mable A. Horsley as assistant.

Prominent girls of the year were: Isabel Atwell Hanna, president of the five Seniors, three of whom were from Maryland; Marguerite Vertner Thompson, president of Sigma Lambda; Sallie Haywood Battle, president of E.A.P.; Meta C. Boykin, president of the Olympic Athletic Association; Georgia Stanton Hales, editor-in-chief of the monthly

Muse. No editor-in-chief of the annual was designated. Esther Rembert was the "cutest" and the "most attractive"; Marjorie Brown, the "prettiest"; Anna Coates Benedict, the "handsomest."

The Niles Medalist of 1907–'08 was Minnie Tamplet Hazard, of the class of 1910, sister of the winner of the medal the preceding year.

The inter-society debate was on the good old southern topic of whether Robert E. Lee did more for the Confederacy than Jefferson Davis. He didn't, according to the victorious E.A.P.'s, Julia Louise McIntyre and Ellen K. Duvall, who defeated Eleanor R. Wilson and Mary Campbell Shuford of Sigma Lambda.

This was the year when the pompadour reached its peak. It became, in a word, incredible in its mammoth proportions, with foundations of large, head-heating "rats." That of Lyman Grimsley was by long odds the most imposing in school. Now that Queen Victoria had been dead for several years, the girls were growing rather daring. They wore narrow "sheath" skirts which, though long, of course, occasionally gave glimpses of openwork stockings and brought on considerable conversation amongst their elders as to what the world was coming to—a question of no perceptible concern to damsels who were singing blithely,

> *Yip—I—Addy—I—Ay—I—Ay,*
> *Yip—I—Addy—I—Ay!*
> *I don't care what becomes of me,*
> *When you play me that sweet melody!*

or who were expressing their adolescent yearnings in "I Hear You Calling Me." When something didn't suit them, they exclaimed in the slang of the day, "Ain't it awful, Mabel!"

"An eye can threaten like a loaded gun" was the quotation in the annual *Muse* applied to Miss Eleanor Walter Thomas, who in the Fall of 1908 became Lady Principal of Saint Mary's, after having taught English there for several years and having given numerous students a genuine taste for their own literature. That this quotation was accurate in the extreme some whom that terrifying eye has withered can rise, even thirty years later, to testify. Deadliest in the memory of Saint Mary's was it upon the occasion when it quelled in an instant a riot in study hall.

One of the teachers was a gentle lady, but she did not know how to handle girls, a fact of which, of course, they were immediately aware. Once while she was supervising Study Hall, in which all the students sat for a few hours in the evening, presumably preparing their lessons for the next day, "Satan found some mischief still" for at least one pair of idle hands. Gently but deliberatedly they pushed a detested text-book off the desk. It fell to the floor with a loud bang. The startling report acted instantly to free the mob spirit, never far below the surface in a youthful crowd, male or female. "Bang!" went a second book in another part of the hall. "Blim-blam!" went more. Feet began to scrape noisily across the floor. The poor lady at the desk was dismayed but impotent, for in a twinkling her little charges were completely out of hand. For several minutes pandemonium reigned, when suddenly a door opened, and a little figure mounted the platform and stood in diminutive but appalling dignity behind the desk. From its big brown eyes darted lightnings as fierce as Jove's. With its paralyzing entrance the storm had abruptly ceased, and in ominous silence the ocular lightnings flashed. Then upon the cringing culprits a little voice, in wrath more awful for its perfect control, pronounced the doom of "restriction." The originally mischievous hands were clasped in prayer.

That was Miss Thomas.

For some years she has been associate professor of English and assistant dean of Western Reserve University, after getting her Ph.D. at Columbia and teaching a year at Lake Erie College, but many of her memories of St. Mary's are still green. The most vivid of these she enumerates as:

"The Faculty presentation of *Alice in Wonderland*. No one who saw them could forget Mr. Cruikshank as the King of Hearts, Miss Lee as the Queen, Miss Schutt as the Duchess, Mr. Owen as the Mad Hatter, Miss Fenner as the weeping Mock Turtle, and Miss Sutton as an inimitable Cheshire Cat. Then came Mr. Cruikshank's brilliant burlesque of *Alice* for the Muse Club to give for the Seniors.

"Our Shakespeare festival on the Tercentenary of Shakespeare's death in 1916.

"The seventy-fifth anniversary celebration with religious, academic, and social observances in 1917. On that occasion the alumnae ramped through halls and grove.

"Our missionary sewing meetings in Lent when I, as inconspicuously as possible, read detective stories to my chapter while they sewed, or the gatherings of the little girls in my room on Sunday evenings while the older girls were having club meetings.

"My institution of a partial student government plan. I wished to reduce chaperonage as irksome for students as well as for faculty, to develop greater independence and sense of responsibility in girls who were really young women in their late teens and early twenties, and to enlist the co-operation of students with faculty—to encourage the *esprit de corps* which had always been resident in St. Mary's. I should like to pay tribute to the sororities and to the upperclassmen as vigorous and loyal supporters of faculty standards of what a St. Mary's girl should and should not do.

"My respect for Mr. Lay and my admiration of what he

did for St. Mary's. No matter how much his predecessors had done toward the making of a great school, Mr. Lay found the necessity of a stiffening of academic standards and discipline. Such a stiffening is never an easy or popular process. Mr. Lay accomplished his task with courage and with unswerving honesty of purpose and integrity. I say all thanks to him, and may his memory be held in perpetual adoration.

"Then there come crowding on me memories of girl after girl who in chief part made St. Mary's what St. Mary's is to me: gifted students like Esther Means, Kate Meares, Nell Wilson, Nell Lewis; the four Thomas girls—quiet Florence, busy Sadie, puzzled Marie, and 'best all-round girl' Arabelle; faithful, devoted little Fannie Stallings and Elise Stiles—the first to die so soon after college, the second to end her life trying to save a child in one of the ship disasters of 1918; and many, many girls with brains and charm, too—Bessie Arthur, Esther Rembert, the Rogersons, the Bordens, Amy Winston, Patsey Smith, and a host of others. And I never forget the little rascals who were always breaking rules which now seem to me very trivial, and the culprits forgivable and lovable.

"I recall, too, with pleasure—pleasure now too poignant —my European trips with St. Mary's girls: of my six summers in England or on the Continent, four were with St. Mary's folk. And St. Mary's used to show friendly interest in those towns of mine and Miss Fenner's.

"I have not mentioned many other memories of the St. Mary's of my day which I hold in common with hundreds and thousands of others—memories of grove and of chapel and especially of persons. There were many of marked individuality whose traits gave color to life at St. Mary's: the charm of Miss Dowd; the high spirits and wit of 'C. F.,' as Miss Fenner called herself; the intense interest of Miss

Sutton; the never-failing kindness, friendliness, and resourcefulness of Mr. Cruikshank; the humility of the scholar in Mr. Stone."

Fresh from Smith, in September 1908 came an attractive blond, so untrammeled in the liberal education there received that during divine services in the Chapel on the holy Sabbath day she sat serenely in the grove and openly sewed —sewed on Sunday!—and the Almighty didn't strike her down! Of such refreshing independence was Miss Georgina Kellogg, and her unconventional behavior put quite a new light upon the higher education of women in at least one youthful mind. If Smith turned them out like that, why, then it might be a college well worth attending.

Miss Bertha May Luney joined the music faculty this year, and Miss Margaret M. Jones came back to Saint Mary's to teach mathematics, after having studied for a year at Columbia and having taught a year afterward in the New York City schools. And Miss "Mittie" Dowd, a lovely person, who had been teaching piano at Saint Mary's, became Director of the Department of Music.

The most important event of the session of 1908–'09 was the legacy which Saint Mary's received from the estate of Miss Eleanor Clement, who had already established a $5,000 scholarship at the school. Miss Clement, as a girl twelve or thirteen years old, had come to Saint Mary's in the 1840's with her mother, Madame Clement, who was Dr. Aldert Smedes' first French teacher. Miss Clement attended Saint Mary's and afterward taught French there for several years. After this, she and her mother lived for a while in Wilmington, N. C., and then opened a girls' school in Germantown, Pa., which was very successful. Miss Clement had died in 1904, and in her will had made Saint Mary's the residuary legatee of her estate after the death of her friend, Miss Osborne, who had been one of her teachers at Saint Mary's, with whom she lived, and to whom she left the bulk

THE REVEREND BENNETT SMEDES
RECTOR, 1877–1899
"Beloved of all who knew him and respected by all with whom he came in contact, the years have shown how well he did his work."

MR. BENNETT SMEDES AND FACULTY

Mr. Bennett chose "a well-selected faculty who were destined not only to maintain the already high scholastic standards of the school but to raise them to higher levels to meet the needs of the emerging South."

of her property. After Miss Osborne's death, Saint Mary's received in 1909 about $30,000.

To the great satisfaction of the enterprising Rector, this legacy made possible the addition of the East and West Wings, the big front porch of Smedes Hall, and Clement Hall, directly in the rear of Smedes, in which are the dining-room and the gymnasium. The cornerstone of these additions was laid on April 3, 1909, and contained a copy of the Bible, The Book of Common Prayer, the Church Hymnal, the *Saint Mary's Bulletin* containing a history of the school, the annual *Muse,* the monthly *Muse,* and the last will and testament of the benefactor.

Though few, if any, Saint Mary's girls of 1908–'09 were so unwomanly as to want to vote, at least suffrage for women was debated at the school this year. But Mary Shuford and Janie DuBose, representing Sigma Lambda, upheld the noblest traditions of home-loving, hearth-tending southern womanhood and easily convinced the judges that the extension of the suffrage to women would not "improve the condition of society." Unfortunate Julia McIntyre and Ida Jean Rogerson who, against all their rearing, had to defend the affirmative, went down in defeat.

So uncommon a conveyance in Raleigh in 1909 was the automobile that when Miss Thomas, Miss Jones, Miss Cribbs, Mr. Cruikshank, and Mr. Hodgson went to Durham in one "in spite of a very high wind" to hear President Eliot of Harvard lecture, they were, according to *The Muse,* "cheered and encouraged by the assembled school who were greatly interested in the trip" which, happily, turned out to be "almost devoid of the usual mishaps and delays that beset motor cars." So far as is known, neither Mr. Cruikshank nor Mr. Hodgson "had to get under, get out and get under, to fix up his automobile," as a song popular a few years later ran.

Three entertainments which delighted the Saint Mary's

girls of this year were Norman Hackett in *Classmates,* a play about West Point; James Young in *Brown of Harvard,* and the Saint Mary's faculty in *Alice in Wonderland.*

The Niles Medalist of 1909 was Georgia Stanton Hales, who also was editor-in-chief of the annual *Muse.* Other prominent girls of the year were: Minnie Leary, president of the Sigma Lambda; Sallie Haywood Battle, president of the Senior class and of E.A.P.; Nell Battle Lewis, president of the Athletic Association; Mary Campbell Shuford, editor-in-chief of the monthly *Muse* and president of the Muse Club. Esther Rembert was still the "most attractive," and Marjorie Brown, still the "prettiest." Mildred Borden, a regal adolescent, was "handsomest."

Wide ruching around the top of high, boned collars was the vogue. Though it seems hardly possible, hats were getting bigger and bigger. In 1908–'09 they were about the size of an umbrella. No greater contrast could be imagined than that between the hats of 1908 and those of 1941. Regardless of grammar and implications which later Freudians might draw, Saint Mary's girls of 1908–'09 were singing, "Next to Your Mother, Who Do You Love?" Other favorites were: "I Wonder Who's Kissing Her Now" and "I've Got Rings on My Fingers and Bells on My Toes."

R. Blinn Owen came to the school in 1909 as teacher of voice and organ and stayed for several years. The girls liked him, and he liked them and entered heartily into the school life. He was a jolly fellow, as well as a good musician, and added to the general gaiety.

In October, 1909, a wedding of much interest to the school took place, when Miss Cribbs' famous curls were covered with a bridal veil and she was married to Mr. Carol Lamb Mann. Her friends at Saint Mary's who regretted losing her were consoled by the fact that she was to live in Raleigh after her marriage.

On April 20, 1910, the Centennial of the anniversary of

the birth of Dr. Aldert Smedes was held at Saint Mary's, when Bishop Robert Strange of the Diocese of East Carolina was the principal speaker, and when Smedes kinfolks and other friends of the school gathered in force.

Society should execute its worst felons, said the victorious E.A.P.'s, Virginia Randolph Bolling Pickel and Nell Battle Lewis, who in the annual debate defeated Janie DuBose and Helen Areson, Sigma Lambdas, who favored life-imprisonment. Twenty-five years later Nell Battle Lewis atoned for her youthful blood-lust by a long crusade against the death penalty in North Carolina in her column, "Incidentally," in the Raleigh *News and Observer.*

Prominent girls of the year were: Rebecca Hill Shields, president of the Senior class; Virginia R. B. Pickel, Niles Medalist; Mary Shuford, president of Sigma Lambda (one term) and editor-in-chief of the annual *Muse;* Lena Payne Everett, president of Sigma Lambda (one term); Agnes Tinsley Harrison, president of the Athletic Association and of the Sketch Club; Mary Owen Green, editor-in-chief of the monthly *Muse;* Virginia Prettyman, president of Sigma; Martha Byrd Spruill, president of Mu; Janie DuBose, "most influential" and "most interesting"; Hortense Jones, "best-looking"; Helen McArthur, "most fascinating."

The annual *Muse* of this year, like those of several preceding, was full of pictures of ephemeral clubs, most of them eating clubs, which were organized chiefly in order to get the names and pictures of the members into the annual. They had such names as W.M.T.E. (We Meet To Eat) and E.T.Y.B. (Eat Till You Bust). Eating on the side was quite an activity in those days. The only place at which refreshments could be bought was "The Little Store," a small grocery near the railroad bridge on Hillsboro Street. Times when girls could get permission to go there were limited, so boxes of food from home were great events and midnight feasts high adventures in those simple days.

The emphasis, indeed, was still upon simplicity, as witness a popular song of the year:

> *Any little girl that's a nice little girl*
> *Is the right little girl for me.*
> *She don't have to look like a girl in a book,*
> *If a good cook she can be.*
> *She don't have to wear rats in her hair,*
> *Or a "straight front X.Y.Z."*
> *Any little girl that's a nice little girl*
> *Is the right little girl for me.*

Saint Mary's girls who went to New York in vacations during the session of 1909–'10 were enthralled by the comic operetta, *The Chocolate Soldier,* and came back to school singing fervently,

> *Come, come, I want you o-o-only!*
> *COME, hero of mine!*

Miss Anna Buxton, teaching English; Miss Helen Urquhart, teaching Latin; and Miss Louise Hill, a graduate of Saint Mary's, assisting in the office, joined the staff of the school when it opened in 1910.

Prominent girls of the year were: Josephine Pearl Tonnoffski, president of the six Seniors, all but one of whom were from Raleigh, Patsey Harry Smith, Niles Medalist; Isabel H. Perry, president of Sigma Lambda; Elizabeth Wood Leary, president of the Altar Guild; Agnes Tinsley Harrison, president of the Athletic Association; Nell Battle Lewis, president of E.A.P. and the Muse Club, editor-in-chief of the annual and monthly *Muse;* Shepherd Leak, "best-looking"; Helen McArthur, "most attractive"; and Amelia Sturgeon, "most popular."

Ruth Critz and Tinsley Harrison, upholding the negative for Sigma Lambda, won the inter-society debate on the query, "Resolved that the modern stage is beneficial rather than harmful." Their defeated opponents of E.A.P. were Elizabeth Leary and Patsey Smith.

Irving Berlin was just coming into popularity at this time, and Saint Mary's girls of 1910–'11 were "crazy about" his big hit, "Alexander's Rag-Time Band." Other favorites of the year were: "The Oceana Roll," "Oh, You Beautiful Doll," "I Want a Girl Just Like the Girl That Married Dear Old Dad," and "Everybody's Doing It." During this session the Parlor was the scene of very strange antics and contortions, for those terpsichorean curiosities, the "Bunny Hug," the "Grizzly Bear," and the "Turkey Trot" were all the rage. Not only were Saint Mary's girls proficient in these, but, with Vernon and Irene Castle as their models, many of them were expert at the new "Fox Trot."

The marriage of Miss Margaret M. Jones and Mr. Ernest Cruikshank, both long associated with Saint Mary's, took place on June 17, 1911, in St. Paul's Chapel at Columbia University, New York City. Mr. and Mrs. Cruikshank returned to the school to live, to the interest and pleasure of the students, among whom their romance had been a lively topic.

The Reverend McNeely DuBose, fourth Rector of Saint Mary's, who had left the school in 1907 to take up parish work in Morganton, N. C., died on April 15, 1911.

In September 1911 Miss Florence Cathaline Davis came to Saint Mary's, to become an integral and important factor in its life for the next three decades. Miss Lily Piemont Skinner was the new French teacher.

Campus leaders of the year were: Patsey Harry Smith, president of the Senior class, of Sketch Club, and of E.A.P. (one term), editor-in-chief of the annual and monthly *Muse*, "most popular," "daintiest"; Mary Brown Butler, Niles

Medalist and "best student"; Mary Hancock Owen, president of Sigma Lambda; Jennie Woodruff, president of the Altar Guild; Evelyn Maxwell, president of Mu; Amabel Conyers Winston, president of Sigma and "handsomest"; Amelia Pinkney Sturgeon, "prettiest" and "most attractive."

Through efforts in behalf of the affirmative by Caroline ("Lina") Ashe Lockhart and Mary Brown Butler of Sigma Lambda against Patsey Smith and Mary Owen of E.A.P., it was decided in the inter-society debate that "the reading of realistic fiction is more profitable to the young than the reading of romantic fiction." In spite of which the young at Saint Mary's continued to prefer the romantic variety.

A third literary society was resurrected this year, Alpha Rho, which in 1907 had existed for the Preps. But its membership now, like that of the other two literary societies, was drawn from the regular school.

"Goodnight, nurse!" was the slang phrase used most by Saint Mary's girls of this day. "Boudoir caps" were a fad with them, and in a photograph of the residents of one of the dormitories in dishabille these caps are practically indistinguishable from the dust-cap worn by Ducky, the dormitory's mascot. The girls of 1911–'12 danced to "When the Midnight Choo-Choo Leaves for Alabam," "Waiting for The Robert E. Lee," "When It's Apple Blossom Time in Normandy," and "Here Comes My Daddy Now." On the walls of the rooms of some of them was a picture of the bathing girl of the year, "September Morn," over which the prurient had stirred up a teapot-tempest. The biggest news story that they read in the papers was that of the sinking of the Titanic.

Two weddings which took place in the Chapel in April, 1913, were of special interest at Saint Mary's because of the connection of the brides with the school. On Wednesday of

Easter Week Annie Webb Cheshire, who was graduated from Saint Mary's in 1903, was married to Dr. Augustine S. Tucker, of Virginia, a medical missionary in China, where Miss Cheshire also had been in the mission field. Officiating at the ceremony were the fathers of the bride and bridegroom, the Right Reverend Joseph Blount Cheshire, Bishop of North Carolina and President of the Board of Trustees of Saint Mary's, and the Right Reverend Beverley D. Tucker, Bishop of Southern Virginia. This combination of large and prominent Episcopal families of North Carolina and Virginia resulted in an almost unlimited collection of kinfolks. Bishop Tucker had thirteen children, and Bishop Cheshire had seven, so the combined relatives were a goodly host, one so large, in fact, that when Augustine, the eldest son of Dr. and Mrs. Tucker, was first brought to this country from China, he seriously inquired, "Mother, is everybody in America my cousin?"

The second of the two weddings in the Chapel in the Spring of 1913 was that of Annie Gales Root to William W. Vass, of Raleigh, which took place on April 30th. Miss Root, a graduate of Saint Mary's of the class of 1903, was a great-granddaughter of the founder of the school, Dr. Aldert Smedes.

Although it had been decided at Saint Mary's as a result of the inter-society debate of 1908–'09 that extension of the suffrage to women would not "improve the condition of society," the question was again debated in 1912–'13, and this time the suffrage cause fared better. American women were to have the vote in seven years, regardless of school debaters, and sentiment for woman suffrage was increasing, even in the South. Mary Brown Butler and Lanie Stanton Hales of Sigma Lambda, upholding the negative of the query, "Resolved: that it is undesirable that women should have the suffrage," defeated Julia Horner Cooper and Julia Washington Allen of E.A.P.

Prominent girls of the year were: Caroline Jones, president of the Senior class, chief monitor, editor-in-chief of the monthly and annual *Muse;* Julia Washington Allen, Niles Medalist; Mary Brown Butler, president of Sigma Lambda; Bessie White, president of E.A.P. (one term) and "handsomest"; Rebecca Kyle, president of E.A.P. (one term); Amabel Conyers Winston, president of Sigma Athletic Association; Evelyn Maxwell, president of Mu Athletic Association; Jennie Woodruff, president of the Altar Guild and "most influential"; Carrie Cleaton, "prettiest."

Francis X. Bushman and J. Warren Kerrigan, of the still-flickering silent movies, were stars popular with Saint Mary's girls. Mary Pickford, whose soubriquet then was "America's Sweetheart," was their queen of the cinema. They sang and danced to Irving Berlin's "International Rag," "He'd Have To Get Under, Get Out and Get Under," and "You Made Me Love.You; I Didn't Want To Do It."

When the students of Saint Mary's assembled in the Chapel for the opening service of the session of 1913–'14, they were stunned. From behind the lectern there looked at them a wholly unfamiliar face, one which had been identified by the Raleigh Police Department, but which was unknown to them. Could it be? . . . Well, maybe it might be . . . Why, yes, it really was—MR. LAY! Previously the Rector had worn a heavy beard and moustache, but while visiting his brother in Colorado in the Summer of 1913, he had shaved them off. Now his countenance was as naked as an onion. So unrecognizable was he that upon returning bare-faced to Raleigh, the first thing he had done was to present himself in the office of the police and identify himself.

Miss Lillian Fenner, sister of Miss Clara, head of the Art Department, became Housekeeper at Saint Mary's in 1913.

For two years previous she had been Assistant Housekeeper there.

Prominent girls of the year were: Myrtle Warren, president of the Senior class and "most influential"; Lanie Stanton Hales, president of Sigma Lambda and of the Sigma Athletic Association, "most popular," "most attractive," "most interesting," and "best talker"; Susie McIver, president of E.A.P. (one term); Margaret Huntington Bottum, president of E.A.P. (one term); Elizabeth Tarry, president of the Altar Guild and of the Dramatic Club; Julia Horner Cooper, president of the Mu Athletic Association; Laura Margaret Hoppe, editor-in-chief of the monthly *Muse;* Annie Sutton Cameron, "best student"; Mary Webber Williams, "prettiest"; Susan Graham Huff, "handsomest." Virginia Lucille Bonner won the Niles Medal.

Three debates were held this year, Alpha Rho winning over both Sigma Lambda and E.A.P., and E.A.P. winning over Sigma Lambda. The subjects were the open shop, Greek letter fraternities, and vocational education. Debaters were: Eliza Davis, Matilda Hancock, Mary Floyd and Katherine Bourne, Alpha Rho; Margaret Bottum, Eliza Skinner, Julia Cooper, and Pensie Warren, E.A.P.; Lanie Hales, Miriam Reynolds, Camelia London, and Courtney Crowder, Sigma Lambda.

Pearl White in "The Perils of Pauline" was the most exciting thing that the girls saw at the movies this year. They were wearing "hobble" skirts, very tight around the bottom; their hats were still tremendous, and their hair, very blowsy over the forehead, was usually twisted into a "Psyche" knot behind. Probably the most important world event of their year was the first radio broadcast, in which Kaiser Wilhelm II of Germany sent a greeting to President Woodrow Wilson, who soon was to become his enemy. At Saint Mary's they were dancing to "When You Wore a Tulip, a Big Yellow Tulip, and I Wore a Big Red Rose."

The war raging in Europe touched the girls of Saint Mary's only lightly. Revolving in their own small circles, they knew and cared little about the great events of the first World War, which their own country was to enter two years later. True, at Christmas time, they helped to stock the "Santa Claus Ship," which carried toys and clothes and food from Americans to the children of the belligerent countries, including Germany, a project originated by a Chicago editor, James H. Keeley. But, for the most part, not even ripples from the great storm reached them.

There were three debates again this year. In various ways their subjects expressed some dubiousness as to so-called progress. It was debated whether the rapid change in fashions was desirable, whether the movies were a greater educational force than the periodicals and, most pertinent at Saint Mary's, whether the girl of 1915 was superior to her grandmother. E.A.P. won two of the debates; Sigma Lambda, one. The debaters were: Ruby Thorn, Courtney Crowder, Eleanor Relyea and Frances Strong, Sigma Lambda; Rena Harding, Josephine Wilson, Alice Latham, and Elsie Alexander, E.A.P.; and Matilda Hancock, Eliza Davis, Robena Carter and Katherine Bourne, Alpha Rho.

Prominent girls of 1914–'15 were: Lanie Hales, president of Sigma Lambda (one term), "most fascinating," "most attractive"; Helen Peoples, president of the Senior class; Courtney Crowder, president of Sigma Lambda (one term); Agnes Hyde Barton, president of E.A.P. (one term), Margaret H. Bottum, president of E.A.P. (one term), editor-in-chief of the monthly and annual *Muse*, "most influential"; Matilda Hancock, president of Alpha Rho; Elizabeth Carrison, president of Mu Athletic Association; Annie Sutton Cameron, president of Sigma Athletic Association, "most ambitious," "best student"; Arabelle Thomas, "best all-round"; Adelyn Barbee, "best looking"; Katharine

Drane, "prettiest." The Niles Medalist was Eliza Dickenson Davis.

There were no more enthusiastic persons in the audiences which cheered David W. Griffith's first big feature movie, "The Birth of a Nation," than the girls of Saint Mary's, most of whom were familiar with the picture's Civil War background from their own family traditions. In the parlor these days they were dancing to a marching song of another war, "Tipperary."

So the stream flowed on, bringing each year new faces, new friendships, new achievements, new hopes. During its flow from 1900 to 1915 three persons had especially vital parts in the life of Saint Mary's: Miss Katie McKimmon, Miss Juliet Sutton, and Miss Lizzie Lee. By their devotion they infused themselves into the very foundations of the place. Hundreds of young lives were affected by them for good.

Miss Katie had custody of the younger girls, and she brought them up in the way they should go, inspecting them with an eagle eye to see that they were properly dressed, inspiring them with her own ideals of southern gentility, and communicating to them something of her own ardent love for the lost Confederate cause. Apropos of the last, it was years before Miss Katie could bring herself to sit through the singing of "The Star-Spangled Banner," and to the end she was not happy in the same room with a picture of Abraham Lincoln.

Through the school's post-office window, thousands of missives passed from the hands of Miss Sutton into those of eager recipients, in most of whom she had keen personal interest. At first as assistant in the Preparatory and Business Departments and later as secretary to the Rector and mistress of the school post-office and book-store, Miss Sutton had manifold duties, which she diligently discharged. But her chief interest was in the girls themselves, those in the school in general, and particularly those in her dormitory and later on her hall. She didn't like them all—she was too human for that—and from her quick and sometimes acidulous tongue those she didn't like were pretty apt to know it. But she liked most of them, and, as troublesome as they often were, they entertained and amused her. To some of them she was devoted, and these returned her affection with interest.

Always the impeccable lady in word and bearing, Miss Lizzie Lee by her gentle influence was long a benediction to the school. Serene and unruffled, she pursued the even tenor of her way through the busy years. Although the pothooks of stenography and the rattling keys of typewriters were her specialties in the Business Department, kindness and innate grace were her specialties, too.

From the banks these three stalwarts for years watched the stream of girlhood flow past them, carrying with it always their interest and their love and enriched by their memory.

5

New Lamps for Old
1915-1930

By Jane Toy Coolidge

IT IS Thursday morning, September 16th, 1915. The opening chapel service is over and the long line of girls has filed back to the School Room for the first assembly of the year. New girls move uneasily, fearful of doing the wrong thing; old girls exchange confident glances. From the platform Miss Thomas looks down upon them all, her dark eyes filled with challenging zest. There is the sparkle of fun in those eyes (the girls she has just chaperoned to the Panama Pacific Exposition will vouch for that) but there is business too. "No joking now," they seem to say; "a new session is upon us. We must set to work."

Miss Katie is near, leaning on the crutch she must use since last year's accident, glad to be back on duty with her primary class; Miss Dowd, refreshed by her winter of study in New York; Miss Fenner, gruff and jolly; Mademoiselle Rudnicka, high-pompadoured, unchangingly Gallic; Mr. Stone, a red rose in his lapel but a harassed look in his eye, the latter, doubtless, a hang-over from superintending the arrival of a hundred girls and their trunks; Miss Lee, white-haired and queenly; Miss Davis, active and energetic. And in the background, the tall, slightly stooping figure of Mr. Cruikshank, his watchful eye on everything, making sure that the wheels turn smoothly as they start on their course.

But Dr. Lay has risen to speak. His deep voice reaches to the last row of the big, crowded room.

"Young ladies," he says, "it gives me great pleasure to welcome you to Saint Mary's School. As the Bishop told you in the Chapel, it is very lonesome here in the summer time and we miss you all very much; it is a real and genuine pleasure to have you back and to be with you once more. I am especially glad to have the privilege of welcoming here the new girls. You have come wondering how you are going to get on, and I wish to say for your encouragement that we have looked you over and think you are a particularly nice looking set of girls. I hope that each one of you will try to do her best to keep up the general average and to improve in such wise as to make a general average improvement for the whole body.

"We are beginning what is for the most of us a new period of work. I think it would help you a little if I use an illustration which I have used before and which is familiar to many of you. You know that when you have to go into cold water, if you wade in slowly, it is one long-drawn-out agony from the tips of your toes to your neck, whereas if you plunge boldly in all at once the deed is done and there is practically no discomfort. It is the same way with your work here. The way to begin is to begin. Let each one of you determine to begin at once as strenuously as possible and not postpone your best endeavors until later on. . . .

"I ask you then to begin at once to try to accomplish the best that is in you, and to take as the one great rule of life here consideration for others, which is the foundation of Christian charity and of true breeding. And I ask you to begin your co-operation right now by helping us in every way to get the work started at once. There are very many of you, and in order to avoid confusion each one must try to do exactly as she is asked, and listen carefully to get clearly in her mind the requests that are made, and then try to carry out these requests in a way that will be considerate of others and enable us all to start off with comfort to everybody."

He stops. For an instant his keen, ice-gray eyes sweep over the assemblage. Have the girls taken in his message? Have they grasped the thing he wants to tell them, the fruit of years of living and teaching that he wishes so earnestly to pass on to these beginners? Some have and some haven't; he is too much of a realist to think that his words of wisdom have fallen on completely fertile soil. He knows girls too well to imagine that. But among the girls before him—bright-eyed, eager, timid, mischievous, wayward, mercurial or phlegmatic, there are some who have grasped his meaning, who will remember his words and be guided by them. Some who will put into practice the principles in which he so firmly and honestly and doggedly and courageously believes. He has started them on their course. The year's work has begun.

It was to be a good year, 1915–'16. Abroad throughout the nation and beyond the Atlantic new currents were in motion, the beginnings of the great tidal wave of change that was to leave no spot in the world untouched when finally it swept upon them, but for this year at least, and for the two that followed, the quiet back-water that was Saint Mary's was undisturbed. Those years marked the culmination of an era in the life of the school. In them the work of Dr. Lay, Mr. Cruikshank, and Miss Thomas came to its full fruition. These three personalities, each so forceful, shaped the school's character and left their imprint on every Saint Mary's girl of the time. It is not an accident that the classes of '15, '16 and '17 stand out as exceptionally strong ones. The fact that the school moved on an even keel, under vigorous and settled leadership, surely played its part.

The Saint Mary's of those years was rich, but the riches were of the spirit. The physical equipment of the school was the inheritance from former years, dear and highly prized but indubitably shabby. Money was scarce, and no wonder; the Summer Bulletin of 1915 gives the reason in its final paragraph: "When one considers the age and size of Saint Mary's, its ample curriculum and extensive educational advantages, its refined tone and high traditions, its excellent health conditions and its *moderate charge of only $300 for all necessary expenses, including laundry and medical fee* (italics mine) one is justified in concluding that it would be hard to find another institution which offers so much for so little." How true, how pathetically true! One smiles at the modest note of pride in the above masterpiece of understatement, but the actual process of keeping up the school on $300 a year per pupil was far from a laughing matter.

There was little money for repairs. A bit of painting each summer, a chary distribution of refurbishment in the most needed spots, that was the extent of physical renovation that could be provided. How carefully and painfully the dollars were stretched to do this only Mr. Cruikshank knew. He put the paint on where it would do most good and took comfort in the thought that brick and mortar can never make a great school, while the things of the spirit can. And the girls, though they shivered sometimes in the vast, high-ceiled rooms of Main Building, and grumbled when the keys of practice pianos stuck, and shuddered when the floors of Senior Hall shook under their feet, never thought of rebelling against these discomforts. They came to regard such shortcomings as the peculiarities of a beloved friend, things to be put up with, joked about, and eventually even to be loved.

And some of the inherited antiquities were fun. Such was the dark, winding secret stairway in Main Building, by which, if you had forgotten to post your name for a bath, you could creep, kimonoed, down to the big, shadowy bathroom on the first floor. There, in one of the seven-foot zinc bathtubs you could usually snatch a bath without reservation. True, only cold water was available, but young blood runs warm, and the sense of adventure that went with the cold plunge made up for its shivers.

When the practice piano allotted you turned out to be a dud, you solved the problem by taking any other piano that happened to be vacant and making your peace with the inspector as best you could. The scanty equipment available for Dramatic Club plays did not cramp their style in the least. Miss Davis may have sighed in secret for more adequate aid to her art, but she never let the girls suspect such longings. She hung the stage with crepe paper roses and wistaria, persuaded Mr. Cullen to haul in small forests of pine and cedar, and tried to make the performance so good that the audience would think only of the actors.

The Rock Buildings were real antiquities. West Rock, sacred to Miss Katie, housed the last of the dormitories, where the youngest pupils, smarting under the indignity of the arrangement, rather than rebelling against its discomfort, led a communal existence. What was the joy of these youngsters, when, coming back for their second year, they were promoted to real rooms!

East Rock was unbelievably crowded. Mr. Cruikshank's office held so many filing cabinets, stacks of books, piles of papers, boxes of samples, and other unnamed heterogeneities that it was hard to see how it could accommodate human beings as well, yet accommodate them it did, and with surprising elasticity. Miss Sutton's office at the left rear end of the hall was a trifle less jammed with inanimate objects, but more apt to be filled with girls. There you went on Monday morning to draw out money for a trip to town, and there, should you be lucky enough to be called to the telephone, you perched on the window sill and talked to your best beau under Miss Sutton's eagle eye and within earshot of Miss Lee in the business room and Dr. Lay in his office across the hall. And the Post Office! Were ever so many girls crowded into such small space as in that tiny room and the corridor outside? True, they overflowed into the covered way, but all the same it was a good thing that East Rock rested on firm foundations of stone, else twice a day over a period of many years its existence would have been threatened.

Plain living and high thinking, that was the philosophy of the school, though no one put it into words. Occasional bursts of luxury were all very well—dinners at the Yarborough Hotel with visiting parents, feasts from generous boxes sent from home, luncheons at the Governor's Mansion for the favored few who had invitations—but from day to day and from month to month fleshly indulgences were definitely not The Thing. They were frowned upon, not only by the faculty, but by the girls who set the tone of the student body. Hard work and high ideals, self-discipline and self-denial, those were the principles upon which the life of the school was based.

Clothes were simple, middy blouses and shapeless, ankle-length skirts being the most popular costume. One shampooed one's own hair, arranged it in a modified pompadour or Psyche knot without benefit of artificial curl, and forgot it unless to add a black ribbon tied straight around the head, crossing the forehead directly over the eyebrows, which was considered a smart touch.

With this heritage from '15, the session of 1915–'16 began. The Rector had received the honorary degree, D.C.L., at Sewanee's Commencement. Dr. Lay's words set the pace for the year. "Plunge in boldly—the way to begin is to begin!" There were only ten Seniors this year, but the calibre of the class was high, and its smallness drew them together. Katherine Bourne, Annie Cameron, Mary Floyd, Selena Galbraith, Frances Geitner, Rena Harding, Susan Lamb, Fannie Stallings, Josephine Wilson, and Helen Wright—how close was their intimacy, how seriously they took their responsibilities, what fun they had in Senior Hall!

Led by these ten capable and energetic Seniors, the school entered upon a golden year. Its outstanding feature was the Shakespeare Tercentenary celebration, an event which gave new and vivid color to the spring term, but even without the Tercentenary the year would have been rich in accomplishment. Each of the traditional entertainments was marked by a new and zestful interpretation. The faculty's dramatization of *Alice in Wonderland* with Miss Thomas as the White Rabbit was one of the high spots. The Carnival, the Hallowe'en party, and the Junior-Senior banquet were others. And throughout the year there flowed from the facile pens of Annie Cameron, Katherine Bourne, and Mr. Cruikshank verses and songs that were to linger as school traditions.

So many of these verses were written, and so great was their appeal, that a special leaflet containing them was incorporated in the annual *Muse*. Among the most popular was a parody on Tit Willow:

On a stool near the mail line our little one sat,
 Wailing "Muse dues, your Muse dues, your MUSE DUES!"
And I said to her, "Fannie dear, what are you at?"
 Wailing "Muse dues, your Muse dues, your Muse dues?"

"Is it pressure of poverty, dearie?" we cried,
  "Or a mean disposition within your inside?"
With a toss of her dear little head she replied,
  "It's Muse dues, your Muse dues, your MUSE DUES!"

and the lines commemorating daily exercise units earned by walks around the grove:

> Most boring thing in this whole school
>   Is units, units, units!
> There's no escape from that dread rule
>   Of units, units, units.
> The sun may shine, the rain may pour
> Be raging hot or ice galore
> But still you have to walk once more
>   Those units, units, units!
>
> Be sure you do not fail to post
>   Your units, units, units.
> For if you do you're surely lost
>   By units, units, units.
> For be assured, if you forget
> You'll have the hardest trial yet,
> For you'll have to do an extra set
>   Of units, units, units!

What a picture those last lines call up! The Exercise Chart inside the School Room door was a huge rectangle of white paper, carefully lined, with the list of students at the left-hand side and beyond each name a series of minute squares in which the symbols W for Walking, G for Gym or Ex for Excused must be daily inserted. It had to be done by each girl in person, and honestly. W meant ten walks around the big outer circle of the grove. Leisurely walks with friends were fun, but if one delayed till the last moment those ten puffing circuits were a real chore.

All over the United States in the spring of 1916 celebrations of the Shakespeare Tercentenary were being held, but nowhere was the commemoration more whole-hearted than at Saint Mary's. For weeks everyone in the school lived, breathed, ate, drank, talked, thought, and dreamed Shakespeare. Behind it all, originating the idea, planning each detail and working indefatigably to carry it out, was Miss Thomas. A devoted Shakespearean scholar, she envisioned a celebration in which every member of the school would take an active and vital part, and her magnetism fired faculty and students with enthusiasm for the enterprise.

The project was divided into three parts: a literary contest which took the place of the annual inter-society debates, the Shakespearean Festival in early May, and the presentation of *As You Like It* at Commencement. In addition a Shakespearean Number of the *Muse* was published. That issue of the Monthly with its stories, essays, and poems on Shakespearean themes, its photographs of Morris dancers and actors in doublet and hose, and its account of the May Day Revels gives ample proof of the fact that for a brief space, at least, all Saint Mary's went truly Elizabethan. But let Miss Thomas tell of it herself:

"The Festival took place in the Grove on the right-hand side of the Auditorium, where there is a natural stage large enough for some two hundred people. About this stage, by 8:15 on May Day, there had collected a goodly crowd of five hundred or more of our friends of the city, when the many arc lights were flashed on and the celebration began with the blowing of trumpets by the two heralds (Velma Jutkins and Hattie Copeland). Rena Harding spoke the prologue, praying for the imagination of the audience to amend all deficiencies (such as skirts substituted for trunks and hoes) and to hear and judge the play with gentleness and kindness.

"There followed the gathering of the village folk, who made way with bows and greetings for the gentry—my lady of the manor, the good town bailiff, the master of the revels, and a numerous train of such Shakespearean characters as Queen Katherine, (Miss Glen) Hamlet (Miss Davis, richly dressed in black velvet), and Ophelia. Among them was Miss Lee, who in silver lace and jewels was a handsome and courtly figure.

"The lady of the manor (Miss Thomas) and the announcer of the sports (Mr. Owen, a true jester in cap and bells and brilliant garb) then set on the revels, in which all gaily joined. During dance and song the festival folk sat in groups on the grass, and between numbers peddlers cried their wares; the hobby-horses, ridden by Annie Cameron and Katherine Bourne, trotted about, and once the constables seized a "pick-purse" and tied him to a tree.

"After the dances 'Her Majesty's Players' presented Act V of *A Midsummer Night's Dream*. The tragic mirth of 'this lamentable comedy' was as delightful as always and forever; truly 'the passion of loud laughter never shed more merry tears.'

"From all sides we learn that our play 'did well beguile the heavy gait of night,' and that we did indeed succeed in re-creating something of the spirit and the detail of the days of the great poet whom we delight to honor, so that our friends could not but obey Puck's appeal to think that in truth they had but slumbered and had dreamed the village gathering, joyous dance and song, fairy revel and progress of stately lord and lady of those golden far-off days were once more real and present, once more of our sober work-a-day world."

Thus the May Day Revels ran their course. Weary Morris dancers and players and courtiers and villagers crept late into their beds, carrying with them the memory of a vivid experience. In that memory two figures stand out—

Miss Thomas and Annie Cameron. Nineteen-fifteen-sixteen was their year. Of Miss Thomas much is said elsewhere, but the story of the year cannot be closed without a word as to Annie Cameron's part in it. Quiet, modest, retiring, she was one who would have been content to remain in the background, but her rare gift as a writer, her strength of character and her devotion to Saint Mary's placed her almost against her will in the forefront of the school's life. There she took her place with unassuming dignity, forgetful of self; no task was too great to be undertaken, and what she undertook she completed, never satisfied until she had given it her best. From her pen verse flowed with what seemed effortless ease, and through all that she wrote, serious, humorous, verse or prose, there runs the common note of love and loyalty to Saint Mary's. Nowhere is this more evident than in the following lines, as filled with poignant meaning today as when she wrote in 1916:

TO SAINT MARY'S CHAPEL

Once more within thy sacred walls
 We meet, but not alone.
The hearts of all who held thee dear
 Meet with us here as one.
We feel their silent blessing
 Upon us as we pray.
The hopes and prayers that once were theirs
 Still live in us today.

For thee they labored, thee they strove,
 They loved thee and passed on,
Leaving to us an heritage
 Of all that they had won.
A sacred charge they gave us
 In trust divine and deep.

Thine honor and thy name they left
  For us to guard and keep.

Thou art to us the token
  Of all we hold most dear,
Mute bond of love unbroken
  Thy sheltering arms we near.
Thou dost our love enkindle,
  Our loyal hearts enroll
In kinship stronger than of blood,
  The kinship of the soul.

And through the discord of the world
  Thy music rising clear,
Dispels the doubt that once we had,
  Casts out our craven fear.
Hopes by defeat once shattered
  And sullied with the dust,
We pledge again in thy dear name,
  In holy love and trust.

Like these who loved and labored,
  Led by thy steadfast light,
We pass from thee with strengthened hands
  To battle for the right.
And as we strive to follow
  The pathway they have trod,
We pray God's peace be ever thine,
  Oh little house of God!

Nineteen hundred and seventeen was heralded as an anniversary year—the seventy-fifth of the school's founding, the fiftieth of Miss Katie's association with Saint Mary's, the twentieth of Church ownership, and Dr. Lay's tenth year as rector. The opening session found the school with a large enrollment and the faculty almost unchanged under the firm guidance of the Lay-Cruikshank-Thomas triumvirate. The academic faculty had not lost a member; Miss Abbott and Miss Shull of the music school had been replaced by Mr. Hagedorn and Miss Thompson; Miss Metcalf's place in Household Arts had been taken by Miss Trowbridge, and in the Infirmary Mrs. Bottum was succeeded by Miss Alexander. The Trustees, alive to the need for an endowment, had inaugurated a campaign to raise $250,000 and entrusted its leadership to the Reverend Francis Osborne. The Alumnae, working zealously, had completed the McKimmon-Iredell Fund of $5000, a tangible tribute of devotion to those two beloved teachers.

Physical changes in the school were the conversion of half of the West Rock dormitory into rooms, and the installation of indirect lighting in the school room and the library. "The lamps," reported the monthly *Muse,* "are attractive in appearance and the lighting both abundant and agreeable. The lights in the library are a gift from the Class of 1912 which had a reunion last May, Miss Patsey Smith and Miss Elizabeth Hughes of Raleigh being the leading spirits."

Two things stand out in the session of 1916–'17, first the Anniversary celebration, and second the wave of patriotic fervor attendant upon our entrance into the war. Always the influence of the past had been strong at Saint Mary's; in this year it was scheduled for a triumphant climax. The program was carried out, yet even as this was being done, the war crisis filled all hearts and minds with new urgencies. Step by step the United States was being drawn into the war, and in its small microcosm Saint Mary's reflected the reaction of the nation as a whole.

War clouds were in the air, but for the fall and winter terms they were remote. The daily activities of the school went on without change. The traditional parties were held, and in addition the Muse Club inaugurated the Circus, complete with ring-master, clowns, acrobats, elephants, sea-lions, side-shows, pop-corn, and pink lemonade. The girls who were at that Circus still remember Madame Trazini, the Living Wonder, the Boneless Woman, and the Head Without a Body. They remember, too, High Culture in Dixie as described by Annie Robinson, large and black in an old-time mammy's costume, and her pointed remarks about the "cemetery" where her daughter obtained that culture. The applause that greeted her equalled that given another actress who appeared in Raleigh just a week later, Maude Adams in *The Little Minister*.

Two other notable artists were heard during the season, Paderewski, to whom music students listened reverently, and Alfred Noyes, who read his poems at Meredith College. The latter, young and charming and very English, made a vivid impression; the influence of his style may be seen in the literary output of Saint Mary's for several years to come.

The Muse Club this year was at the height of its power. What an honor it was to betake one's self to the curtained secrecy of the Muse Room on Sunday evening, there under Mr. Cruikshank's tutelage to plan activities which later the whole school would share! Mr. Cruikshank spoke earnestly; his listeners hung raptly on every word. They were, his confidences intimated, the elect of the school; theirs was the responsibility of leading the student body in the right way. *Noblesse oblige.* No girl who shared in those meetings failed to feel the power of the spell, to leave the Muse Room fired with high resolve, and what is more, oftener than not to make aspiration a reality.

Other clubs there were, too, less lofty in purpose, gatherings of kindred spirits intimate and free from care. The Follies, the Merry-makers, and those mysterious alphabetical identifications S.O.C., B.D., T.I.B., S.D., D.G.S. and T.S.S.—what hours of fun those names recall! To the clubs' natural fascination was added the charm of fruit that was, if not actually forbidden, certainly not altogether approved by the authorities. It was known that in high quarters clubs were condemned as cliquish. This was their final year; soon the edict was to go forth sending them the way of their predecessors, the sororities, but for this last year club members revelled in their joys.

Joys there were a-plenty in the fall of 1916, pleasures in which the whole school joined. The Halloween party made history with its colored wedding (Miss Fenner and Mrs. Cruikshank as bride and groom, Miss Lil Fenner and Miss Alexander attendants) Mr. and Mrs. Owen as the Campbell kids, and the Seniors as nursery rhyme characters under the guidance of Alice Latham as Mother Goose. But more serious matters were afoot. Stories of suffering in Europe touched all hearts and stirred hands to action. Belgian Relief work was begun, and a bazaar was held in the parlor, each girl preparing a gift to be sold, and more than $100 was realized. At Christmas the exchange of gifts was foregone and the money saved contributed to the Belgian Fund. Later a First Aid class was formed, teachers and girls studying their manuals together. When examinations were held, great was the thrill of those girls whose marks were higher than their teachers'. The star performers were Miss Thompson and Agnes Pratt, with 100 per cent each.

The months wore on and war fever mounted daily. Hearts were keyed high, nerves stretched taut with anticipation, half fearful, half exultant. On April 3rd, three days before the United States declared war on Germany, Dr. Lay addressed the student body at a special meeting after dinner in the school room.

"No country has ever pursued the course taken by

America in the past two years," he said, "in the firm conviction that war is not the right method by which to overturn wrong. This great country has been patient, temperate, moderate in the face of insult. On no one has the responsibility and anxiety of this time of sufferance borne more heavily than on our President. What shall we do to show our sympathy and loyalty to him?"

Three hours later, at 9:30, the school room was again crowded with girls, towsled now after their study period, but no less enthusiastic. Alice Latham, President of the Senior Class, stood before the assemblage and read:

April 3, 1917.

Mrs. Wm. G. McAdoo,
1719 Massachusetts Ave.
Washington, D. C.

The students of Saint Mary's have tonight adopted unanimously the following resolution:

We, the girls and teachers of Saint Mary's School wish, through you, to extend to our President our wholehearted sympathy for him in this crisis and to pledge to him and to our country our loyal service.

It has been with deepest admiration that we have watched and applauded each move that he has made in his wise guidance of our country and his firm championship.

Signed,
Alice Latham, President Senior Class
Katharine Drane, President Junior Class
Estelle Ravenel, President Sophomore Class
Nancy Woolford, President Freshman Class
Nettie Daniels, President Sub-Freshman Class
Eleanor W. Thomas, for the Faculty
George W. Lay, Rector.

"It is in order that a motion be made to adopt the resolution."

The motion was made.

"Any seconding of the motion?"

The school came to its feet clamorously; the adoption was by rising vote. And the voters continued to rise. Up they climbed on benches and desks and lifted up shouts and yells as an outlet for pent-up feelings, feelings that sprang from vaguely defined fears of what was to happen soon, and from heightened emotion at the call of patriotism.

There is small wonder that the answer to this telegram to Mrs. McAdoo was delayed. The wonder is that in those portentous days an answer came at all.

>Washington, D. C.
>April 14, 1917
>
>Alice Latham, President Senior Class
>Saint Mary's School, Raleigh, N. C.
>
>Have not had an opportunity until today to show your splendid telegram to my father. He has asked me to send you his deep appreciation and warm thanks for your message, and to say that such a pledge of faith and service does much to cheer and encourage him.
>
>I send my thanks and my love to my school.
>
>Eleanor Wilson McAdoo

War had been declared. Fateful days were upon us. It seemed strange now deliberately to focus attention on the past, yet the Anniversary Celebration was scheduled for May 11th and was not to be laid aside. War was a fact, but none the less true was the school's seventy-five years of high accomplishment. Incongruous, then, though it seemed, it was truly fitting that when war furor was at its height, commemoration should have been made of Saint Mary's achievement in the enduring arts of peace.

The celebration included an address by Emilie Watts McVea, beloved alumna and former Lady Principal of Saint Mary's, now president of Sweet Briar College. There was a special session of the Literary Societies at which the prize winning selections of the year's contest were read, "Three Scenes from the Life of Saint Mary's" by Katherine Drane and "The Thirteen Originals" by Aline Hughes; addresses were made by representatives of the societies, and songs written for the occasion were sung with gusto—"To Find Mr. Cruikshank," "Happy and Innocent," and "The Old Swing on Senior Hall."

The Anniversary Pageant picturing the past and present life of the school was presented by the student body with the assistance of groups of alumnae; it included dances, figure drills, living pictures, and plays. The celebration ended with an evening performance of the Gilbert and Sullivan opera "Patience," beautifully given by the Chorus Class under Mr. Owen's direction. Truly, for all who were present, May 11th and 12th, 1917, were full and memorable days.

Commencement followed close upon them, and tearful goodbyes were said to the fifteen graduates, Virginia C. Allen, Virginia P. Allen, Emma Badham, Frances Cheatham, Jeanet Fairley, Georgia Foster, Elmyra Jenkins, Golda Judd, Alice Latham, Eva Peele, Eleanor Relyea, Annie Robinson, Nellie Rose, Rubie Thorn, and Ethel Yates. It was the occasion of another parting as well, for word had gone out that Miss Thomas was not to return in the fall. Wide-eyed in dazed surprise girls stared at one another. It couldn't, it just couldn't be true! So vital, so integral a part of Saint Mary's had Miss Thomas become in her seventeen years as Lady Principal that it was hard to conceive of the school without her.

Deep indeed was the universal sense of loss, for Saint Mary's debt to Eleanor Walters Thomas was great. Scholarship she had brought to the school, and firm integrity of character, and the magic gift of a glowing personality that illumined her every word and act. Girls who came after her day knew her as a legend; to those who were under her tutelage she was a force whose influence is with them still. One of these, Aline Hughes, has expressed what many others feel:

"There is a snapshot in my kodak album which brings Saint Mary's back to me in a rush of memory—those exciting, busy, happy days. It is a picture of 'our Miss Thomas.' She is seated alone on one of the lower steps leading to Main Building, now Smedes Hall, a small but potent figure. There is no hat on her soft, wavy brown hair, worn in a loose pompadour. She is crouched down, elbow on knee, fist supporting her cheek, looking straight into the camera. She is not smiling, but there is the impression that a twinkle might not be far away. It is so natural a pose that I can almost hear her soft, clear voice, with her clipped way of saying 'S'nt Mary's,' always a little strange to us who were accustomed to sing broadly 'Sai-aint Mary's, wherever thy daughters may be, etc.'

"Among all the hubbub and clamour of excitable girls she lived her quiet life somewhat aloof. She had no intimates, although the respectful admiration and affection of the school were hers. A few Seniors were in her confidence, chatting and laughing with our Lady Principal to the admiring astonishment of younger students. To most of the girls she was a figure apart, clever, witty, amusing, fair but stern with all. She was often seen in serious conferences with the Rector, Dr. Lay; and more frequently she and Mr. Cruikshank would stand beside a bench in the grove, he stooping from his great height, one foot propped on the bench, his long arms gesticulating. It was one of our favorite groups for we loved them both even though we smiled at the contrast in their appearance.

"Miss Thomas had an apartment in Main Building overlooking the grove of oak trees. Her living room there was used as an office where she interviewed the sinners and those who had problems at certain stated hours. At those times the bench outside her door was crowded with quaking girls, for Miss Thomas' eyes could flash, and she drew the truth out of one as if it were a sore tooth and she the dentist. It was, however, a pleasant room with an open fireplace and books and comfortable chairs. Once I went there for a conference about a paper I was to read in my Junior year. Her kindness and her clear mind were equally helpful to me and made the room seem no longer a place of judgment. I have known the room as a warm and friendly spot on Sunday evenings when she gathered some of the prep department girls there to read 'A Window in Thrums' and 'Sentimental Tommy.'

"She was kind to these youngsters from the dormitory, with an understanding of their mischief and sympathy for their occasional bouts of homesickness; but she was not sentimental over them or over anything else. If one of them threw pepper in the dormitory to make the others sneeze, she was sure to be punished for it, but she was made to feel that this was justice and no unfriendliness, and Miss Thomas' eyes could not quite hide a twinkle.

"Her sense of humor was keen and she had a very quick wit which delighted the students in her brief talks in assembly hall, adding spice to the otherwise dull bread of notices and rules. But Miss Thomas was not a smiling person. Her outlook on life was serious, clear-eyed, idealistic. Her small person had a simple dignity even as she walked about the school, hatless, her coat hanging loose upon her shoulders. I can see her now in the crown and velvets of the Lady of the Manor at our Shakespearean Festival.

"She was one of the best teachers I've ever known. In the first place, she was a scholar herself and she taught English literature as one who knew and loved it. Her reading of poetry was like music. Parrot-like recitations she would only allow from dull students; if she thought a girl capable of more she lashed at her with tongue and wit until the sluggish mind caught the spark and flashed back in reply. She filled us with respect for herself and enthusiasm for the subject. Her rare compliment was like an accolade. It has always been a source of regret to me that Miss Thomas did not return in my Senior year and that we were deprived then of her inspiring influence and her friendship."

> *Hail to our boys in France!*
> *Hail to the cause of right!*
> *We love and honor them,*
> *Support the cause for which they fight!*

All through the school in the spring of 1918 you could hear those words. The Chorus Class sang them, jauntily repeating "boys in France" at the end of the first line; they were hummed in covered ways and corridors, and when groups gathered around the piano in the evening, somebody was sure to start them. "Hail to Our Boys in France" shared honors with "K-k-k Katie," "Joan of Arc," "Keep the Home Fires Burning," and "Over There." It was a good song and it was our very own. Mr. Owen had composed the music, the words were from Aline Hughes' pen. Nineteen-seventeen—eighteen was our war year; its spirit is in that song.

"Honor the boys in France! Pitch in and work here at home! Let every girl do her bit to win the war!" There was no joking about it; we were in deadly earnest. "Slacker" was the most contemned word in the school vocabulary, and in spite of all the weakness of the flesh, slackers were few. Patriotism burned at white heat.

Work for the Red Cross was first in the list of war-time activities. The school was 100 per cent in membership and in contributions to the War Fund. Surgical dressings were made in the Muse Room under Miss Lee's supervision, Louise Toler directing, Jane Ruffin and Mary Mullins in charge of tables. ("Muggins," the best monkey who ever climbed a rope in the circus, how swiftly her agile fingers rolled bandages now!) Knitting needles clicked from West Rock to Senior Hall, and the output of sweaters, socks, helmets, eye-pads, wristlets, and washcloths was something to be proud of.

Thrift-stamp teams were organized and rivaled each other in patriotic hoarding—and in the choice of ferocious names, "Kaiser Killers," "The Stamp Act," "Lick'ems," "Hun Hunters," and "S.O.T.K." (Stamp out the Kaiser). Meatless and Wheatless days were kept conscientiously and with surprisingly little grumbling. Even more surprisingly, an Anti-Candy Club was formed. At parties only the simplest refreshments were served, often none at all. It was a time of high ideals and self-denial, with the elation of whole-hearted effort for the Cause.

With spring came war gardening and clean-up work. Teams of volunteers were formed to join in the cultivation of a school garden and in caring for the grounds. Pairs of girls carrying mowers, rakes, and sickles became a familiar sight in the grove; weed pullers grew grubby-handed and red of face as they struggled in the garden back of the dining hall, and in every breast was the proud consciousness that Saint Mary's was doing her part.

These war activities were carried on in spare time. Regular school work went on as usual. The faculty, with the exception of the Lady Principal, was almost the same as the previous year. Miss Agnes Barton, a member of the class of 1915, replaced Miss Julia Allen, and Miss Lillian Fenner was succeeded as housekeeper by Mrs. Marriott, who came in the fall of 1917 to begin her long and valued association with the school. In the spring Miss Urquart, who had been in charge of Latin for five years, received an emergency call to National Red Cross Headquarters and was released from teaching to take up this work.

As Lady Principal and teacher of English literature Miss Lucy G. Hester undertook the difficult task of filling Miss Thomas' place. She was to remain at Saint Mary's for only one year, and by the girls who knew her she will always be mentally associated with the fifty-first psalm, the memorizing of which she meted out as punishment for minor offenses. Stern and unbending, handsomely dressed in dark purple, she would sit at her desk, prayer-book in hand, while one by one the sinners stood before her and declaimed:

"Have mercy upon me, O God, after thy great goodness; according to the multitude of thy mercies do away mine offenses.

"Wash me thoroughly of my wickedness and cleanse me from my sin."

On one occasion, if memory serves me, the entire student body was convicted of noisiness in assembly, and the penitential verses assigned to them all. If she did not already know that psalm by heart, surely by the time the sentence was carried out its words must have been engraved upon the Lady Principal's memory. It is possible that such a multitude of miserable sinners overwhelmed her; she bore with them for one year, then vanished from the Saint Mary's horizon.

In spite of war work the regular program of school activities was carried on with little change. New interest in the literary societies was stimulated by a revision of the system limiting their number to two. Alpha Rho, being the youngest society, was abolished and its members divided between Sigma Lambda and E.A.P. The monthly

Muse was edited by these in turn, and they vied with each other in supplying worthy material. Stories and poems poured in, most of them romantic presentations of wartime themes. Through the *Muse's* pages gallant boys in khaki marched to victory or death, lay in muddy trenches lit by bursting star shells, or were blissfully united with long-lost loves. There were reflections of the war's impact on school life as well. Mary Yellott, who had taken Annie Cameron's place as school poet, wrote:

> *"And have you bought your Thrift Stamp yet?*
>   *No? Well, I have it here.*
> *Oh come, you know you have the change—*
>   *It's just a quarter, dear.*
> *You want your quarter for ice-cream?*
>   *It would be nice, but how*
> *Then is the Kaiser to be licked?*
>   *And think, the cream's for now,*
> *But if you get your stamp today*
>   *In nineteen-twenty-three*
> *You'll get your quarter back again*
>   *With interest, you see."*
>
> *And so the stamp is sold, and so*
>   *You go without your cream.*
> *But you've helped to lick the Kaiser*
>   *And bring triumph to your team!*

Saint Mary's war year drew to its close. The annual *Muse,* bound for economy's sake in cardboard instead of leather, was dedicated:

To
Esther Barnwell Means, 1904
now with the Y.W.C.A. in France

NEW LAMPS FOR OLD

to
Dorothy Valentine Brown, 1910–11
Red Cross Nurse in France

and to
All Saint Mary's girls at home and abroad
who are devoting their time and their energy
with unselfish zeal
to the great cause of our country.

The ten war Seniors, Katharine Drane, Bessie Folk, Aline Hughes, Helen Laughinghouse, Helen Mason, Maude Miller, Henrietta Morgan, Novella Moye, Gertrude Pleasants, Agnes Pratt and Estelle Ravenel, carried the daisy chain out into the grove and sang "Goodby School, We're Through." The war chapter was at an end, for its influence was to touch but lightly the opening weeks of the next fall. And though the girls of 1917–'18 did not know it, a far more important era of the school's history had also closed. Before another term began Dr. Lay, after eleven years of staunch and fruitful service, was to leave Saint Mary's.

Coming to Saint Mary's in 1907, Dr. Lay brought to the school gifts of a high order—a keen and penetrating mind, forthright honesty of word and deed, and an indomitable will. An educator of long experience, he had a very definite vision of the Church School's function, a vision in which high spiritual ideals were translated into actuality by mental discipline. Laxness of thought, slackness in the performance of duty he would not tolerate. Intensely practical, he saw in the homely virtues of promptness, exactitude, and diligence the essentials of character building, and these he demanded from the girls under his tutelage.

Regular attendance at classes, chapel, and assembly he insisted upon, even when indulgent parents wished their daughters excused for pleasure excursions; this rule sometimes caused heart-aches, but his firmness in enforcing it did much to foster sound habits of study and to weld the school into a strong and cohesive entity. To Dr. Lay Duty was, in very truth, the sublimest of words; in devotion to it he spared neither himself nor others, and on the solid granite bedrock of that devotion Saint Mary's stood firmly grounded during his eleven years as its head.

With dogged perseverance and unflagging energy, he gave to Saint Mary's always of his very best. When in the summer of 1918 he terminated his rectorship, he left behind him an institution vastly stronger, sounder, and more efficient than the one to which in 1907 he had come. And in the hearts of all who knew him there he left the memory of a true leader of the Church Militant, strong of faith, courageous in action, unswervingly true to his ideal.

The opening of the 1918–'19 term found the school under new leadership. Dr. Warren W. Way, beloved rector of Saint Luke's Church in Salisbury, North Carolina, had been called to take Dr. Lay's place. Born in Irvington, Illinois, Dr. Way had received his training at Hobart College, the General Theological Seminary, and the University of Chicago. He had served as assistant at All Angels' Church, New York City, as missionary in Illinois, and as rector of Grace Church, Cortland, New York, before going to Salisbury. Mrs. Way had been Miss Louisa Atkinson Smith of Staunton, Virginia, and their family consisted of three children, Evelyn, Roger, and Warren, Jr. The Ways moved into the rectory during the summer of 1918, and Dr. Way took over the guidance of the school.

At the same time Miss Alice Edwards Jones, a teacher of long experience in private schools and former head of the Latin Department of Winthrop College, became Lady Principal. There were numerous changes in the faculty as well; Miss Thornton, Miss Dennis, Miss Southwick, Miss Bierce, Miss Giddens, Miss Sheppard, and Miss Meares entered upon their association with Saint Mary's. Of these, Sue Kyle Southwick's tenure of office was to be the longest, her place in the affections of the school family the most enduring. A true artist, a skilled teacher of piano, and a bright and charming figure, she endeared herself to pupils and faculty alike, and to a wide circle of music lovers throughout the state.

The school's enrollment this year was the largest in history, the number of resident pupils passing the 200 mark. New faces were everywhere, new adjustments had to be made. And with it all, during the second week of the term an unheralded visitor made its appearance—Spanish influenza.

From the army training camp at State College where thousands of soldiers were learning to operate those strange new war vehicles, tanks, came the first word of the pestilence. Rumors of its terrors fell upon startled, incredulous ears; surely, steady-headed girls and teachers told each other, these reports were exaggerated; at any rate, serious though the epidemic might be, it was still remote. The words "Spanish influenza" had a distant, alien sound. And then overnight all remoteness was gone; Saint Mary's was in the grip of the flu.

Every bed in the Infirmary was filled, new ones were crowded in wherever possible, and West Wing was transformed into a hospital. Nurses were imported as long as they were available, but with State College, the Tank Camp, and the city of Raleigh stricken, soon no nurses were to be had. Teachers volunteered for nursing duty, readily accepting new and arduous tasks. Yet each day the number of those able to carry on the work was fewer; morning and evening lines formed at the Infirmary where Miss Alexander took temperatures, and daily the lines grew shorter as increasing numbers were ordered to bed.

Classes were suspended and parents notified that their

daughters were free to come home; there was a general exodus of all well enough to go, girls from a distance being allowed to visit friends nearby. As soon as patients recovered they, too, were sent home to convalesce, and the remaining school family settled down to battle out the siege. Miss Alexander, Dr. Knox and Dr. Root ably led the fight, and all who were able helped to carry on.

The servant staff was depleted and there was much arduous work to be done; heavy trays had to be carried from the Dining Hall to West Wing; necessities and comforts had to be supplied to the sufferers, and spirits had to be kept up. Miss Jones was in the forefront of the fight. To be given an alcohol rub by the Lady Principal might have seemed under ordinary circumstances a strange experience, but circumstances were not ordinary now, and such ministrations were accepted most gratefully.

The epidemic wore itself out. By the middle of October it was safe to call back the students and resume the regular routine. The crisis had been successfully met, yet it left in its wake a train of problems. Reorganization of the year's program under a shortened schedule made the session of 1918–'19 a difficult one for the leaders of the school.

A month has passed. It is early of a cold November morning. Outside the stars are shining and all is quiet. Inside the school buildings it is still quieter, for all the girls are snuggling under blankets and dreaming, some of days not wheatless or meatless, others of the far-off day when He will come back from France.

Suddenly a shrill, piercing noise breaks in upon the dreams. Girls sit up in bed and listen. The noise grows louder and louder. Factory whistles, automobile horns, bells. What can it be? Is there a fire? No red glow shows against the sky but the clamor still increases. Automobiles are dashing down Hillsboro Street; groups of people are clustered on the sidewalks. Then through the darkness come newsboys crying "Extra! Extra!"

We can hear them as they come nearer and nearer. One is in the grove and we strain our ears to catch the words "Extra! Extra! The war am over now for sure! We done woke up Peace!" Peace. Can it be true? We are stunned, dazed. We have almost forgotten how we felt before the war. We cannot realize that the boys aren't fighting any more, that they are safe.

But there is no time to ponder. Lights have sprung on in the halls and everybody is dressing, throwing on sweaters and coats and rushing out. Already some girls are in the grove running around and yelling. There! That last shoestring pops, but we can't stop for that. We tuck it in somehow and dash out to the grove.

What a strange sight meets our eyes! In front of Main Building is a crowd of girls, but goodness! can they be the same ones we saw in the parlor last night? these girls with hair screwed into tight knots and sweaters flung hastily over shoulders? Yes, they are the same. Perhaps it is the glow upon their faces, the awed look in their eyes that has changed them. Eyes are shining with suspicious brightness, and one girl is crying even as she smiles. No wonder, for her brother is in a German prison camp and now she knows that he is safe.

Someone has started a snake dance in the grove. In the gray light of the dawn a long string of girls with joined hands is dancing around. We all join in that mad dance. More girls come out, yelling and beating on dustpans. Finally we stop, breathless, and discover that our arms are around a girl's neck. We hug each other violently, and when we finally break apart, find that we don't even know each other's names.

But see! Over in the east there is a rosy glow. In a moment the rim of the sun peeps through the trees. Keevie Wilkes has brought out the flag and we find ourselves gathered around the flagpole. The Stars and Stripes rise against a pale sky. We are silent now, and a great solemnity comes over us. Every hand goes up in salute. Someone starts the Star-Spangled Banner, and how we sing! Never before have the familiar notes seemed so beautiful; this dawn has given them new meaning; as we sing them our hearts throb with joy and thankfulness and peace.

Thus Armistice Day came to Saint Mary's. Elation filled the air. Peace—and victory. The war had been won. Before us lay a brave new world. Happy days, those, days of joy and triumph and trust.

Following upon this elation came the reality of hard work. The time lost by the influenza epidemic had to be made up. Holidays were curtailed and the school swung into its stride. Dr. Way made history by introducing the first innovation of his regime, chapel caps. Pie-shaped triangles of black serge were distributed to each girl and assembled into head coverings of startling individuality, creations that proved treasure trove for school wits. Chasing lost chapel caps and the substitution of unnamable objects became a favorite sport.

> *Three little kittens, they lost their mittens,*
> *A great and tragic mishap.*
> *Though that's very sad, it's not half as bad*
> *As losing your last chapel cap!*

But the caps had come to stay, and at Easter the school blossomed into white ones.

Spats, also, became an important article of apparel. The flu had put authorities on their guard, and the edict went forth that no girl should appear with ankles unprotected. The high-shoe era still prevailed, but daring souls were already rebelling against it, and spats proved the answer to

NEW LAMPS FOR OLD

the problem. During the coldest months still another addition to the wardrobe was recommended, woolen petticoats; knitted or flannel, every girl was urged to provide herself with one. We were taking no chances of getting flu again!

Gradually the numerous new faculty members settled down into Saint Mary's ways; constantly the teachers of longer standing strove to maintain the traditions of past years. Miss Katie, Miss Dowd, Mr. Stone, Miss Fenner, Miss Lee, Miss Sutton, Miss Bottum and Miss Davis, these now were the link between the old order and the new. And above all, it was upon Mr. Cruikshank that the burden fell. It was a year of change. The new administration was established and new policies introduced. Slowly the old order was passing, and the death of Mrs. Iredell, so deeply loved by generations of Saint Mary's girls, was a milestone in the path of the change.

The graduating class of 1919 numbered thirteen, Bertha Albertson, Helen Battle, Elizabeth Bowne, Nina Burke, Marian Drane, Josephine Erwin, Margaret Fallon, Mildred Kirtland, Elizabeth Kitchen, Ellen Lay, Louise Toler, Elizabeth Waddell and Mary C. Wilson. "Pep" was the popular word of the year, and the class was a pepful one. Its Senior Minstrel Show, given with Mr. Owen's help, was a (literally) howling success, and the Hallowe'en impersonation of the arrival of the flu germ turned tragedy into comedy. The 1919 School Party, under Senior supervision, was notable for the introduction of "Sweet William," destined to become a classic. Written by Mary Yellott, it gives apt expression to the universal affection for Mr. Stone. Who can forget the song so eloquently sung and acted in pantomime by Elizabeth Waddell and Ellen Lay?

> *When first I saw Sweet William*
> *'Twas when I left the train.*
> *In one of his hands he took my bag,*

In 'tother he twirled his cane.
He asked me for a quarter
And kindly took my check.
I was so thankful to him that
I 'most fell on his neck!
But there were 'most a dozen more
And checks and bags there galore,
So he looked once at me,
And then turned him to flee,
Leaving me for the once the floor!

When next I saw Sweet William
'Twas in the History Room.
He wore stuck in his button hole
A red rose full in bloom.
The very first thing he asked me,
I really did not know.
But he said "That's right," and then he talked
On the theme for an hour or so—
With a pause every now and then
And then he'd start off again.
When his "What?" oft is heard
We just fill in the word—
Oh, Sweet William's the sweetest of men!

The summer of 1919 was a busy one at Saint Mary's. The pounding of hammers, the whine of saws, and the slap-slap of plasterers' trowels filled the air. Main Building was being remodelled, thanks to the generosity of Mr. W. A. Erwin of Durham, and was henceforth to be known as Smedes Hall in honor of the founders and as a tribute to Mrs. Erwin, the former Sadie Smedes, youngest daughter of Dr. Aldert Smedes.

When the girls arrived in September, they stared admiringly at the transformation that had taken place. One of them tells about it in the monthly *Muse:*

"As we entered Main Building, now Smedes Hall, the change from the one to the other was at once apparent. Blazing light and startling whiteness first attracted our attention, which however, was soon claimed by the handsome new mahogany furniture, especially the mirror, which we have since found most useful for last minute arranging of hats and chapel caps. Gone the broad, low staircase and the little, dark, crooked stairs behind it, and in their place a new spiral stairway winding artistically up to the third floor, with a skylight of generous proportions lighting it all the way.

"The lobby on the second floor is an addition which came in very conveniently for the first joint meeting of the Literary Societies, for other entertainments and the nightly half-hour of dancing during the first weeks of school. This spacious hall almost took the place of our beloved parlor, which was then closed, but on the third Saturday night was reopened to an admiring throng. The predominant note in its color scheme is brown, shading from the soft tan of the paper to the rich mahogany of the great beams across the ceiling.

"All over the building rooms have been newly plastered or papered, and many new rooms have been added. The tiled baths are a luxury we never expected to indulge in at Saint Mary's!

"The cement basement of last year has undergone numerous changes. . . . In West Rock the lingering remnant of the old dormitory has been divided into airy, comfortable rooms. And in East Rock, the former Teachers' Sitting Room now bears a placard denoting it as the Office where on week days a crowd of impatient girls may be found waiting to see Mr. Cruikshank, and on Saturday evenings a group of equally impatient young men waiting to see 'er— Mr. Way.'

"The walls and woodwork of the Infirmary have been

painted with an ivory tint, the dear desire of 'Miss Alec's' heart, and the whole effect of the interior is greatly softened and brightened.

"The enlarged Laundry has been provided with a number of *new electric irons,* and the prompt delivery of our laundry bears witness to the effect that they are being put to good use. We have little fear of the coming cold weather as a much larger and more efficient heating plant has been installed, and many new radiators have taken the place of the old ones.

"Senior Hall is now being used entirely for students' rooms, while driven from house and home the Cruikshanks have sought refuge where best they might find it. They had expected to be comfortably settled in their new house by the time school opened, but when we arrived a little heap of bricks out by the Auditorium was the only indication of the fact. Among all the improvements at Saint Mary's we think there was none more urgently needed than a comfortable home for the Business Manager and his family, and when the cottage is completed, in our opinion it will be the greatest improvement of all."

Changes had taken place in the school family as well as in its buildings. Mrs. Carolina V. Perkins had come from the Cathedral School in Washington to be Lady Principal. Mr. R. Blinn Owen, beloved for his gusto, his artistic enthusiasm and his flowing black tie, had given up the directorship of music and Dr. William H. Jones, less effervescent but equally proficient, had assumed that post. He was to become, as the years went by, one of the most loved and valued members of the faculty.

Miss Trowbridge's calm presence in the Household Arts Department was replaced by Miss Leggett. Miss Shearer and Miss Quackenbos took over French and Spanish, Miss Searle and Miss Loulie Wilson assumed Mathematics and Latin. Miss Anne Neave took Dorothy Ambler's place as office secretary and Miss Talbot succeeded Katherine McDowell as housekeeper. And a class of twenty-five members took possession of Senior Hall. Lucy London Anderson, Katherine Batts, Millicent Blanton, Nina Cooper, Rainsford Glass, Mary Hoke, Nancy Lay, Jane Ruffin, Eleanor Sublett and Mary Yellott were among them. The Class of 1920 was proud of its size and strength, quite sure (as is every other class) that it was truly remarkable. Certainly it entered upon the year's activities with enthusiasm, and carried them through to a successful close.

The monthly *Muse,* under Mary Yellott's efficient editorship, was published with hitherto unequalled regularity, eight issues appearing. Of these six were in the hands of the Literary Societies, each society filling three numbers which were judged against each other as a feature of the annual contest. Interest in the societies ran high, rising to fever pitch when both Sigma Lambda and E.A.P. chose Rudyard Kipling as the subject for rival Model Meetings, and when the secret leaked out each stoutly refused to relinquish her choice. Feeling was intense; disaster threatened, but Mr. Kipling himself saved the day. Tactful arbitration by faculty advisers brought out the fact that his prolific pen could supply an evening's entertainment both for E.A.P. and Sigma Lambdas, and the contest went on undisturbed.

Under Mary Hoke and Rainsford Glass (better known as Moke and Rene) rivalry between the athletic associations was equally keen. The walls of the gym resounded to:

> *With a vevo! With a vivo!*
> *With a vevo, vivo, vum!*
> *Johnny get a rat trap*
> *Bigger than a cat trap!*
> *Johnny get a cat trap*
> *Bigger than a rat trap!*
> *Hannibal, Cannibal*

LIFE AT SAINT MARY'S
> Sis Boom Bah!
> Mu Team, Mu Team!
> Rah! Rah! Rah!

and to the high, lilting sound of

> *Sigma girls are high-minded!*
> *B'lieve to my soul they're double-j'inted!*
> *They play ball and don't mind it—*
>   *All day long!*

Katherine Batts ably guided the Junior Auxiliary, and the eight girls who had been delegates to the summer conference at Blue Ridge brought back inspiration that gave the work new impetus. In connection with this an item in the monthly *Muse* for April, 1920 is interesting:

"The Inter-Chapter Meeting of the Junior Auxiliary held in the Parlor on Sunday evening was under the direction of the Blue Ridge delegates. Katherine Batts, the President, opened the meeting, and the Rector introduced the first speaker, George Denny, a Carolina delegate and an admirable example of what Blue Ridge does for boys."

We wonder if the editor of the *Muse,* in checking this copy, felt premonitory twinges of the heart—for as is well known to all Saint Mary's girls of the time, Mary Yellott was to become Mrs. George V. Denny, Jr.

The Class of 1920 was fortunate in having Mr. Cruikshank as its adviser, nor was the title an honorary one. Adviser he was in the fullest sense of the word, helper, monitor, and friend. No problem was too great or too small to be brought to him, and burdened though he was with a thousand duties, he never failed to produce for these girls the miracle of his whole-hearted interest.

Yes, the Class of '20 was lucky and its members knew it. They might sit for hours on the wooden storage chests in

EMILIE WATTS McVEA

"Wherever she moved, things came alive!"

"MISS KATIE" Mc-KIMMON

"Her presence was like a benediction upon the school."

JULIET BRISCOE SUTTON

". . . a part of the life at Saint Mary's during all administrations except the first."

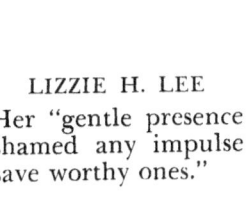

LIZZIE H. LEE

Her "gentle presence shamed any impulse save worthy ones."

THE REVEREND McNEELY
DuBOSE

RECTOR, 1903–1907

Succeeding his cousin, Dr. Bratton, as Head of the School, Dr. DuBose "served Saint Mary's devotedly for four years."

THE REVEREND THEODORE DuBOSE BRATTON

RECTOR, 1899–1903

Under his leadership "enrollment increased, the Rectory and Senior Hall were built, and the curriculum reorganized as that of a college."

Senior Hall rebuilding the world—or the school—nearer to their hearts' desire, but never did these verbal reconstructions touch three people—Miss Lee, whose gentle presence shamed any impulses save worthy ones, Nancy Lay, their versatile and much loved president—and Mr. Cruikshank. Not by one iota would they have altered any one of these.

The year saw no epoch-making phenomena but it brought a number of minor events and innovations worthy of note. Dr. Way established the School Council, a tentative move towards student government; the chapel line was arranged according to height, and Fire Drills were instituted. (The latter lent a new interest to dull days; alarms at unexpected moments signalled a frantic exodus to the grove and an even more frantic counting off by numbers. At one such count-off the seniors, to their consternation, found Miss Lee missing. A courier dispatched to Senior Hall returned with the shocking message that Miss Lee said she was already burned up so they'd have to proceed without her.)

Miss Dowd, so long identified with music at Saint Mary's, had gradually withdrawn from her work in it, finally leaving the school in 1920. Never was a teacher more deeply loved, more highly respected. By all who felt her influence she will be remembered as a shining example of the fact that an artist can be as well a very great lady.

In the spring an influenza scare caused a lengthy quarantine of the school, and a "Little Store" was started in the basement to take the place of the one usually visited on Hillsboro Street. Florence Stone's wedding in the Chapel excited much romantic interest, and two daring Seniors secreted themselves in the recesses of the organ to witness it. At long last the Cruikshanks were able to move into their new brick cottage. A March week-end holiday was instituted, and Seniors from far away were allowed to go home with friends living nearby. Nineteen-twenty came to its close. The twenty-five Seniors went their various ways, yet six of them were to meet again in the fall when they went to Chapel Hill to continue their studies at the University. This was the first class to make such a large-scale migration. The convenience of the arrangement and its successful results were to make such transfers more and more common in the years to come.

Days of change were upon the school. To no one was this more apparent than to Dr. Way, and he bent all his energies toward the development of a greater Saint Mary's. He saw the need of increasing the school's physical equipment and realized that to do this an adequate endowment was essential. Thus, in the early 1920's the campaign for the endowment fund was pressed strenuously forward. When in January, 1920, Reverend Francis Osborne gave up his connection with it, the firm of Tamblyn and Brown was entrusted with the organization of a national campaign.

But the burden of the work fell upon alumnae and church people of the Carolinas. Dr. Way labored unceasingly, and he was aided by the Reverend A. C. D. Noe and the Reverend C. H. Bascom. Gifts of $5000 from Mr. Erwin A. Holt of Burlington and $1000 from Mrs. Annie Gray Nash Sprunt of Wilmington gave an impetus to the campaign; in South Carolina the diocesan authorities assumed $30,000 as their share of the whole and made an initial payment of $5000. In 1923 the Diocese of North Carolina voted an annual gift of $5000 to the school, to be continued for a five-year period, and there were gifts too numerous to mention from classes, groups of friends and individuals. The dioceses of North and South Carolina, the alumnae, and the public at large were being aroused to the need of giving the school material support, and for this awakening Dr. Way was largely responsible.

In the organization of the school itself Dr. Way's progressive spirit was ever ready to introduce changes. In 1920–'21 he created the office of Academic Head and called Miss Ophelia Stone to occupy it. Mrs. Perkins continued as Lady Principal, but Miss Stone took over the teaching of English literature and supervison of the girls' scholastic programs. She organized the College Club, which put new emphasis on continued study after graduation. Miss Stone remained at Saint Mary's only one year, being succeeded by Miss Sara Turner.

It was an era of swift and numerous changes in the faculty. Miss Cone, Miss Cummings, Miss Hesse, Miss Spofford, Miss Ballou, Miss Kretschmer, Miss Moorfield, Miss Cooke, Miss Mildred Morgan, Miss Weeks, Miss Abbott, Miss Mathison, Miss Moffatt, Miss McCausland, Miss Prosser, Miss Harrison, Miss Reigart, Miss Spenser, Miss Suydam, Miss Prather, Miss Houchen, Miss Crofut, Miss Cobb, Miss Force and Mrs. Judd—these passed in rapid succession through the school. To the girls whom she taught, the name of each one bears its special significance, but on the permanent body of the school as a whole such temporary abidings could leave little impression. The contrast with the old, settled order was marked.

Teachers came and went in those early years of the twenties, and the character of the student body began to show small signs of change. The trend was toward a gayer, more carefree spirit, greater indulgence in luxuries, more elaborate dress. The authorities tried to stem the tide, but rules, however sternly enforced, could not alter the spirit of the day. Dr. Way, in one of his reports, speaks of combatting "the feverish folly of these trying times." The need for such combat was apparent to the older generation, but all over the world post-war Youth was shouting to be served.

The youth of Saint Mary's, sheltered within the grove,

found outlet for its exuberance in minor flights of freedom. Hair was elaborately ratted into vast puffs extending rearward in mountainous projections. Later, perhaps because the ratting process had taken its toll, bobbing set in. Noses were coated chalky white with powder; cosmetics were smuggled in and used in spite of Mrs. Perkins' tearful protests against the evils of "rou-ou-ou-ging." Beige or flesh-colored stockings were introduced, and some daring spirits, when forbidden to appear in the streets of Raleigh with legs so conspicuously adorned, left the school on Monday morning wearing black stockings and surreptitiously changed to light ones in the privacy of Boylan Pearce's ladies' room.

Dresses, especially evening gowns, became more elaborate. Where formerly most of these had been made at home, they were now bought ready-made. Materials were richer; chiffon velvets, heavy satins, and quantities of gold and silver laces were used. The *Muse* blossomed forth in full-length photographs that looked like representations of Follies' beauties. These lavish costumes demanded appropriate settings for their display, and the Junior Senior banquet, disdaining the old simplicities of the Muse Room, moved to the new splendors of the Sir Walter Hotel.

These transitions belonged to the early 'twenties, but before they took place another change of vastly deeper import had come about. In the summer of 1921 Mr. Cruikshank gave up his connection with the school.

Since 1903 the personality of Ernest Cruikshank had been woven into the fabric of Saint Mary's life. Teachers, pupils, servants—all members of the school family—had turned to him instinctively for advice and help on all occasions, and had never been disappointed. To each and every one he listened, but it was to the girls that he gave himself most completely. I think it was because the unquenchable youth in his heart called out in kinship to them. Hundreds of girls felt this kinship of the spirit, and one of them, Annie Cameron, has expressed it:

"One memory of Saint Mary's effaces or rather sums up all the rest, the memory of Mr. Cruikshank. Indeed he has always been to me synonymous with all that is best and finest and most lovable about Saint Mary's. His office seemed to me the heart and center of the school, and I have never ceased to miss him when I go back.

"I can see him now, unhurried and unperturbed amidst piles and mountains of work, completely unruffled in the face of countless interruptions and endless irritations, never losing for a moment his quiet patience, his keen sense of humor, his pleasant, friendly manner, his warm personal interest in each one who came to him for help and advice, and his deep kindness, his gentleness and real sympathy in any trouble.

"I remember the pleasant walks we used to have with him on Sunday afternoons, going out behind State Hospital to where the new lake was being made, or rambling through the woods that used to stretch down Saint Mary's Street back of the Methodist Orphanage, or walking out towards Dr. Lewis' house.

"I can feel again the drowsy warmth of the Chapel on our return, and the invincible sleepiness that would creep over one coming into it fresh from a long walk in the sharp air of a late fall afternoon.

Other memories come. I see him at Muse Meetings, never preaching to us but challenging us with some situation to be met or some activity undertaken for the good of the school. And I am sure we would just about as soon have died as to have failed to measure up to what he expected of us.

"And Muse Parties! What delightful, mysterious, exciting and much-to-be-envied affairs they were! And what a good time, I'm sure, he had planning them and springing his little surprises!

"Again I hear him, deeply touched, telling us of a Mission that Father Harrison was holding at Christ Church, and suggesting that we go. We did go, and then again to an early service there which I am sure was an experience and a memory that none of us would part with.

"No, there was nobody quite like Mr. Cruikshank. I loved Miss Thomas, I loved Mr. Stone, I loved Miss Sutton. I thoroughly enjoyed Miss Fenner. I reverenced Miss Katie, I liked Miss Dowd and Miss Lee and many others, but there was nobody like Mr. Cruikshank, and I will always be thankful that I had the good fortune to attend Saint Mary's for four years during that 'golden age,' the time when he was there.

"And do you know, when any situation arises that involves either being or not being loyal to Saint Mary's, the first thought that crosses my mind is 'What would Mr. Cruikshank think if I didn't do so-and-so?'"

Few teachers leave behind them greater memorials than this. Saint Mary's was fortunate, indeed, for eighteen years to have claimed such a one as her own.

The graduates of 1921 were the last to know Mr. Cruikshank's guidance, the last to enjoy the intimate delights of the Muse Club. With the going of its leader, the club was discontinued, but for this final season it functioned happily. Frances Venable was its chairman, Susan Collier business manager, Dorothy Kirtland an able and enthusiastic class president, and Katherine Waddell its poet. To the last named we owe a rhymed history of the year:

> *The first few days of schooldom*
> *Were hectic, quite, last fall,*
> *Matriculation, schedules,*

NEW LAMPS FOR OLD

And homesickness and all.
But when we once were settled
  And wits were sharpened keen,
We stopped our studies long enough
  To play at Hallowe'en.

The Goblins and the Fairies
  Came flocking to the gym
The seniors chilled our backbones
  As ghosts in moonlight dim.
The next event was Christmas,
  But lots occurred between,
For all the "babies" bobbed their hair
  And tall ones, too, I ween.

The Seniors' play at Christmas time
  Surprised us one and all,
We didn't know the Senior Class
  Possessed a Christmas Doll.
Down in the gym the Christmas tree
  A festive scene and gay;
The carols in the early morn—
  And we were off next day.

The same old train that took us off,
  Alas, soon brought us back,
And after us by parcel post
  Came things we'd failed to pack.
And then exams, those dread exams!
  We crammed and did our best,
But when we flunked we thought 'twas time
  We took a little rest.

Infirmary blues, we had them then,
  The worst you've ever seen.

*They grew and grew, diphtheria too—
    Resulted—quarantine.
Oh well, the worst of times will pass,
    And brighter days will come—
The holidays on March the tenth
    Spelled H-O-M-E, home.*

*Oh how the days of April flew,
    And then the days of May.
On rocks and walls the roses bloomed,
    And springtime came to stay.*

*And so Commencement day is here,
    And with the last sweet note
"Jerusalem, High tower," we sing,
    A lump comes in our throat.*

*We love our friends, the dear old grove,
    Each minute more and more.
And then the school year Twenty-one
    And all its fun is o'er!*

Two new features were introduced into the school program this year, Stunt Night and the May Festival. For the former, all organizations joined in an evening's entertainment for charity, and the sophomore class' trial of Mary Louise Everett by the faculty on the charge of breaking a door on third floor was the triumph of the occasion. Shrieks of appreciative laughter greeted the appearance of Miss St. John (Elizabeth Tucker) who "glided" across the floor weeping bitter tears for the victim, and Miss Shearer's (Dorothy Nixon) vigorous protest "Me non!" to every word Judge Perkins spoke.

May Day with its Queen, court attendants, jester and costumed folk dancers, was a colorful addition to the spring. Commencement was saddened by the knowledge that Mr. and Mrs. Cruikshank, Ernest, Jr., Mary Pride, and Olive, would no longer be in the Cottage when the next session began. It was the end of an era. Mr. Cruikshank's eighteen years at Saint Mary's had passed into history.

Taking over the office of Secretary and Business Manager, Mr. Albert W. Tucker came to the school in the summer of 1921. And in September there arrived Miss Sara Turner as Academic Head and Miss Bertha A. Morgan as Lady Principal.

Miss Morgan was a marked contrast to her predecessor. Mrs. Perkins had been the perfect picture of a gentle Victorian lady; the waywardness of her charges brought anguished tremors to her voice as she pleaded with them to mend their ways, and her mild brown eyes seemed always filled with shocked surprise at the doings of the post-war generation. No such surprise troubled Miss Morgan. Intimate knowledge of girls had put an end to that, and she wasted no words in pleading with them. To command was her way, and to exact obedience. Her coming to the school was like a fresh northern breeze, breath-taking at first, but invigorating and wholesome. Inevitably, with the first appearance of her initials on a permission slip she was known as BAM, and to the whole school Bam became the symbol of Discipline with a big D.

"Miss Bertha A. Morgan has come to school to stay.
She chases up the chapel caps and scares the rouge away.
She takes the canned food from our rooms and throws away our gum,
And watches us with sharpest eye and tries to stop our fun.
And all we bad school children gather 'bout her after school,
And listen just as quiet as mice to many and many a rule,

As to rubbers, gloves and other things she tells us all
   about;
And Miss Morgan's going to get you if you don't watch
   out!"

Mischief makers had met their match, and joke about her though they might, there was in even the most rebellious hearts a genuine respect for one who had proven so redoubtable. Respect was to grow into admiration and friendship. Bam became a name to be used not fearfully or derisively, but with affection.

Miss Turner, too, proved a real power in the school. Hers was the task of directing each girl's course of study, and to it she brought capabilities of a high order. As a teacher of English she was scholarly and forceful, and her friendly spirit was to endear her to girls of succeeding years. Under her leadership was organized the Pan-Archon Council composed of presidents of classes and heads of organizations, its purpose being to integrate student activities and so to replace, as far as was possible, the old Muse Club.

Appropriately enough, twenty-two girls graduated in 1922. Mary Louise Everett was their president; the class included Julia Winston Ashworth, Evelina Beckwith, Lenore Powell, Elizabeth Lawrence, and Mary Wiatt Yarborough. They were a happy group of Seniors, and Louise Eggleston has left us an alphabet descriptive of their day:

A's for Assembly—we have every day!
But A's for the Annual, the Muse Board would say.
B is for Basketball—get in the game,
You may come out alive but you won't look the same.
C is for chapel caps, car fare and Crushes;
A glimpse of the last brings us tremors and blushes.
D's for DETENTION, most terrible fate,

NEW LAMPS FOR OLD

But on Saturday night D means only "date."
E's for Exams; when they come twice a year
Our head's full of nothing, our heart's full of fear.

F is for French and Friday and fish,
That they'd not come so often sincerely we wish!
G is for Gym and Geometry too,
You just guess which we like, we will leave it to you.
H is for Hash—a most savory thing
And also for holidays, Christmas and spring.
J is for joy, the kind that is spread
On third floor "Main" before going to bed.
K is for kisses, to crushes most dear
When they're telling each other goodnight on the stair.

L is for letters for me and for you
With all kinds of sweet things and checks maybe, too.
M is Miss Morgan and Monday and Mu
And music and money and Main Building, too.
N is for nights when we've nothing to do,
And also for "nuts"—and we know quite a few.
O is for overshoes, worn in the snow.
We got them for ninety-eight cents, don't you know.
P is for powder and also for paint
They help little girlies to be what they ain't!
Q is for quiet—that's just what we all
Try hard to preserve as we go through the hall.

R is for rouge and too much on your cheek
Makes an "R" for Restriction the very next week.
S is for "Sweet William" of History fame
And it also means Sigma, a jolly good name.
T is for the Tuckers, they're fine one and all,
And for tennis and teachers and telephone call.
U is umbrellas—nobody's got 'em,

And lots of "unheard-of-things" known to Miss Bottum.
V is for volley ball, played every day
And also Vacation that's coming in May.
W's for Whitehead—she shoots quite a line
And hears from cute sailors, fourteen at a time.
X is for exercise—marked on a chart,
To avoid restriction you must do your part.
Y is for yells that are heard at a game,
From the Sigmas and Mus when the score is the same.
Z is for zero, a mark very rare,
For who ever heard of us failing up here?
Etc. is all of the things we don't know—
And I guess they would fill up a volume or so!

Since 1903 one small, dark figure had played a continuous, if modest, role in the life of Saint Mary's—little Ducky, the waitress. Now in 1922 she was to make her exit. No longer would her crinkly smile bring cheer to the tables she served so willingly; no longer would groups of girls stand entranced in dormitory halls watching her pat out the rhythm of her little dance and recite in singsong voice the "Ba-ker-shad-y-lad-y" she had learned as a spelling stint so long ago. No more would the favored few who sat at her table eat ice cream and cake at her yearly party behind the auditorium. Ducky, who to generations of girls seemed ageless, had grown old. Cheery to the last, she made a brave exit, bobbed her final curtsey, kissed the hands of the "chillen" she loved best, and declared with dignity "Your kindness will never be forgotten!" The silver pitcher that was her gift from the school was small token, indeed, of the affection in which she was held; its polished sides were no whit brighter than the shining spirit of the little brown woman who had been a part of Saint Mary's for so many years.

Grief came to the school in the autumn of 1922 when

the death of Mr. Cruikshank touched all hearts with sorrow. Though he had left Saint Mary's, his spirit was a living reality there; the knowledge that he had died came as a stunning blow. That he should be buried from the Chapel was fitting indeed, and that Dr. Lay, his co-worker for so many years, should come to assist at the service was equally so. This last solemn tribute Saint Mary's could pay to her friend.

The year brought to a climax the Endowment Campaign. In the Close of the National Cathedral in Washington an elaborate pageant, The Cross Triumphant, was given for the benefit of Saint Mary's. Later the same pageant was produced at the school, under the direction of Miss Davis, bringing together many groups of alumnae and stimulating interest in the campaign. Dr. Way was able to announce that the school debt of $40,000 had been liquidated, a new laundry and central heating plant installed, and an endowment fund created. He never ceased in his efforts to publicize the school's needs and to raise the funds that were to supply them. In 1923 Saint Mary's High School department was accredited, a definite step towards the academic standardization that was the trend of the times.

Nineteen-twenty-three brought Student Government to the Seniors, an enterprising class of twenty-nine members among whom were Elise Ballard, Betsey Ballou, Daisy Cooper, Addie Huske, Elizabeth Hickerson and Lucy Lay. Martha Best was their president.

One of the class, Sophie Eggleston, in looking back on the year says: "I don't remember events, I only remember faces, impressions, fleeting moments—things like Miss Fenner looking through her thick glasses in the Art Room and calling us 'monkeys'—hunting my chapel cap, cleaning up our rooms at the last minute on Saturday afternoon, buying a new outfit at spring holidays—the smell of the Infirmary and the hot holls for breakfast. How lovely Mary Louise Everett was, and how many clothes Martha Best had. The portraits in the parlor and the discussion of whose grandmother's hair and hands belonged to the girls in the Confirmation picture. All these things flit through my mind when I think of Saint Mary's." Pleasant, tranquil memories, these. Nineteen-twenty-three was a tranquil year.

Nineteen-twenty-four and twenty-five continued in the same vein. Under the firm guidance of Miss Morgan and Miss Turner the routine of school life proceeded smoothly —too smoothly, perhaps, for some adventurous spirits, as is shown by one student's account of those days:

"The thing that stands out most vividly in my recollection is that I was *forever* being campused for things one doesn't *do* at Saint Mary's. I might say I was in an almost continual state of being campused for doing things I shouldn't, things quite innocent and harmless in their small way, but still Things! Like waking up too late to dress properly, which necessitated rolling up the legs of your pajamas, throwing on a coat and dashing to breakfast, hoping to high heaven that this rather extraordinary dishabille will pass unnoticed by THOSE WHO MATTER, and to your great consternation realizing that your pajama legs have come unrolled *spang* in front of Miss Bertha Morgan!

"I remember the longest 'stretch' I ever did at Saint Mary's. It was in the spring. I was awfully tired of classes, hated the sight of books, and above all, wanted to do something Different. Well, I did it all right, something the school thought a bit *too* different. I got a bottle of blond hair dye and dyed my locks. Now I am naturally a dark brunette and the dye turned my black hair a sort of salmon pink—not blond, not even pale brown, but SALMON

PINK! Well, you can imagine how I looked. Miss Morgan took one look at me and almost turned a back flip. When she had recovered sufficiently, she decided I was no fit advertisement for Saint Mary's School, and so for *weeks* (at the time it seemed like a good thirty years to me) I 'did time' on the campus until all the dye had worn off."

No, one didn't trifle with Miss Morgan. Her hands were firm upon the reins, and she held unswervingly to her course. Yet the treats she planned for her charges showed an understanding of their yearnings—as when the whole school, even those on the restricted list, was allowed to go to the movies for a Christmas present, when the "little store" privilege was granted to all pupils, and when the Honor Roll students were given a royal feast at a special table in the dining hall. Katherine Morris wrote:

> *Here's to Her—*
> *Tall and slender*
> *but—not fair,*
> *hornrimmed glasses*
> *'n dark brown hair.*
> *Eyes that 'right straight*
> *through you cut*
> *'n make you feel*
> *like a perfect Nut.*
>
> *Her face is stern*
> *but then she smiles*
> *'n she even tries*
> *to change the styles.*
> *She restricts you for*
> *a long, long year—*
> *'n then she up*
> *'n calls you 'dear'!*

> She's always here,
> 'n always there,
> 'n can catch you
> almost anywhere.
> She is stern
> 'n she is strict—
> but to Miss Morgan
> You bet—We'll Stick.

A number of new features were introduced into the life of the school during these years. The appearance of the choir in veils added a striking note to Sunday chapel services. In the Dramatic Club, Miss Davis, ever alert to progress, introduced the workshop method of play production under which every member had an opportunity to learn something of scenic design, sound effects, direction and stage management. New clubs sprang up and displayed their pictures in the year book—the Elizabethans, the Doctors' Daughters, the Only Childs' and the Ministers' Daughters. This last group wore the gayest of paper caps and boasted the motto "there's a little bit of bad in every good little girl." And, most striking change of all, the annual *Muse* became in 1925 the *Stagecoach*.

Katherine Fisher was president of the Class of 1924, and among its twenty-one members were Mary Powell, Clare Spence, Mildred Waddell, Eugenia Trexler, and Eleanor Yarborough. The following year, 1925, sent forth twenty-six graduates with Catherine Menzies, Betty Ragland, Katherine Johnson, Bettie Fell, Virginia Lay, Ellen Mellick, Kalista Hood and Whitney Holt among their number.

Nineteen twenty-five marked a notable milestone in the school's progress, the appointment of women to the Board of Trustees. For years there had been a growing sentiment in favor of this step. The alumnae, led by the New York

THE REVEREND GEORGE WILLIAM LAY
RECTOR, 1907–1918

". . . energetic, brusquely honest, invariably just, and sincerely interested in education." Once, returning clean-shaven after a vacation, he was almost unrecognizable, as these pictures show.

THE REVEREND WARREN WADE WAY
RECTOR, 1918–1932
Coming to Saint Mary's from Saint Luke's Church, Salisbury, N. C., Mr. Way "continued the sound educational policy of Dr. Lay, and organized the expanding school as a junior college."

NEW LAMPS FOR OLD

chapter, had clamored for it as far back as 1918, and Emilie Watts McVea had given the movement her active support. Now at last the objective was attained and two women, both old Saint Mary's girls, Mrs. T. W. Bickett of Raleigh and Mrs. Walter D. Toy of Chapel Hill, took their places on the Board.

This year marked the last appearance of a title which since the days of the founders had been taken for granted as a part of Saint Mary's, but which fell on modern ears with a quaintly Victorian sound. The Lady Principal became Dean of Students, and in September, 1925, Miss Catherine Albertson assumed this office.

Notable gifts were made to the school during this period —$5000 from Mrs. Bessie Smedes Leak for the establishment of a scholarship in memory of her sister, Mrs. Annie Smedes Root; $1750 for a student loan fund from the children of Mrs. Julia Johnston Andrews; $500 from the Masonic Body of North Carolina, also for student loans; $500 from the Class of 1920 towards the purchase of a new organ; two handsome marble seats placed in the grove by the New York Alumnae Chapter; and from Mr. B. N. Duke of Durham a trust fund of $25,000, the income of which was to be continuously applied to the benefit of Saint Mary's. To these gifts were added the constant contributions of alumnae both as individuals and in chapter groups; space does not allow their listing, but their extent may be seen from the fact that by the fall of 1926 a total of $2277 had been given by alumnae towards the organ fund. Proof positive this was of the alumnae's awareness of the school's needs and of their generous rallying to her support.

Skirts were going up, boyish bobs were coming in. Beige stockings were accepted now, and spats had vanished into the limbo of the departed. Middy blouses were seen only in the gym; there, with long black stockings and voluminous serge bloomers, they were still *de rigeur*.

It was the era of waist lines that struck one at the hips, of tight *cloche* hats pressed down over the ears. Striped hose for sports wear were a sprightly novelty, and without approval of the authorities, stockings were rolled below the knees. These were the fashion notes of 1926; to them Saint Mary's added her own individual touch. "Styles in chapel caps," says the Bulletin, "are more subdued than last year, and of a flat character. The blanket safety pin so much in vogue last season at the side or back of the cap has been replaced by less conspicuous clasps. *Harding* is sponsoring embroidery on top of cap, the personal touch being gained by application of the wearer's name in all prevailing colors. Fruits and flowers embroidered in pastel shades are equally chic. Whether embellishments of flat artificial holly as sponsored by N. Cooper last December will be worn again is still a matter of dispute in designing circles."

The opening of the swimming pool was the great event of 1925–'26. Long awaited, and long delayed by rock encountered in the excavation, it became an actuality on March 1, and a new and popular sport was added to the athletic program. Great was the rejoicing among the students, and equally great the satisfaction of the administration in the achievement of this step in progress towards a truly modern Saint Mary's.

The thirty-eight members of the year's graduating class were proud of their large number, and they made history by adopting still another member, Mrs. E. B. Lawrence of Raleigh, who as the mother of Ann Lawrence, one of their class, had endeared herself to them all. Miss Ruef, beloved teacher of French, was their adviser, and they claimed Mr. Stone as sponsor. Marion Lee, Ruth Loaring Clark, Alicia Platt, Dorothy Dougherty, Sylbert Pendleton, Cleave Shore, Martha Dabney Jones, Margaret Bullitt, and Sara

Purrington were of this class. They were the first seniors under Miss Albertson's gentle guidance; Miss Shapcott, Miss Grant, Miss Houchen, and Madam Simbolotti were others of the faculty they knew. Miss Frances Bottum, for so long an earnest and devoted member of the school family, was not with them this year, having gone on a leave of absence which was to prove a permanent parting from Saint Mary's. Her post in the Science Laboratory was taken by Miss Slaught, but her other contributions to school life —illustrations for countless *Muses,* and help with literary society programs, willingly given year after year, could not be so easily supplied.

Following close upon the 1926 Commencement, a great loss came to Saint Mary's in the death of Miss Clara Fenner. To generations of pupils dating as far back as 1892, she had been the presiding genius of the Art Studio; the humorous twinkle of her eye, the often repeated admonition, "use your ounce," and her instructions, as pungently phrased as they were keenly practical, had given the studio a character all its own. It was a place of hard work joyfully accomplished, of labor lightened by good humor and the spirit of fun. This was Miss Fenner's own spirit; there was in it a kind of gallantry that communicated itself to her pupils and to the scores of girls whom for successive summers she introduced to the delights of Europe. In Miss Fenner herself, even through the trials of a last painful illness, this spirit persisted to the end.

During the summer of 1926 a new organ was installed in the chapel, and shortly after the opening of the fall session, it was dedicated to the memory of Dr. Bennett Smedes. To the alumnae who had given so generously towards the purchase of the instrument, and to all members of the school family who were to share daily in its enjoyment, this was a very real satisfaction.

The session of 1926–'27 added two new organizations to

the list of student activities—the school orchestra and Latin Club or *Senatus Populisque Romanus*. In the fall the school thrilled to the melodies of *Rose Marie* and *The Student Prince,* and Thanksgiving was celebrated by seeing Robert Mantell in *Julius Caesar* at the State Theatre. Athletics were made compulsory; instead of "signing up" as heretofore for an hour's exercise, each girl was required to choose some form of sport and attend daily practices. Spring brought an unusually lovely May Festival, with Mary Dickerson reigning over a court complete with maids of honor, heralds, flower girls, and jester. Later in May came a new and startling ceremony, the Letter Club Initiation, which the Bulletin described as follows:

"Saturday night, May 21st, brought forth some queer happenings in school. After the school party everyone went to her room feeling sad, but soon this sadness was broken in upon by a series of mysterious events. A solemn procession passed under the windows winding in and out between buildings, finally disappearing in the darkness. Who were they, and what on earth were they doing? It was discovered at length that they were girls being initiated into the Letter Club.

"Over the week-end the mystery was almost forgotten, but Tuesday the outcome of it took place. About four o'clock that afternoon strange things were happening out in front of Smedes. Girls with umbrellas and wearing slickers were tramping about in spite of the fact that the sun was shining and the sky was cloudless. Anyone walking down the path was barked at by two girls under the stone benches. Another two girls, blindfolded, were trying to feed each other bananas.

"Back and forth through the crowd a small girl was stamping, clad in waist-high rubber boots and a dress on backwards. She carried a long rubber speaking tube, which she made use of to the annoyance of her victims. A sturdy sentinel paced round and round carrying a broom over her shoulder and wearing an exaggerated dunce cap with a feather in it. She was approached by a girl who insisted on shaking hands and saying that she was Mary Queen of Scots and came over in 1492.

"One girl wearing a huge yellow ribbon on her much-frizzled hair was diligently sweeping the front walk with a maple leaf, while another paid her respects to each onlooker by holding out an egg and saying 'cackle, cackle!' in a dignified and sober manner. Wonder upon wonder, girls were seen to pass their dearest friends without a word or a look, and all that day Senior Hall knew few visitors!

"The initiations afforded much amusement throughout the school, and after all the poor victims had only a short while to suffer, for with the sound of the six o'clock bell all their troubles ended, and they were full-fledged members of the enviable Letter Club."

Commencement in 1927 brought thirty-three seniors to the Chapel to receive their diplomas from Bishop Cheshire. Mela Royall, Fannie Bryan Aiken, Genevieve Dando, Laura MacDonald, Martha Thigpen, Helen Dortch, Frances Marriner, Mary Margaret Muse, Mary Thurman, and Sallie Satterthwaite were among those who stepped forth from the grove as alumnae.

Expansion was in the air. These were boom days. The whole nation was riding high on a wave of optimism, and Saint Mary's felt the impact of its surge. For some years there had been discussion of making Saint Mary's a full four-year college. Now, spurred by the spirit of the times, the movement increased and the question became imminent.

Some of those most vitally interested in Saint Mary's felt the proposed expansion to be in keeping with her progress. Of these, Dr. Way was the leader. Others equally devoted to her welfare felt that as a school and Junior College Saint

Mary's fulfilled her essential function. Earnestly the trustees deliberated upon the issue, and in the end the opinion of the latter group prevailed. No extension of the school's curriculum was undertaken, but rather a strengthening of the present course to meet the highest standards in its field. Succeeding years were to confirm the wisdom of the choice, and a gratifying forward step was achieved when, in the autumn of 1927, Saint Mary's was accredited as a Junior College by the Association of Secondary Schools and Colleges of the Southern States.

The eighty-sixth opening found Bishop Cheshire once more in the Chapel chancel, but now, as he announced in his address of welcome, he was taking the place of Bishop Penick, newly appointed President of the Board of Trustees. For thirty years Bishop Cheshire had held that post; now, with a sense of duty well done, he was relinquishing its responsibilities to a younger man, but for some years to come Saint Mary's was still to know the privilege of his patriarchal presence.

Taking Miss Turner's place as Academic Head, Miss Virginia Henry Holt came this year to enter upon a brief but highly successful period of service. Other additions to the faculty were Miss Lineberry, Miss Terrill, Miss Bohannon, Miss Hohn, and Mrs. Frank Nash. Mrs. Nash, an experienced librarian, was to bring about a real reconstruction of the Library; this was a large undertaking since for years the Library had been the step-child among the school's facilities. Now through systematic cataloguing and advantageous rearrangement, its usefulness was to be greatly increased, and a sound foundation laid for the truly modern library that it was to become. The process of modernization was a long and laborious one, yet from the moment Mrs. Nash stepped into the Library, it took on new life. From a rather dreary spot it became an oasis bright with flowers. Its ordered quiet was an invitation to

NEW LAMPS FOR OLD

study, and the girls soon discovered in the new librarian a helpful adviser and a sympathetic friend. Serene and gracious and lovely, Mrs. Nash won the admiration of all who came to know her.

There were twenty-eight seniors in 1927–'28, among them Phoebe Harding, Helen Andrus, Josephine Battle, Mary Katherine Duff, Sara Falkener, Ree Garrett, Sarah Glover, Elizabeth Platt, Pattie Smith, and Erma Williams. Theirs was the last class to inhabit the old Senior Hall, the last to know as its adviser, Mr. Stone.

For in January, 1928, just a week after he had met his pupils in the History Room, there came to the school the grievous shock of Mr. Stone's sudden death. That he would have chosen to go thus quietly and quickly, his mind alert, his enjoyment of life and of people as keen as ever, there is little doubt. Always young in spirit, he was never to grow old.

His last pupils, even as those of earlier days, were to remember him head erect, shoulders thrust jauntily back, a twinkle of fun in his eye, his lips under his cropped mustache curving in the hint of a smile. For twenty-five years Saint Mary's girls had known him so. They had delighted in his wit, marvelled at his vast fund of knowledge, and revered the high principles that were an integral part of his character. Devotion to duty and a high sense of honor ruled his life, but there was no dourness in his practice of these virtues. Rather he wore them gaily, debonairly, like a cavalier's cloak, investing them with some of the charm that was his own. His sympathy and understanding and affection for his pupils was deep-rooted and genuine. The girls who sat in his classes, and went with him for long walks on Sunday afternoons, and listened when in the Rector's absence he read the chapel services, felt this in his every word and deed. Small wonder that they returned his affection a hundredfold. Mary Theresa Lawrence, one of those who knew him last, expressed the feeling of the whole school when she wrote:

IN MEMORY OF WILLIAM ENOS STONE
You would be first to bid us not to mourn,
You'd chide when our unbidden tears would fall,
And tell us that, although our hearts are torn,
Our grief, when shared, is not a grief at all.
Still lives the fragrance of the withered flower,
Long glows the mellowed light from vanished sun;
So is it now with us in this sad hour,
Your memory—for we loved you—every one.
Your love for us, like brightly burning star
That brighter grows with coming of the dawn,
Shall shed a benediction from afar,
A blessing that shall follow on and on.

Old girls returning in September, 1928 opened their eyes wide in pleasure at the sight of the new Senior-Junior Hall. They had known that it was in the process of building, had studied the plans posted on the bulletin board in the Covered Way the winter before, had watched the Infirmary being moved westward to make room for it, and had seen the foundations laid in the spring. Yet all this foreknowledge had failed to prepare them for the delightful actuality that was Holt Hall. The new brick building, three-storied and with pleasingly simple lines, fitted into its place behind West Wing as though it had always been there; its beauty and completeness exceeded even their rosiest dreams.

Inside, the cream-colored woodwork, hardwood floors and luxurious tiled baths with showers made the new building seem more like a beautiful home than a school dormitory. The attractive reception hall and living room, the kitchens complete with electric stoves and irons, the bedrooms boasting dressers with full-length mirrors—all these and countless other features won universal admiration. To this admiration was added sincere and heartfelt gratitude to the donor, Mr. Lawrence S. Holt, whose generous gift made possible this beautiful memorial to Margaret Locke Erwin Holt.

The opening of school was saddened by the passing of one who to generations of girls had symbolized the very heart and soul of Saint Mary's. Miss Katie was gone. From Fayetteville, where she spent the summer months, she had written to her friends "I am comfortable and content here, but I am longing and waiting for school to open. I am going back on September 15th." On that day her frail body was resting in the Chapel, the spot she loved most on earth, and gathered round her were Saint Mary's friends of all ages.

Countless tributes have been paid to Miss Katie. Many, happily, came before her death, in the period when full of years and of honor, her presence was like a benediction upon the school. Hundreds of the girls who felt her influence have expressed what that influence meant; their tributes are summed up in the following familiar lines:

TO MISS KATIE

To long for truth, to try to realize
The highest that we see—that is the noblest
Living, and that, dear friend, in all these years,
Your high sincerity, your love of love,
Your hatred of deceit and scorn of all pretense
  Have helped us to desire.

  Thinking of you,
We know that love and truth are real,
That God and good are the eternal verities.
Noisy ambition, hard won fame, the wish

> For recognition even of worthy work,
> Beside these vital truths fade into nothingness.
> To do good, and to distribute of your love
> And of your strength to them that need,
> That has been your life. And with such service
> God is pleased.

On the roll of Saint Mary's daughters there is no name more distinguished than that of Emilie Watts McVea, the writer of these lines. Her death, which came a few months before Miss Katie's, in June, 1928, was a tragic loss not only to Saint Mary's but to the whole educational world, in which she was a truly outstanding figure.

Twenty-six members of the class of 1929 took up their abode in newly finished Holt Hall and entered upon a happy year. Among their number were Jaquelin Drane, Emily Badham, Margaret Cameron, Nannie Crowder, Clyde Duncan, Jeannette Gilkey, Kate Kitchin and Virginia Taylor. Their Senior Vaudeville was a high spot of the year, and one of its acts, "Pokie Huntus," will be long remembered by all who took part in it. The Tacky Party was a hilarious occasion; the Christmas presentation of *Bracebridge Hall*, the May Festival at which Mary Neville was crowned queen, and Miss Albertson's hayride for the seniors were other colorful events.

Two new sports were added to the athletic program this year, hockey and riding. The Riding Club, organized under Miss Shapcott's influence, gave pleasure to an enthusiastic group of horsewomen. Twice a week Mr. Bacheler's blue Ford drew up before Smedes Hall, the riders piled in and were whisked away to the stable where Sue and Gray Dawn and other spirited steeds awaited them.

Nineteen-twenty-nine saw the achievement of a long desired goal, the appointment of a full-time Alumnae Secretary. Mela Royall of the class of 1927 was the first to hold this position, and her work in building up the alumnae organization was most valuable.

The fall of 1929 found the nation staggering under the Crash, yet for the time being Saint Mary's went her quiet way undisturbed. Later she, too, was to feel the consequences of those chaotic days, but now their tragedy touched her lightly. The school year had an auspicious beginning with a large enrollment and a graduating class of thirty-four. Among the members of this class were Elizabeth Webb, Blanche Hanff, Roxana Eaton, Em Green, Margaret Powell, Mary Stockard, Martha Thomas and Caroline Tucker. "So far we have done rather well in making our influence felt throughout the school," their representative wrote early in the term, "but on one occasion we failed, when we undertook to stamp out the chewing gum epidemic!" (Schoolgirl nature, apparently, changes little with the years.)

The Juniors were an active group. "Of course we are burdened with work," they reported, "but we feel our importance a great deal and enjoy throwing our privileges in the faces of underclassmen. One of our greatest privileges is being in Mr. Guess's History Class, and it is especially enjoyable for those who sit in the back rows, for it is to them that he addresses most of his conversation. Although he seldom says more than 'Please cease all communications in the rear of the room and become quiet,' we puff with pride at this attention."

The Sophomores admitted that some of their number had been disappointed to discover that they were not Juniors, but said that the interesting character of their classes made up for this. "We have English to the tune of the laundresses singing, for into Miss Cooke's classroom float old familiar songs sung in harmony, making a perfect setting for the tragedy of *Hamlet*. We also have our History to the music (?) of the practice halls."

The Freshmen prided themselves upon their sophistication and chose Nancy Boxley as a president who would represent them with poise and dignity. The Preps were most cheerful under Rosine Raoul's leadership and reported naively: "The school seems surprised at the number of attractive and intelligent girls who are Preps this year. Heretofore a Prep has been rather looked down upon, but we can assure you that the opinion has justly changed this year." History repeats itself nowhere more emphatically than at boarding school. When in all the years between 1915 and 1930, were not Seniors, Juniors, Sophomores, Freshmen and Preps just like that?

But there were differences, too. A new era was on the way. "Every evening," says the *Bulletin*, "one sees a continual stream of girls making a bee line for the second floor of East Wing. *A radio has appeared in Harriet Stowers' room.*" The radio age was here, nor were the girls of 1929–'30 to remain listeners only. Later in the year the school made its debut on the air, broadcasting a program over Station WPTF. Great was the excitement as the Glee Club piled into the bus which took them to the station, even greater the thrill of their performance there and the flattering telephone and telegraph messages that rewarded it. Mr. Jones allowed his musicians the even more satisfying reward of a visit to the California Fruit Store on the way home; there they revelled in sundaes and sodas, more sundaes and sodas, and still more, until in amazement at the extent and variety of bizarre combinations, he asked if they wouldn't like some ham and eggs. Marconi had made a new world but he had not touched the schoolgirl appetite.

Radio might replace singing around the parlor piano, Commencement marshalls wear trailing, beruffled dresses or brief skirts and boyish berets, class poems be written in rhymed couplets or the free-est of free verse. The Saint

Mary's girl of 1930 might appear very different from her sister of '15, but essentially the two were close together. The years between them had seen vast changes in the world; never before had so short a space of time brought such a revolution in manners, customs, modes of thought and of life. Yet the 1930 class notes quoted above might with equal truth have appeared in 1915.

Plus ça change, plus c'est la même chose. True this is of the school-girl heart, true of a hundred years of life at Saint Mary's. Wars, depressions, and social revolutions go their way, but behind the sheltering grove of oaks Saint Mary's and Saint Mary's girls remain the same. It is a heartening thought.

6

"Onward and Upward"
1930–1942

By Anna Brooke Allan

IT WAS a morning in May in the year 1930. Bishop Penick was speaking to the graduating class and to the "old girls" who had come back for the Commencement alumnae meeting. He was setting forth once more the ideals of Saint Mary's and quoting from the histories of the school during the sixties to show again that the traditional heart of Saint Mary's remains unchanged, no matter how greatly fashions in girls and language and customs may vary. The Senior Class of 1930 must have been very happy to feel on that day that they were a part of the Saint Mary's which is timeless—which is "unchanged by change" —and at the same time to feel in their hearts that "We represent the latest edition—the fullest development to date —in fashions of girls, language, and customs." It was their class that in the fall had produced with a great deal of satisfaction a skit called "Then and Now," showing the contrast between the quaint little girls of fifty years earlier and the smart young moderns of 1930. It was they who had been accorded two extra "movie cuts" to see George Arliss in *Disraeli,* and Mary Pickford and Douglas Fairbanks in *The*

Taming of the Shrew. Once that year the University of North Carolina Glee Club had given a concert at Saint Mary's and had danced with the Seniors afterwards at the Rectory! In the spring they had been present at the tea in the parlor in honor of Bishop Cheshire's eightieth birthday. That same year, also, some of them had gone with Mr. Jones and the choir to see the floodlights turned on the State Capitol for the first time—that was at the Golden Light Jubilee in honor of Thomas A. Edison—and they had been allowed to leave the school dining room early that evening that they might secure their seats near the platform to hear the music. Some of them with the sciences classes had attended the lecture at State College on "The Making of Rayon." Others had gone to see *Good News.* And nearly all had been among the five busloads from the school who enjoyed the State Fair under the guidance of Mr. William Guess, who happened to be the Gentleman-of-the-Day.

More than a decade has passed since the Class of 1930 received Bishop Penick's benediction. In the pages that follow I want to recall what has happened at Saint Mary's during the years since then. While I was there as a student in the early thirties, my generation, like every other generation of school girls, lived from day to day—studying, eating, making excursions, planning and promoting projects that were our "school life," playing and laughing and loving; but all that while we hardly realized that we were going to take away from school anything more than the "sweet memories" which we sang about in the first verse of the Alma Mater. It has only been since graduation that the second verse of the Alma Mater has become significant. Only now, when we look back on our experience, can we see how well Saint Mary's "cared for her daughters"; only now can we truly tell of the "happy instructions."

We see when we look back that the period in the school's

history from 1930 to the present time has been one of true growth, worthy of the heritage that belongs to Saint Mary's. The beginning of the thirties found the school affected by the economic depression which forced many privately operated and endowed schools and colleges throughout the country to close their doors; but Saint Mary's weathered the storm, and the beginning of the forties found it filled again to capacity. During the decade Mrs. Ernest Cruikshank was made President. The courses in music, art, home economics, expression, and business became available without additional tuition charges; and the academic department kept pace with the times, the standards being steadily raised, particularly in the college courses. Building and remodelling made considerable changes in the face of the school. Mr. William Erwin, whose marriage to a Saint Mary's girl is described elsewhere, died, leaving a legacy of $25,000, which facilitated much of this change. Several generations of students strove for the perfection of a student government based on the honor system. These are only a few of the chapters in the progress of Saint Mary's during the thirties; there are more, and yet always along with the new, the best of the old lives on.

The first three years of the decade witnessed many annual events familiar to girls who came before that time and to those who have come since. The years opened with the seniors on hand to welcome the new girls as they arrived. Soon after schedules had been settled, came the Old Girl-New Girl party; and a few days later every new girl found in her mail-box a note, inviting her to be a member either of the Sigma or the Mu athletic association; that night in the gymnasium the athletic program got under way with the annual Bloomer Party and basketball game. (The Bloomer Party, by the way, is no longer called a Bloomer Party, for the kinship between the modern "gym-suit" and the old middy and bloomer is hardly perceptible.) Class-

"ONWARD AND UPWARD" 211

work soon started in earnest, and it seemed no time before the Christmas festivities came, followed by vacation and exams and a new term. On Easter morning the entire school family arose early, dressed themselves in white, and went together to the chapel to take part in the most beautiful service of the year. Commencement season included, besides the main events: recitals and exhibits, class day in the grove, and step singing in front of Smedes Hall.

But among the annual traditional events of those first three years were a few which no longer occur; I remember the last of the Senior Vaudevilles (1933–'34) created and produced entirely by the seniors. It was a play called *Much Ado About Nubbing*, the scene of which was a certain boarding school and the characters mostly "you-know-who" in disguise. Also there was at one time, but is no more, the fashion show of the *Stage Coach* staff. Early in the year it was the custom for the two literary societies to vie with each other to present the better program at a "model meeting." In those days everyone in school belonged to one or the other of the literary societies.

The Year 1932 was marked by the loss of a number of friends who had given largely of themselves to Saint Mary's. On December 27 the Right Reverend Joseph Blount Cheshire, beloved Bishop of North Carolina, died at the age of eighty-two. He had believed and had said that Saint Mary's School was the most important work in his diocese, and his loss was keenly felt by the school. In August death claimed the Reverend George W. Lay, who had been Rector from 1907 to 1918, and under whose administration, Saint Mary's had made its most significant educational advance. At the end of the session 1931–'32, the Reverend Warren W. Way resigned the position he had held for fourteen years as Rector of Saint Mary's, to return to parish work. He had continued the sound educational policy of Mr. Lay, and his had been the work of organizing the expanding school as a junior college. The same year the school lost two other valuable members of the administrative staff, Miss Virginia Holt, Academic Head and teacher of English, now at Chatham Hall in Virginia, and Miss Katherine Albertson, Dean of Students, who has since been engaged in research and writing, especially in the field of history of Eastern Carolina.

The opening of the ninety-first session of Saint Mary's in 1932–'33 was unique up to that time. Theretofore, the Heads of the school had been clergymen, who had used their gifts in the educating of young women. Then at last there came out of their work a woman who could carry it on. In 1932 a Saint Mary's graduate was called to be Principal and Academic Head of the School. It was as if planters, sowing anew each year and harvesting much that was fine, had at last produced a prize plant, one from which the seeds would drop again into the soil to perpetuate the growth of the field. The "prize plant" of course was Margaret Jones, now Mrs. Ernest Cruikshank, President of Saint Mary's School and Junior College. Taking over the administration of any school in the critical year 1932–'33 presented some difficulties. The enrollment at Saint Mary's had dropped to ninety-eight boarding students and a somewhat decreased day school. Funds for physical repairs were limited. The perplexingly rapid post-war changes during the preceding decade had made it hard for school authorities everywhere to make a wise adjustment of their social regulations. Mrs. Cruikshank, together with the Board of Trustees and the school's Business Manager, Mr. Albert W. Tucker, steered the school through the financial crisis, and by the session of 1936–'37 it was again filled to capacity, as it has been ever since. The academic progress has been steadily complemented with physical expansion to care for the restored and increased enrollment. The coming of Mrs.

"ONWARD AND UPWARD"

Cruikshank marks the beginning of a new chapter in the School's history.

In looking back it is interesting to see that a 1931–32 issue of the *Bulletin* carried an editorial entitled "A Saint Mary's Utopia," which pictured a number of innovations in school activities; the editor's dream of membership in limited literary societies on a competitive basis was made a reality the following year. She also imagined that student officers might be elected and trained in the spring of the year preceding their terms, instead of in the fall after many of the old officers who could have helped them had left school. Honorary teams and clubs and more competition in athletics and in scholarship were suggested. Trivial changes these may seem to be, and yet how important they are in a school community where morale depends so largely upon interest in, and a feeling of responsibility for, intramural activities. I do not know where that editor is now, but I believe she would be interested to know to what extent some of her dreams have come to pass and what other things, undreamed of then, have come about during recent years.

Any alumna who has longed in vain to build her own house, adding or renovating as the years demand, may take vicarious pleasure in the recent physical progress at Saint Mary's—which is still going on. If she likes to hang new curtains or knock down walls, make an outdoor fireplace or devise a plan for more closet space, rehabilitate unused rooms or cut a new driveway—it doesn't matter what—Saint Mary's under Mrs. Cruikshank has done all these things and more besides. The growth of the boarding department from ninety-eight students to two hundred and twenty has naturally caused a stir within the walls. The third floor of Smedes and of the adjoining Wings (which were not used at all when I was a student in 1933–34) are now one long hall with newborn rooms, complete with new, more substantial walls and attractive maple furniture. The second floor of East Rock was re-opened in 1934. West Rock was at one stage furnished and decorated by the Alumnae Association to provide an office for the alumnae secretary and rooms in which visiting alumnae and friends of the school could stay over night. The school turned it back into a dormitory in 1935–36, re-imbursing the Association for what had been put into it.

Two kitchens on the second and third floors of Holt Hall, which had been equipped partly by the gift of the Class of '31, were converted into bedrooms, and a new super-kitchen and utility room for Holt was carved out of the southern end of the fourth floor attic. (The first-floor kitchen is still in use as such and comes in handy when there are parties in Holt Hall parlor.) Old Senior Hall, after having been condemned and boarded up for several years, came to life again in 1934 and 1935 and now provides a pleasant home for the chaplain and his family, with rooms for faculty members upstairs. Before the completion of the first-floor apartment the chaplain and his wife lived for a year and a half on the second floor of Smedes Hall. It was necessary for the Reverend Mr. Fletcher to whistle as he ascended the stairs to his study and then wait patiently for the "all clear" signal from the girls above.

In the spring of 1935 the Recreation Room under Smedes porch was opened. The Little Store counter and the day students' debris gave way to ping-pong table, victrola, and card tables; the seniors made curtains for the windows. But the Recreation Room in 1940 became the Day Students' Room again, and the post office was moved from East Rock into Smedes' ground-floor central hall, leaving East Rock streamlined for the administrative offices and free from the raids of mail-seekers.

In the fall of 1937, returning students were surprised to

find that a Music Building had sprung up on the hockey field, a putty-colored, one storey clapboard structure containing practice rooms and three ample studios. Later another studio was added. There are sixteen practice pianos in their separate rooms with the daily schedules of who-practices-at-what-time tacked on each door, just as there used to be when the practice rooms opened into the covered-way connecting the Library with the central buildings. East of the Music Building there is a new supplies and storage building; and the lot north of the dining room and gymnasium, which was formerly not used at all, has been graded to serve as the athletic field.

The most thrilling by far, however, of the new physical aspects is the transformed Library, which now occupies the whole first floor of the Art Building except a small hall way for the staircase. I shall never forget my first sight of it from one of the double doorways (which used to be one of Mr. Guess's classroom windows). The familiar partitions had vanished, and I could look across to the windows on the opposite side of the building. Between me and those windows were space, shiny new tables and chairs, cool green woodwork, and the latest in lighting fixtures. The books were around the walls. As the librarian explained to me the arrangement of the great double room and called my attention to the new circulation desk, the glassed-off office, and the basement stairway, my mind kept going back, trying to find the old library room with its alcove, originally the gymnasium and kindergarten room, now swallowed up in the new greater library, along with the two classrooms I had known best. Those Art Building classrooms have been replaced by a rejuvenated ground floor in West Wing, which now contains four large classrooms and a hall room where the choir may vest without fear of the old ever-recurrent calamity of involving at least three white cottas a week with the inky mimeograph roller. (The choir has been wearing cottas, cassocks, and caps instead of veils since early in the decade.)

Started with a gift from the Class of '39 for an outdoor fireplace, a log cabin for recreation has been built in the grove behind the President's House (the Rectory), to the northwest of the infirmary. The outdoor oven, which faces north, is there just as the Class of '39 wanted it, but it has the unusual advantage of having a log house built around the southern opening of its chimney.

Nearly every September returning students discover a newly completed painting job, the most conspicuous of the decade probably having been that of 1934, when the white walls of Holt Hall bedrooms became cream, light green, or watermelon pink. New telephone booths are standing in various corners of the school; and there are also watercoolers, in which unfortunately the younger generation (and sometimes their elders) have tried occasionally to store food, soft drinks, and flowers. In the summer of 1940 a sprinkler system was installed in the old buildings to cancel the fire hazard, but I hope the students will still be subjected to midnight fire drills. The fire drills were excellent for discipline and would serve to counteract the dangerous "modern" tendency that allows students to choose freely what they want to do without impressing upon them that they have to do some things in this world whether they want to or not.

Whether they want to or not at Saint Mary's, however, some of the girls must do their studying in the Study Hall, formerly called the School Room, though not any longer in the great-room-of-hard-desks that I knew. The room is the same, but the new chairs and reading tables and superscientific lighting remind one of the kind of thing one used to describe in fantastic English-M compositions which were called "The Saint Mary's of the Future" or "Saint Mary's

Five Hundred Years Hence." Such has been the progress of the outward and visible aspects of Saint Mary's.

The curriculum also has undergone a metamorphosis since the "original thirteen" and "some day scholars" of 1842 entered the doors of what is now Smedes Hall for a general education suitable for girls. The demand for the college course since its establishment in 1900 has increased until at the present time the enrollment in the three high school classses for which work is offered is only about one fourth of the total registration. The present graduating classes number in the fifties. The development of the college work has been in keeping with twentieth century currents in women's education throughout the country. Every year the value of the junior college is becoming more apparent, as the four-year colleges find themselves torn between the demand to make their intellectual wares available to a larger number and the necessity of keeping their degrees from becoming empty symbols that can be had for the price of four years' tuition. The junior college course of Saint Mary's, complete in itself, is designed to fill the needs of the large majority of students; but at the same time it gives sound preparation to the students who plan to continue their studying in a four-year college.

With modern transportation and communication pressing the outside world into the campus, the scope of institutional education has expanded. The "original thirteen" would be amazed to see some of the antennae which now project from the courses they knew. One may go with the French class to a French motion picture, or with the psychology class to a series of lectures in Raleigh, or with the English class to a play, or with the science class to look for wild life or to visit the museum. A student may go to Durham or to Chapel Hill, or in Raleigh to the State Library, the Olivia Rainey Library, the Civic Music Concerts, the Woman's Club Series, or to various programs at State College. She may easily "wander afar out of sight of the grove" and still be back in time for "light bell." There is also within the school a full program of outside speakers and musicians. And the radio in the last fifteen years has brought the world not only to the classroom but even to the student's bedside.

But though the modern student is expected to receive passively and digest an almost overwhelming mass of "education," there is still active work to do, over and above class work. In addition to the college composition classes, there are two student publications besides the annual. The *Bulletin*, after an era of being a quarterly summary of school events, has now in addition revived the old *Muse* in the form of a student literary section. The *Grapevine*, semimonthly mimeographed gossip sheet of 1936-1937, has been re-born as the *Belles of Saint Mary's*, a four-page, first-rate collegiate newspaper, a member of the Associated Collegiate Press. It includes school news, student reaction to world news, editorials, personal items, features, a Faculty Corner, and columns—both serious and frivolous. Classes within classes, or rather beyond classes, are the various academic departmental clubs: the French Club, the Deutscher Verein, the Political Science Club, and the two rival literary societies, which have once more become writing groups. (Incidentally, the *Belles of Saint Mary's* of March 11, 1941, announces that the Deutscher Verein is collecting tinfoil and soap for the British.)

Perhaps the most significant manifestation of the academic progress of Saint Mary's is the growing importance of the Library in the life of the school. I wish that every alumna might have had a copy of the 1937-1938 Commencement Number of the *Bulletin,* in which appeared Mrs. Harlan C. Brown's article on "The Saint Mary's School Library—A Century of Progress." Since 1930 when the library totaled 4,574 books, growth has been steady;

gifts in the form of private collections of books, and funds for the acquisition of new books have swelled the collection. At the suggestion of Miss Florence Slater and in memory of Elizabeth Dancy Battle, in November, 1934, the library of the late Louise Floyd Wickham, consisting of 1206 volumes, was bequeathed to Saint Mary's. During 1933-'37 the raising of a memorial fund was sponsored by Mrs. J. S. Holmes, Miss Susan Marshall, and Miss Betsy Montgomery, in memory of Emilie Watts McVea (at Saint Mary's many years). One hundred and eighty contributions were used to purchase 225 books, of which the largest number were English literature; also from Miss McVea's personal library eighteen books were added to this gift. Those in charge of the executive end, the organization, the buying of books, the cataloguing and clerical work have set an enviable record; and to crown their efforts came the award in 1937 of the Carnegie Corporation grant of $4,500, followed by the expansion and remodelling of the Library to accommodate the books (and students) that had overflowed into the halls, classrooms, dormitories, infirmary, and the "outdoor reading room." The number of books in the library in June 1940 was about eight thousand, and the magazine subscriptions, fifty.

The academic work, though it occupies the foremost place, is not the only program offered at Saint Mary's. The five special departments and physical education supply ample outlets for other interests and talents. There are departments of Art, Music, Business, Dramatics, and Home Economics.

Though I never belonged to the inner circle who had the run of the Art Studio and the privilege of working under Miss Harris, I was always glad that the biology class had to go through the studio to reach the laboratory. And how doubly pleasant were the play rehearsals held in the art room during the midwinter months in 1933-'34 when the auditorium was sometimes too cold to work in. Eighteen lucky girls took art in 1936–'37; the number jumped to forty-seven the next year when the art course was offered without extra charge. While art students are learning art history and appreciation, however, other students are apprehending through them a valuable dilution of their knowledge.

This process of apprehending other students' lessons while trying to comprehend your own goes on wherever there are specialized fields in a school, but it is especially noticeable where there is a department of music. Since the departmental courses have been offered without extra charge, music no longer belongs to only a few advanced pupils or even to only the large number of girls who "take." It belongs to everyone in school. More and more girls each year look forward to the concerts in Raleigh and to the student and faculty concerts. It must have been very gratifying to Mr. Jones to have so many come to the chapel in the late afternoons during midyear examination week to hear him play the organ. No one who has attended Saint Mary's since 1919 can think of music there without gathering to her heart and mind the memory of Mr. William H. Jones, whose death in February, 1940, at the age of sixty-nine, ended twenty-one years of faithful and invaluable service to the school. He was the beloved associate of the faculty and the dear delight of the student body. His announcement that choir practice would be as usual, though it was the same each week, was indispensable. I remember that when he would start to leave the dining room without having made his announcement, there would be a muffled bedlam until, sensing that something was wrong, he would turn back. Then, though every girl in the room could have pronounced his words before he said them, he would give his usual announcement amidst the suppressed glee of the triumphant student body. Mr. Jones, besides being our teacher and director of music at Saint Mary's, was a director in the Civic Music Association and for many years organist at Christ Church, and director of the Saint Cecilia Society in Raleigh and the Raleigh Male Chorus. A graduate of old Trinity College (Duke), he had studied four years in Berlin, had taught at the Pomfret School for Boys, Connecticut, and had been organist in Norfolk at St. Paul's Church and at others. He had come to Saint Mary's soon after returning from overseas.

I remember how Mr. Jones felt about girls' smoking. He was a great smoker himself, but when some of the students begged for smoking privileges, he would be very sad and would say quietly and with deep feeling: "Putting a cigarette in a woman's mouth is like putting mud on a lily."

The *Belles of Saint Mary's* (February 23, 1940) said editorially of Mr. Jones:

"He was not merely an organist and a teacher. He had a rare ability to give much of himself and his deep knowledge to his music. What he found, he made his own, enriched, and gave back with the enviable stamp of his intelligence. If he was classical in his sympathies, he was broad in repertoire and understanding, and artistically colorful in his work. His teaching was patient, his knowledge encyclopaedic, his touch encouraging and understanding.

"As a person he was genial, kind, and tolerant. The whole student body loved and admired him. They benefited by his learning, and borrowed freely of his library and his mind. They liked his puckish wit, his bright joviality, and through his informality found his generous friendship. They will long remember the deep contentment of his vesper music, nor soon forget his personal grace . . .

". . . Thoughtfulness added considerably to his stature. His summer trips narrated themselves briefly through post cards from various places. Often friends found their interests remembered through books or papers or presents which he left them in their absence.

"His touch was sure, and enduring."

Inseparable from Mr. Jones' personality was his studio, for many years on the northwest corner of the West Wing ground floor. There in addition to his music were his countless books, his pictures and the world war posters he had brought back from France, and a few sturdy ashtrays. There he taught and studied and read; there were the choir practices, council sessions, and faculty meetings; and there also for a number of years the Raleigh Male Chorus assembled. The students enjoyed the Chorus's concerts immensely, but they gleaned especial pleasure on rehearsal nights when the men's voices resounded through the halls and rooms near the studio. I remember once during evening study-hall when we were hot and restless at our desks in the big room in Smedes Hall, the time came for the Chorus to disband for the evening. Just outside the study-hall window a quartet paused to render their own harmonized version of "How'm I doing? Hey, hey—twee, twee, twee—twa, twa"—decidedly off the regular program. The spell over the quiet room was broken. If the teacher on the platform had not been more alert than we, we might have taken her by surprise and rushed to the window before her look forbade it; as it was, we sat where we were and listened.

A chosen group had the privilege of presenting the Gilbert and Sullivan operetta each spring, but the tunes and as many words as could be caught were on everyone else's lips also, during the whole of the second semester. Fortunate, too, were those who held the coveted places in the choir; but those who were left outside of Glee Club and Choir could still forget their inhibitions and pour forth their songs at step sings and on bus rides. In 1936–'37, thirty-eight pupils took music lessons; under the new no-extra-charge policy the next year the number increased to ninety-eight.

While many girls at Saint Mary's are learning what to do with a piano keyboard, many others are fingering the keyboard of a typewriter. The business department, since its beginning in 1897 under the direction of Miss Lizzie Lee, has developed with the needs of the times. Up until the day she retired in 1936, Miss Lee turned out well-trained graduates whose success was a credit to her able teaching and management. The girls of the thirties will remember her as a gentle, gracious lady with lace at her throat and with snow-white, curly hair. Her bedroom, well filled with hundreds of neatly arranged, dainty little objects, seemed a world apart from the other rooms in Holt Hall. You could visit with Miss Lee and sit in one of her chairs and talk with her, just as you might with someone at home; whereas, in any other room on her hall, you would sprawl on the bed or sit on the floor and call to someone two doors down if you felt like it. To the girls, there seemed to be about Miss Lee the charming air of long gone yesterdays, inexplicably mixed with something that made her "one of us." In the interchange between pupils and teacher, no fine shade of meaning, nothing, was lost in the gulf of years between; she was our age—yet wise and gentle and tolerant.

Closely associated with Miss Lee and bound to her by the ties of a long friendship, was Miss Juliet Sutton. Miss Sutton also taught in the business department at one time, along with her thousand-and-one other duties. When she completed her forty-second year of service at Saint Mary's in June 1940, the *North Carolina Churchman* (June 15, 1940) carried the story of the farewell dinner in her honor:

"Miss Juliet Sutton, after nearly forty-two years of active service to Saint Mary's School and Junior College, retired at the end of this school year.

"Dinner at Saint Mary's on Thursday evening, May 16, was a special occasion in her honor. Unaware that a party for her was on foot, Miss Sutton said with characteristic dryness when two corsages arrived for her in the late afternoon, 'Why, it's not my birthday or anything.'

". . . The students . . . sang at dinner the song with which they honor special guests on any occasion, but even the extraordinary spirit and enthusiasm which they put into it did not seem to make Miss Sutton realize that the party was especially for her.

"Dessert was served in the parlor where Miss Sutton has for many years, in her own phrase, 'Kept the night.' To many generations of school girls, Miss Sutton 'on duty in the parlor' is as much a part of the stately room as the portraits on the wall. Mrs. Cruikshank, President of Saint Mary's, spoke a few dignified and sincere words of tribute to Miss Sutton. After calling attenting to Miss Sutton's long and faithful service to the school, to her loyalty in supporting its interests, Mrs. Cruikshank mentioned the fact that because of a 'certain pungent quality of personality all her own, and because of her discriminating friendships, Miss Sutton has won a place in the hearts of literally thousands of girls.'

"A beautiful pin, a circle of matched pearls set in gold, was presented by Mrs. Cruikshank to Miss Sutton, as a gift from the students, faculty, and officers of Saint Mary's.

. . . . . .

"Miss Sutton, the daughter of a Pittsboro clergyman, came to Saint Mary's first as a student. She became a member of the staff the year that Dr. Bennett Smedes, second rector of the school, died. The many and varied posts that she has filled have brought her into intimate contact with practically every girl who has been at Saint Mary's for forty-two years. She has assisted in the dormitories and the business department; she was secretary to the rectors; she

"ONWARD AND UPWARD"

has recorded (and remembered) the grades of students, and has had charge of the post office. In short, Miss Sutton has been a part of the life at Saint Mary's during all the administrations except the first.

" 'You couldn't run a school now as they did then,' Miss Sutton once said in reference to the changes in strict discipline which she has seen in four decades. Always young in spirit, Miss Sutton herself has changed with the times."

Another person who will always be young, though generations of students may come and go, is Miss Florence Davis, whose name is synonymous with the Expression Department of Saint Mary's. Neither in her work nor in her personal life does she give in to the temptation to live in the past or to rest comfortably on past accomplishments. Every fall she returns to Saint Mary's after her summer study, erupting with ideas and full of plans for the dramatics season; but her winter's work does not depend for inspiration upon what she gathers in the summer. She feels strongly the importance of going forward day by day, week by week, keeping abreast of (and sometimes ahead of) not only all that goes on within the school but also activity in the town of Raleigh, in the state, and beyond—especially in the realm of the theatre. She will not stage a play unless it is a good play in the first place, and in the second place a finished production, even if it takes months to finish it to her satisfaction. Along with the care she gives to dramatics she manages "permission slips," the girls' invitations, and all the work of a social dean of resident students. Consequently, throughout all her waking hours, she has "Work To Do." She does it—and she loves it!

I remember the try-outs for the Dramatic Club, held in the Auditorium early in the year. Miss Davis called the new girls one-by-one to the stage to display what they could do, or could not do, with pantomime. Then from the back of the auditorium, she would ask for their names and addresses, and the extent of their experience or interest in a half-dozen different phases of stage-craft. When the afternoon was over, everyone was happy, for all the girls who had "tried out" had been admitted to the Club, and Miss Davis was armed for the rest of the year with notes on each new member's special leanings and aptitudes.

As the time for a play drew near, the atmosphere at rehearsals grew tense. More frequently Miss Davis would tap with her stick at the back of the auditorium to signify that the lines should be repeated. For dress rehearsals there were always visitors, usually members of the faculty; but for *Cradle Song* two Sisters came to help with the convent clothes and manners. When the day of a play came, people were running back and forth, setting the stage all through the morning and afternoon. Already Miss Davis had secured the familiar piece of rich brocade—one of the downtown stores had had this same remnant on hand for several years and was always willing to lend it to Miss Davis whenever she found a place for it on the stage. The cast had early supper—special delicacies—and costuming and make-up were underway before sundown. The cast insisted that they were allowing too much time to dress, but Miss Davis was firm on that point and five minutes before the curtain rose, when all was ready—and just ready—they always realized that she had estimated correctly the amount of time needed.

The two high spots of the dramatics season were, and are, the Carolina Dramatic Association's State Tournament at Chapel Hill and the Shakespearean play at Commencement. I do not believe the thrill of any other Dramatic Club excursion from Saint Mary's can match that of the trip to Chapel Hill in the spring of 1934. The cast was convinced (secretly) that the Saint Mary's play was a "washout." Miss Davis alone seemed not discouraged, and we suspected that perhaps her optimism was for the benefit of our downcast spirits. We saw other plays in the Playmakers' Theatre at Chapel Hill in the morning and evening and presented our own in the afternoon. We did *Les Précieuses Ridicules*. It went better than we had expected, but we were not sure whether it was on a par with *The Man Who Married a Dumb Wife,* produced by a rival group. Nevertheless, when the awards were announced at the end of the evening session, first place among junior college groups went to Saint Mary's. Our spirits zoomed and stayed for days in the stratosphere. When we got back to Raleigh long after midnight, we went en masse to awaken Mrs. Cruikshank to tell her that we had won the prize. She shared our happiness—and our surprise. This was the first of many Festival plaques won by Miss Davis's plays. Another time I remember we were not so fortunate. The stage was set, or at least almost set, for tragedy. The curtain went up on a quiet living room containing a family into whose midst death was already stepping. But alas! the electrician had not heard the warning and there he was in the center of the stage tinkering with the table lamp. Realizing his predicament, he uttered an inappropriate exclamation and bolted through the window, leaving behind him a disconcerted "family" and an amused audience.

Speaking of "disconcerted families," I believe Saint Mary's offers an excellent antidote for them in real life through its home economics classes—cooking and sewing. The biscuits I have tasted at the end of one of the "laboratory periods" would be a source of pride to any bride. Every year the sewing pupils compete in State College's intercollegiate and interschool dressmaking contest. The fabrics used are supplied by the textile students at State, and at their annual fashion show awards are made for the best results in making dresses of these fabrics.

Competition at Saint Mary's on the whole, however, is intra-mural. Gym, for instance, implies much more than the course of two one-hour periods a week. One season follows another: hockey, swimming, basketball, volley ball, baseball, and tennis; and Sigma and Mu teams compete from September till June. The enthusiasm of the most enthusiastic has not waned in the past decade, but possibly there are fewer enthusiasts, the old border line cases having turned to other activities and to taking advantage of the increase in the number of "town" privileges. In the fall of 1937 new sports included kickball, shuffle board, hit-pin baseball, paddle tennis, darts, quoits tennis, and zel-ball. (If you are seventeen or seventy-seven, you'll get a good laugh out of zel-ball.) A new coat of varnish appeared on the gym floor that same year, and hairdryers were installed for swimmers.

Dancing through the decade has gone from "aesthetic" to "natural" in 1930–1931, to "creative" in 1932–1933, to "modern." Folk dancing and Morris dancing have flourished.

The latest innovation in the department is the excursion to the bowling alley in the afternoon. Memorable annual events include: Play Day, held each year on a different campus, to which schools and colleges from all over the state send groups; Posture Week, when one is allowed to slump only in the privacy of one's own room; the Faculty-Student Basketball Game, in which the faculty usually cheat outrageously; and May Day. Of the succession of Saint Mary's May Days Letty Lassiter Wilder of the class of 1935 has written:

"The history of Saint Mary's May Days tells of vacillation between a formal May Day with an impressive procession of attendants, maids of honor, ladies of the court, and heralds and pages and recently a May Day of considerably less pomp, more vitality and ingenuity. On several occasions the two schools of thought have compromised with each other for a particularly successful pageant. In the

"ONWARD AND UPWARD" 229

twenties there were maypoles and magnificent queens; dresses were gorgeous; flowers, elegant. Rumors flew as to the sums expended on dresses of the attendants, the maids of honor, and the queen.

"But by 1932, lush days were long past. The depression had settled even upon May Day at Saint Mary's. For two years there was no dancing on the green. In 1934 efforts were made to keep May Day expenses slight for the 'Corner' was not yet turned. Withal it was a delightful pageant. The dance group was used more than ever before. In addition to the May Pole and other folk dancing, 1935 witnessed a break with May Day tradition. There was no white satin and no pastel dresses for the ladies of the court. The queen wore a Grecian costume as did everyone participating in May Day, for the theme centered around Orpheus and Eurydice. The Greek influence lasted through 1936. Both in 1935 and 1936 creative dancing was strongly emphasized. In 1937 and 1938 pastel gowned courts were ruled over by queens in lovely full-skirted white dresses.

"The theme of May Day in 1939 was derived from Milton's 'L'Allegro.' The dance department was highly successful in working out dances from the poem, and also from Masefield's 'Cargoes' in 1940."

The activities I have been discussing so far represent organized departments of the curriculum. A picture of what the school has been in the last ten years would not be complete without some mention of another activity, the very important, though extra-curricular, Student Government. Briefly, the present organization is as follows: the Honor Council, which is made up of the Student Government officers, class presidents, and class representatives, serves as a judicial body, has general oversight of the workings of the Student Government Association, and seeks to maintain a high level of student conduct; the Legislative Body, composed of seven members of the faculty and fifteen students, has the power to initiate legislation pertaining to social and dormitory regulations and to pass upon suggestions from the students; the Hall Council has charge of dormitory reports; and various student committees take care of orientation for the new girls, issuing the handbook, managing the Student Drive, keeping the grounds neat, appointing hostesses and pages for social occasions, and regulating the school dances. However, one must not imagine that the Student Government, as outlined in the current handbook, came swiftly and painlessly into being. It has suffered temporary stagnation, apparent defeat, and agonizing rebirth, and it has never reached perfection even momentarily; but it has come a long journey since 1930, and with each new generation of students, the struggle for its development goes on. Many students in that struggle have experienced for the first time the heartbreaks that come from a youthful striving to impose a theoretically perfect system on imperfect creatures. And from the experience they have come out wiser, humbler, more tolerant and kindly, and with a deeper love for those imperfect creatures and a faith which looks far beyond that in any utopian system of government as an all-powerful cure-all in itself.

Many students of the thirties will remember with pain the elaborate induction services, attempted at one time by the Student Government. We dressed in white and made pledges, one by one, on the stage of the Auditorium; but the ceremony was long and hot and monotonous, and after we had watched our classmates' rigid solemnity for two hours, the desire to laugh stole over us. After that year's crop of students was inducted, everyone breathed a sigh of relief, and the method was abandoned. The Pan Archon Council rose and fell in 1934–1935. It added to the Honor Council the heads of other organizations, but as the Honor Council girls were already interested members of the other organizations its value in our relatively small student body did not warrant its survival. The Classification System for some reason was sickly from birth and never reached maturity. A student's "class" depended on everything from academic success to punctuality, personal appearance, and loyalty. It was theoretically a comprehensive evaluation of each person as a member of the school community. Social privileges and study hour regulations varied for members of Classes A, B, C, etc., the "class" membership being announced quarterly.

An indirect outgrowth of the Student Government Association is the Order of the Circle (founded in 1937–38), an honorary club which represents a significant advance in student-responsibility for school affairs and in the value placed on scholarship. Its purpose, quoting from the Student Handbook, is "to promote a spirit of cooperation among the students and between faculty and students by the cultivation of high ideals of fellowship, service, citizenship, and scholarship, and to assist new students in finding their places in school life and activities." Any of the alumnae who have lived through eras when the would-be studious were considered somewhat leprous, and when "anyone-who-was-anyone" proved it by trying to "get by with" things, will watch with interest the work and influence of the Circle during the next decade.

Along with the development of student government, the introduction of the six-day week for juniors and seniors, the growth of the college department, and the steady improvement of the calibre of the college work under the wise direction of the President, the social regulations have been adjusted gradually to make for a healthier proportion of off-campus recreation without allowing the school program to suffer. An increase in the number of town and movie privileges has decreased the old feeling of obligation to take advantage of *every* one available. Week-ends still have to be weighed and chosen with discrimination; yet graduation finds happy memories of visits and dances mingled with other happy memories of school days.

But off-campus recreation has not done away with the traditional social life within the school by any means. From the Old Girl-New Girl party in September until the final "School Party" when the seniors do not hesitate to make fools of themselves and others for the entertainment of the rest of the school, the seasons and holidays are marked by fitting celebrations. The juniors entertain as spookily as possible in the gymnasium at Halloween—and clean sheets are at a premium the following week. The seniors give the Christmas pageant in the chapel on the night before the holidays and sing carols on the campus early the next morning. The giving of impudent "Christmas presents" with saucy or sarcastic verses attached has recently been abandoned. An attempt was made to establish an annual faculty show, but the faculty are still trying to live down the first one, since which they have never fully recovered their dignity in the eyes of the students who laughed at them.

Paralleling the activity and spirit within the school are the work and fellowship of the alumnae. The Alumnae Association, which has been since its beginning an aid and a source of pride to Saint Mary's, entered a new era in 1929 with the appointment of the first full-time executive secretary. Besides increasing the effectiveness of the organization, the alumnae secretaries have established and encouraged chapters in different towns, got in touch with many former students who had drifted away, and kept members informed of the progress of the school, drawing the "old girls" closely together. The alumnae have been interested in serving the school in various ways. For many years the organ which is now in the chapel was their project. The Alumnae House in West Rock, enthusiastically planned, beautifully decorated, and graciously relinquished when the school needed the building for a dormitory, was the work of many old girls, guided by the special care of Miss Esdale Shaw, twice President of the Association, and member of the Board of Trustees. The redecoration of the Parlor, a room rich in history, filled with the happy associations of all generations, and beautiful in its own right, was irresistible as an alumnae project; and the result has been more than satisfying to old and young. In 1937 Fannie B. Aiken, Saint Mary's '27, gave as a memorial to her grandmother (Fannie B. Aiken, 1872), and her aunt (Fannie B. Aiken, 1885), a large mirror which was placed in the entrance hall of Smedes Building. But the greatest service of the alumnae, and the evidence most indicative of their love for the school, has been the gift of their daughters. According to the Saint Mary's *Bulletin,* which always carries a section dealing with alumnae news and the Association's activity, fifty-eight descendants of old girls were enrolled in 1939–40.

It has been gratifying to see the number of old girls who have come back to visit on any and all occasions—for a minute, for an afternoon, for a week-end—but the school is fortunate in having had a number of alumnae come back to stay, the most notable return being that of Mrs. Ernest Cruikshank. Three of the girls of the thirties have already come back during the decade to serve in the capacity of Alumnae Secretary. Alice Alexander, now Mrs. Charles Connor of New York City, a graduate of Smith College, was Secretary from 1935 to 1937. She is the lady whose pictures in *Vogue* many Saint Mary's alumnae watch for each month; and she is as lovely in every way as her pictures. Kate Spruill, now Mrs. William Harrison of Rocky Mount, returned after her graduation from Hollins in 1937. We of the first generation who know Kate challenge the second hundred years to produce another such daughter as she. And now Sarah Vann (Saint Mary's 1930–32), who received her secretarial training at Katherine Gibbs, has been carrying on the good work since September, 1940, and has been working with the alumnae for a fitting celebration of the school's one hundredth anniversary.

Hundreds of alumnae look back on their school days and say "I loved Saint Mary's; I loved the place; I loved the girls, etc." I am one of those hundreds, but I do not want anyone to entertain for a moment the idea that I loved the girls at Saint Mary's the minute I laid eyes on them—I didn't. When I arrived in the fall of 1933, it seemed as if every other new girl discovered at least a second cousin as soon as she arrived, or else her mother's roommate's niece would turn up and be an old girl and probably a senior. I felt that I alone was unknown and unappreciated. Later I found I was kin-somehow-through-marriage to a girl who was related to everyone else in school, but by that time lessons and activities had started. There was no more time then for "Who do you know?" and "Do you remember that summer?"—and when the next breathing spell came around, everyone knew everyone else and remembered everything. Also we knew all about people we had never seen—especially certain very attractive young men. Maria Drane Temple tells me that not long after her graduation she spoke on the street one day, as if to an old friend, to a man she thought she knew. When he looked baffled, she realized that he was "The One" whose picture had hung in the room across the hall from hers for two years at Saint Mary's. She knew his name, his face, his most famous words, but this was their first actual encounter.

When I look back on my two student years at Saint Mary's, I cannot remember distinctly what we could do or how many times a week we could do it; I just remember what we did do. But at the time—at least at first—I felt sorely oppressed by regulations. "They read us the rules by installments," I wrote in my first letter home, "so that we can digest one batch before being floored with another," and further, "We have to have a signed list of everyone we can go out with or see in Raleigh. Can you think of anyone besides —————— who might ask me out? You might try suggesting that I be allowed to use my own judgment, but [mournfully] I doubt if it would do any good." (Incidentally, it did "do some good.") But my second letter home was in a different vein: "This is the swellest place. I'm so glad I came here. We can go down town or to the little store across the street almost any afternoon without a chaperon. . . . We have to go to study hall every night, but if our grades are o. k. at the end of this month, we can start studying in our rooms. . . . I'm gaining weight every day in spite of the fact that I eat only one piece of bread at every meal." (Perhaps the going down town or to the Little Store almost any afternoon had something to do with the weight, but I didn't think of it at the time.) My happiness was about complete by the third week when forty-one of us went on a special bus to a football game at Chapel Hill. "We sat on the Davidson side during the first half," I wrote to my mother, "and on the Carolina side during the second. (The girls complained of the *sun in their eyes* during the first half.)" I remember clearly now, and I evidently suspected at the time, that the sun was not the real reason for moving. Many girls were always fortunate enough to find brothers, cousins, young uncles, and so on, on the Carolina side of the stadium.

There are at least five aspects of institutional life which may be considered timeless in our school history. For instance, one could write an account of "The Manifestations of an (Unacademic) Interest in Man Through a Hundred Years of Saint Mary's," or a chapter on "A Decade of Eating Between Meals," or the "Vicissitudes of Living Within One's Allowance." Or one could toss off "Notes of Comparison and Contrast in a Century of Spontaneous Recreation and Unpremeditated Ribaldry," or an essay "On Going on Excursions Beyond the Deadline: A) Legally, B) Illegally." The latest developments in these phases of school life follow naturally the preceding chapters, the reader taking into consideration, of course, the inescapable pressure of greyhound busses, radio, modern bakery machinery, Toddle Houses, vitamins, and the evolution of a conception of female education which is in keeping with the new place of woman, economically and socially, in a rapidly changing world.

First let us consider Eating, during the past decade—as a form of recreation. Unscheduled eating has through the years caused temporary elation, followed usually by regret, and often accompanied by just a touch of shame (to the extent that the eaters prefer to do their Worst secretly with only their nearest friends). It seems that as far back as the sixties (when war-time food was none too plentiful or varied), Mary Ruffin and two other girls "somehow got hold of twenty-one eggs, had them cooked, took them to the woods, and ate them all." The "Feeds" of the thirties (or binges, bats, jags, or sprees—I can't find out what the latest term is) consist usually of less protein, more carbohydrates. One fond grandmother a few years ago sent her granddaughter five dollars with which to entertain her friends on her birthday. The granddaughter turned over in her mind several possible plans, including ice-cream for the hall, or movies on Monday afternoon; but she finally settled on asking two intimates to accompany her to Staudt's Bakery for the afternoon, and at that place, among them the three disposed of the total sum. The girls usually celebrated birthdays with food between study hall and bedtime. Ice-cream cups were supplied by members of the hall and anything from cake to fried chicken or sour balls was added from boxes sent from home, or through the generosity of hungry roommates. Over and over again we would solemnly give up eating bread at meal time, and occasionally when we faced the fact that bread at meal time had little to do with our ever increasing weight, we would resolve to forego the wares of the stores on the other side of Hillsboro Street and of the Little Store run by the Seniors under the front porch of Smedes Hall. But resolutions were soon forgotten, and stylish slimness was seldom achieved. By the fall of 1933 dieting in the dining room beyond reasonable limits had been banned and anyone who persisted in this practice was sent to the infirmary. As nearly as I can gather, the "anti-diet rule" was enacted as the result of a sad experience at some previous Christmas. It seems that about two weeks before the holiday nearly everyone who felt too fat had signed an oath to eat practically nothing for the duration of the session, in order that she might be lovely looking at Christmas time and incidentally might fit once more into the evening dresses on hand. This vanity being an incentive, all had gone well until the girls sat down at table for the traditional Christmas banquet the last night before the close of school. Every Saint Mary's girl remembers those Christmas banquets and can guess what went on in the minds of the dieters; anyone who has made the mistake of eating heavily after two weeks of starvation can guess what went on in the stomachs of the dieters. One by one they had left the dining room before the banquet was half over.

In my own day, I think that for every dieter, there were at least two double-eaters, judging from the ordering done for the Senior Little Store. One girl came regularly right behind the candy man's weekly visit and purchased outright a carton of Heath Bars. The proceeds from the Little Store that year bought an electric victrola and furnished the Recreation Room under Smedes Hall porch.

When I went back to Saint Mary's for the year 1937–'38, I was in charge of a table in the dining room. Shortly before Christmas my girls announced that it was time to turn their attentions to dieting for the usual reasons. "Ah," thought I, "I shall be coöperative and under my kindly guidance this dieting will be kept on a sensible basis." I offered to take the responsibility for deciding what they should do without at each meal, and guaranteed a slow and steady loss of weight. The girls were eager to begin. The arrangement was to proceed along scientific and businesslike lines. Discussion was to be reduced to a minimum; my casual directions were to be final. For two and a half days I dictated briefly at the beginning of each meal. Wistful glances were exchanged among the seven girls but there was never a word of complaint. On the third day I chanced to be down town shopping. I had not been hungry between meals during those days because, of course, I always ate the extra desserts at the table. I passed by a bakery and looked smugly in through the broad glass window. On the other side of the glass seven familiar faces looked out at me from behind chocolate éclairs, cream puffs, buns, and doughnuts. Dieting was not mentioned at the table again.

Eating, however, was but one of the forms of recreation. From the beginning, I believe, Saint Mary's girls "wandered afar out of sight of the grove" mostly during the summer months and after school days were over, and of course on a few special occasions like the day of the State Fair and the time of the annual excursion to the State Hospital. At one time (long ago) the Christmas holiday was three days; not many went home then. With distances cut down by faster transportation, holidays and week-ends were made practicable and are now considered inalienable right.

"Going out" has become simpler, but I believe no less exciting than formerly when outings were rarer. There is still the turmoil of getting ready; and in spite of wise pronouncements against borrowing, one is still likely to wear one's roommate's hat if it is more becoming than one's own.

"ONWARD AND UPWARD"

If anyone questions the beauty and romance of a forty-two passenger bus, she should see one, all lights aglow, roll into the Saint Mary's gate, past the summer house, around the drive, up to the steps of Smedes, where forty-two eager young girls are watching for it. The bus stops; the door opens; the scramble for seats begins. There is always singing on a bus trip. Sometimes, I remember, we were allowed to sing while riding through the down-town section, if the songs we selected were in good taste and not too loud. Right well I recall also, the occasions when our group was coming out of the Theatre at Chapel Hill after performances of the Carolina Playmakers. The rest of the audience scattered this way and that, taking paths across the campus or searching the side streets for their automobiles. The Saint Mary's bus was always at the curb, waiting. It was much to be desired that a goodly showing of the University students would linger at the bus windows until we were off, and the departure was always happily delayed for five or ten minutes, while Miss Davis stood in the doorway of the bus, calling the roll to be sure that no one was left behind.

Besides bus trips there were also shorter expeditions, for which we had to fall back on the use of our feet. We would walk two-by-two in a line that extended the length of a block or more. We did not like this so well; we felt too conspicuous. During my first year at Saint Mary's the students presented a petition (which was granted) that they be allowed to walk in "clumps." They thought that way it would look to a passerby as if the sidewalks just *happened* to be particularly conjested at a given spot at a given moment.

With opportunities for going beyond the campus boundaries, one may readily see that the student of the thirties had ample opportunity to exercise her ability to manage her personal finances, to relate her spending to her allowance, to balance her budget—or to fail to balance it, as the case might be. Valuable lessons were learned at Mr. A. W. Tucker's office window in the hall of East Rock. At the window we deposited our spending money each month and drew it out as needed, learning all the while slowly and painfully that respect is due to Office Hours and that overdrawn accounts are to be avoided. Mr. Tucker not only helped us individually to keep our account books in order and explained to us the mysterious things that business men know and school girls do not know, but it was he also who shouldered the responsibility of the transactions of Club funds, class funds, football excursions, and dozens of other group activities. And all of this of course was in addition to the splendid job he was doing (and is still doing) in handling the business end of the administration of the school. He demanded of the students with no uncertainty businesslike exactness in all dealings, but I think he had an especially soft spot in his heart for those who were puzzled and distraught by the complexities of ways and means.

Frequent calls for help and lists of items that couldn't be done without, as they appear in one student's letters home, will probably strike a familiar note in the minds of other ex-students and their parents. "I'm afraid I'm living beyond my means because my money is practically gone," she wrote in October, 1933. "I spent $6.10 on second-hand books and $2.35 on furnishings for the room . . . the trip to Carolina [Chapel Hill] cost $1.50. On top of all this do you think I might go to see *Green Pastures* on the fourteenth? Seats are $1.10 and $1.65. Also my radio is broken and I suppose I'll have to have it fixed."

"Thank you so much for the check. It came just as——— [my roommate] realized she hadn't another penny to lend me, so now she's borrowing till her check comes. Such is life. I don't know where it all goes."

And later: "I purchased some navy blue shoes . . . I had to pay $1.00 for my undergarment for creative dancing in the May fete, will have to pay $1.00 for my soft shoes when they come. My clown costume for tumbling is going to cost about $2.50 on account of the great amount of material. The tax for the Junior-Senior dance is $2.00. It must be paid by the 17th of this month. My trip to Chapel Hill including evening session ticket at 50¢ [Dramatic Festival] and lunch and dinner only cost 90¢ . . . I've become a very expensive child to support."

And during the following session: "Thanks so much for the money. I now have an abundance. I hope it will last until Christmas. I've long since given up eating between meals." And later: "I'm leaving on the 8:20 train. Please send motherly advice and money." And so on and on through the years—

I am going to try not to say much about the interest of the girls of the thirties in young men (called in the student handbook "dates"), for I believe the older generations always think the younger generation has its mind too much on men. The modern girl is supposed to be a bit more matter-of-fact about it all, but she still runs to the windows when the State College students serenade from the grove after a great football victory. And she regrets exceedingly that there has been no occasion for a repetition of anything like the thrilling rescue by the College students at the time of the Saint Mary's Infirmary fire in bygone days. The thirties have seen, however, two interesting developments: The Saint Mary's Dances, and the evolution of the Date.

The first Saint Mary's dance, the Senior Dance, was given on the night of December 10, 1932, the year Mrs. Cruikshank was made Head of the School. It was hailed at once as a New Tradition; and every year since then has seen the occasion eagerly anticipated and happily remembered. The Seniors spent days getting the gymnasium ready for its debut as a ballroom, and when the evening came they danced under a blue crepe-paper ribboned ceiling, set with silver stars. The horizon was a procession of red, green, and yellow housetops in the snow. Until almost midnight the girls and boys danced to the music of the "State Collegians." The underclassmen listened from their dormitory windows at first, then advanced to the downstairs doorways; then, growing bolder and being covered by the night, some stepped beyond the threshholds into the open space between the dormitories and the gymnasium. It was only a matter of seconds before they were all clustered at the gymnasium windows, looking at the bright scene within and forgetting to breathe in their excitement. The first of the Junior-Senior dances followed in the spring, and the old Junior-Senior banquet gave way to another New Tradition. The decorating of the gymnasium has always been an important part of the festivities, girls from all classes taking part. The walls have been hidden periodically behind New York skylines, colorful marine life, laughing comic strip characters, and snow covered fir trees.

I remember my senior year: the hour for the guests to arrive was approaching and the gymnasium was not ready. Supper time had come and gone unnoticed, and still we worked on in our gym-suits and sneakers. We finished with only minutes to spare and ran to get into our evening dresses, which of course had been ready for days. Having returned to the gymnasium after an exhaustingly short interval, fully transformed as we thought, we decided to use the last thirty seconds in practicing shaking hands, with our best receiving line manners. Alas! as we touched each other's hands, we realized that every hand was parched and bristling with the remains of the flour and lime which had been used for "snow" on the scenery. With panic such as only the twentieth century readers of American advertisements can feel, we ran to our rooms again to search out lotions and creams to repair the damage. The evening started with a little confusion, but ended naturally with the semi-

ERNEST CRUIKSHANK

"A man of fine mind and peculiar charm. . . . As long as he stayed at Saint Mary's [1903–1921], he was the main cog in the machinery of its administration and a powerful factor in the student life."

MARGARET JONES CRUIKSHANK
PRESIDENT, 1932–

"... her mind and spirit ... can be recognized in the school's advance ... in the progress which on the surface might seem to have 'just happened.'"

annual positive declaration of "Absolutely the best time I *ever* had in my *life*."

I remember before other dances the feeling of waiting, half-fearfully, half-joyfully in our dormitories for the first guests to arrive. Everyone was ready, and one by one the juniors and seniors would be summoned to the parlor by a breathless underclassman. "Yours is here, Madge," she would call from the stairway, and Madge would wait a few minutes before going down so as not to seem too eager. We were somewhat subdued during that hour before the dance, being afraid that maybe we were expecting too much—maybe this dance wouldn't be as good as the ones the year before. But after the dance there was no restraint. We said good night to the boys in the gymnasium, and while giving them time to reach the gates, we tried to smother Mrs. Cruikshank with our joy. Then we went together back to our halls to talk to each other—all at the same time at the tops of our voices—until the hall-teacher could get us into our own rooms and comparatively quiet, a difficult task for her on such a night.

Many a lasting friendship, started at a Saint Mary's dance, was nurtured in Smedes Hall on subsequent Saturday nights. The boys arrived at eight o'clock, usually having been warned beforehand to be prompt because time was limited. If they came early, they waited on the front porch or talked to the Lady of the Day until the doors were officially opened. Every boy registered in a ledger on the parlor table, putting his name beside that of the girl whom he had come to see. This "Date Book" sometimes made interesting reading during the week.

In the fall of 1933 one could choose whether she would entertain in the parlor or at a double-desk in the big study hall. I believe the desks were usually preferred, though sometimes there were many couples ranged around the long seats that skirt the parlor walls. The Lady of the Day took turns sitting at the end of the parlor and at the desk on the platform in the front of the study hall. She had a bell which she would ring at 9:25 as a signal for all to begin saying good night during the five minutes of grace that remained before the stroke of 9:30, when all boys should have reached the doorway. She could also ring the bell during the evening if anyone had a tendency to sit on his spine or put his feet on the furniture or in any other way behave unseemingly, but I don't remember that she ever did.

Since those days the schedule has been readjusted so that a young man may now visit from eight to ten. I think no one sits on the rostrum in study hall any more. For a few years dates enjoyed ping pong, dancing, and bridge in the Recreation Room under Smedes Hall front porch, and one of the youngest generations pressed the gymnasium into service on Saturday nights. Now, just in time to be recorded in the first hundred years' history of the school, has come a student's description of the latest privilege. The *Belles of Saint Mary's* of March 18, 1941, carried the following news item:

"Now to senior dignity is added the unique privilege of walking down the path with a handsome boy—even a cousin will do if you can dig one up—crossing the 'bloody boulevard' of Hillsboro Street, boarding a bus, faring forth decidedly unchaperoned into a nighttime city for a 'pitcher-show' and (if the date's piggie bank holds out) food at the California-or-somewhere. Then the handsome lad may escort his dignified, entertained, cosmopolitan young lady back to her *alma mater*—not later than ten o'clock . . . How pleased our Peter [Progress] must be with himself. How ultra-modern he must feel when he sees a smart young couple stroll gaily off campus for three hours of exciting freedom, and remembers how—'twas not so long ago—

those ancient moderns of Saint Mary's looked forward to a Saturday night hour in the parlor with their beaux, provided it did not take the gentlemen the entire hour to secure visiting permission from the powers that were."

Back in the autumn of 1934 a certain girl was allowed the unusual privilege of having a date in the parlor on Sunday night, because the caller had come from a great distance expecting to see her. A younger girl from the adjoining hall, thinking the parlor empty, decided to make a dash—in her night clothes—over to the west side of the building. She had reached the middle of the great parlor floor when she realized her mistake, and overcome with sudden consciousness of her undress, she uttered a squeal loud enough to attract the attention even of the portraits, and fled back to her room, attempting an unnecessary explanation over her shoulder. I do not know who of the three youthful players in that scene was most embarrassed.

I wish Tempe Neal could see Saint Mary's grove on a Sunday afternoon this year. Tempe, you will remember, was the little girl who sent her mother a copy of the Blessner lithograph of Saint Mary's when it was first issued, the one with the stagecoach in the foreground. She wrote an explanation on the back of the picture, the concluding statement of which was, "There are most too many gentlemen about." As far as I have been able to discover, there are only two male figures represented, other than Mr. Blessner himself, the coach driver, and several small children. Tempe would be interested to see in the 1939–'40 Handbook, the following paragraph:

"On Sunday afternoons girls may sign up in the parlor to entertain their dates on the front campus, weather permitting. Bounds for dates on campus are . . . etc." I understand that this form of entertainment has been well-attended, weather permitting.

LIFE AT SAINT MARY'S

When anyone looks back on her school days, she remembers a whole realm of activity, spontaneous, unplanned and unsupervised—pleasures outside the curriculum, outside the extra-curricular activities, not outlined in the catalogue nor mentioned in the handbook. Inspiration for this kind of activity comes when one least expects it—sometimes when one is doing nothing in particular, but just as often when one is in the midst of studying and certainly should not stop. But come the inspiration has, I am sure, for a hundred years to Saint Mary's girls. In the year 1933–34 a friendly rivalry between the First Floor of Holt Hall and the Third Floor took up most of our spare time. While a girl from the Third Floor was secretly greasing the door knobs on the first floor, a First Floor-ite would probably be piling up the full laundry bags against the door of an unsuspecting Third Floor-ite. When the unsuspecting Third Floor-ite would come out of her room, the bags would fall in upon her and she would have to return them to the bottom of the stairs to be collected for the laundry. This kind of incident was only a minor skirmish in a delightful war that dragged on from September till June.

Saturday nights often brought forth demonstrations of the effectiveness of costumes and make-up: unidentifiable ghosts were likely to appear at your window, or vamps with spit curls and heavy eye-shadowing might knock at your door and pay a short visit, giving you a sample of what they considered tough, night-clubbish conversation. Sometimes a game of sardines developed, and one girl would hide herself on a dark stairway, or under a bed, or in a bath tub; as each girl found her, she would quietly climb into the same hiding place until all were re-united and usually at the point of suffocation and exhaustion from trying to suppress their giggles. Every year there was the usual number of Ouija board and table tapping sessions, with the amazing results not uncommon in girls' schools where everyone mysteriously knows everything about everyone else's private affairs. Some groups always enjoyed singing on the steps of Holt or in the grove when the weather began to get warm and the afternoons long. Intermittently a little cooking would be attempted in the Holt Hall kitchens, but I can't remember with what success if any. I do remember the black coffee we wasted a good deal of time struggling with during examination week. It was cooked thoroughly in a frying pan and strained through a handkerchief before serving. Tea was a better means of uplifting the constitution and the disposition. We had a corporation of four tea-drinkers, each member owning her own cup and saucer, which had been chosen with care from the patterns carried in the local five-and-ten-cent stores. How well I remember finding one afternoon a note under my door: "Miss Rosalie McNeil—at home—tea—soon—you bring the butter." I believe Mrs. Naylor in the Infirmary kindly supplied us with butter that day. Of course it was understood always that we bring our own cups.

In the late spring a good part of one's unscheduled time was spent in sunburning on the back campus. If one rigged up an umbrella over the head, one could also write a term paper while tanning—if conversation was not too distracting. In the fall there were leaf piles to jump into and usually, at least once a year, a snow came to disorganize completely the Regular Life for a day or two. At any hour in any season there were Bull Sessions, impromptu discussions of uncertain length, with a few orations included, arising from a chance remark. Year after year the things which are considered most important about *Life* are thrashed out. Perhaps there is more emphasis on social reforms one year and on war and peace the next, but eternally conversation can fall back on death and immortality and love and marriage and Human-Nature-in-General—also on specific examples of human nature, which are often interesting but dangerous topics.

Perhaps the only Bull Sessions entirely free from the more dangerous aspects are the well-known ones held at the Rectory on Sunday nights. Understanding that one of the best ways to reach young people is to let them tell you what they think, Mr. Kloman instituted these discussions when he came in 1935 to serve as chaplain for the school. Mrs. Kloman sees to it that there is a supply of homemade cookies which make the girls realize that there is something lacking about bakery food, after all. The hospitality of the Kloman household has become as characteristic of Saint Mary's as chapel and morning mail. Profitable and pleasant as the academic life is, by its very nature it is a cloistered one anywhere; the more artificial elements of "school life" at Saint Mary's have been greatly alleviated by Mr. and Mrs. Kloman's generosity in sharing their home with students and faculty. There, one is likely to meet delightful people of all ages and from all places.

Considering classes and activities, organized and spontaneous, the reader may well ask whether Saint Mary's girls do any studying other than in the daily evening study hall. The answer is Yes. In May, 1935, I wrote to my mother as follows:

"I have finished my French term paper and my English term paper, have still my chemistry seminar to finish and my logic term paper to begin, The Merchant of Venice to memorize, the chemistry notebook to do, all kinds of school functions and commencement doings to get ready for, and several books to read, to say nothing of my regular lessons, and every afternoon filled with either dramatic rehearsals or Orpheus and Euridyce, the May Day Festival."

Though sometimes obstacles were involved, we went to all kinds of ends to get the necessary work accomplished. Some people were able to study before breakfast; others who tried it went to sleep again immediately or they arrived at the "silly stage." (People in the "silly stage" decide eventually that nothing really matters and then they go to bed again.) The only plan of early morning work I could follow was to get up very early, do something mechanical like re-copying a paper, and return to bed for several hours of sleep before really meeting the day. The advantage in this excellent plan was that one woke up at half past seven and found the paper copied without any memory of having done it; however, there was always the danger that one would wake up and find the paper not copied and would have no recollection of having heard the alarm go off. But there were other methods. At more than one double-header basket ball game, where one half of one game is sandwiched between the two halves of the other, several players worked like mad at their books during the half when they were not on the floor. I think I never went to a play rehearsal without at least one lesson to do between exits and entrances.

There were various methods of working after light bell, such for instance as that time-honored device of getting into the bathtub with blanket and pillows. If someone said wearily, "And I will lie in Abraham's Bosom all the night," she meant that she was planning to climb into a blanket-nest under her bed for a little studying after hours. The light was hidden by the bed covering which hung to the floor on all sides, but since all ventilation was cut off, it was necessary to come out of the Bosom frequently for air. One could, and sometimes did, take a chance on brazenly leaving the lights on after time and studying in a civilized manner at the desk. A girl usually preferred being told by Miss Lalor that she looked like a "stewed owl" after a sleepless night to risking a "goose-egg" in Miss Lalor's grade book on an unprepared hygiene recitation. But (as Miss Lalor herself pointed out) girls who resembled stewed owls often thought like stewed owls also, and received the famous Lalor goose-eggs in spite of their studying.

The most universally utilized of all Times-not-intended-for-study was the Morning Walk. This was a five or ten minute period preceding the morning assembly, during which we were required to walk in the grove for some reason which had to do with the circulation of the blood. Someone reading aloud or to herself could be steered safely up and down the path, fulfilling the first requirement of Morning Walk, which was to "keep moving." After a while we got to the point where we could write a little as we moved; but this morning period was best adapted to memorizing. There is no question that we used a good bit of our legitimate study-time for irrelevant pursuits. Yet, in the end, I think we paid back fully the time we had stolen from study periods—though we had to steal the time wherewith to pay in the ways I have described. The final result of this misappropriation of time was fuller days and nights—and now, fuller memories—than we should probably have had, had we walked passively in the ways of our schedule.

When the "old girls" look back on a day at Saint Mary's, they remember the fury of the bells at seven A.M., followed after an infinitesimal, split second by the blaring forth of someone's victrola down the hall; then the rush for breakfast, the stampede through the covered way for mail, the day brim-full of activity—tragedy and triumph; dancing in the parlor after supper; study, a half-hour of revelry, and finally bed. But under it all was a deeper current. We did not speak of it often—only sometimes in the late hours after light bell. It came to the surface when someone else was in trouble or we saw it rise in others when we needed help. We felt it especially in our chapel; it was louder than the music, brighter than the candle light. It was that love, which is the "heritage pure, an experience wholesome and sweet." Intermingled with the memories of the variety of experience that was "school life" are memories of chapel services, work on the altar guild, the child at the Thompson Orphanage whom we never saw but to whom we sent clothes and presents through our League, the girls at Saint Mary's on the Mountain, and the unknown occupants of "our bed" at Rex Hospital. In addition to the League, there is now also the Doctors' Daughters Club, founded by our nurse, Mrs. Naylor, for the purpose of service. It has been busy with Thanksgiving and Christmas baskets, knitting, and relief for the war-sufferers of China. The Order of the Circle is directing the school's British War Relief Program.

Through the tapestry that is Saint Mary's from 1930 to 1942 run the threads of personalities, interwoven with events, inseparable from the whole—invaluable, constant. For lack of space I have been able to mention only a few. Two more stand out in my mind—two who are not linked with any one activity or department. One is the Right Reverend Edwin A. Penick, Bishop of North Carolina since 1933 and Bishop Co-adjutor before that time. His confirmation services and Commencement messages have been an inspiration to the Saint Mary's girls of the thirties. Even when we did not see him, he was near to us. His home, Ravenscroft, on the southeast corner of the campus, not only symbolizes the nearness of his spiritual qualities but also holds, for every Saint Mary's girl to be aware of, a family whose relationships with one another have established a precious ideal.

The second is the Reverend Joseph Fletcher, Chaplain from 1932 to 1935. On the teacher's platform, in the pulpit, or at the dinner table, Mr. Fletcher was vital and stimulating. One could agree with him or disagree with him, but one could not ignore the issues, spiritual and social, which he threw at his classes and congregation. The June editorial of the 1934–'35 *Bulletin* said: "The most important thing we have carried away [from Saint Mary's] with us is that which Mr. Fletcher has endeavored to make us realize— that there is a world outside the walls of Saint Mary's . . . a great field waiting for us . . . in which we can apply . . . the lessons we have learned." Mr. Fletcher tried to help us understand some of the problems of that greater world outside and he tried to make us practice our lessons well while we were in school. He was a man who, if he found incongruity between certain existing conditions and the teachings of Jesus Christ, was not afraid to say so. When the Cincinnati School of Applied Religion gained his services, not only Saint Mary's but the whole of North Carolina suffered a loss.

In speaking of personalities, I come at last to Mrs. Ernest Cruikshank, to whom all of us since 1932 owe the greatest debt of gratitude for what the school was to us. I know I have not done justice to the latest chapter in the history of the school; for her sake I wish I might have. At some future date I hope it will be done.

Mrs. Ernest Cruikshank (Margaret Jones she was then) was born in Hillsboro, North Carolina, the daughter of Halcott Pride and Olive Echols Jones. She first attended the school of Misses Nash and Kolloch in Hillsboro and later entered Saint Mary's Academy in Raleigh, where she studied for three and a half years, being graduated valedictorian of the class of 1896, at the age of seventeen. She was an excellent student, particularly outstanding in mathematics. A few years ago, one who had taught her confided in some of the girls of the thirties: "Margaret without knowing it was a great comfort to me, for when the students asked me questions for which I was unprepared (as students sometimes do, you know), I would ask Margaret Jones to put the problem in question on the blackboard; then I would ask if there was still a question. And if there was, I

"ONWARD AND UPWARD"

would ask Margaret please to explain her work. She never failed me!"

Mrs. Cruikshank has never entirely given up her teaching of mathematics; she continued it when she became a member of the faculty at Saint Mary's, and in the New York City high schools. Again, although she was no longer teaching regularly after her marriage and when her children were young, she was pressed into service at Saint Mary's in the year 1917–'18. Now, as President, though her days are full, she still does not fail those who come to her in their need. More than one of my contemporaries, who was desperate about the complexities of college algebra, came back to the dormitory after an "extra evening" at Mrs. Cruikshank's house, feeling calmer and wiser, and everlastingly grateful.

Not long after her graduation at Saint Mary's, Miss Jones spent a year in Alabama at the home of her older brother, and at the age of eighteen she returned to Saint Mary's as a teacher. Although she taught girls with whom she had studied two years before, and although some of the students were as old as if not older than she, those who knew her then say that the girls never took advantage of those former contacts or of her age. She was earnest but patient, and was, I gather, a kind of godsend to girls who had been frightened or discouraged by mathematical difficulties. One of her former pupils remembers when Miss Jones used to teach on the ground floor of Smedes, in what is now the business classroom. At that time one could enter the covered way which joins East Rock with Smedes, only by going through the classroom. Consequently, on rainy days the situation was likely to be difficult. At the crucial point of the explanation a knock would come upon the door and then, "Please, may I pass through, Miss Jones?" And usually after that distraction, the steps in the problem which had just been explained would have to be reviewed.

The students would no sooner have found themselves again when another knock would be heard and the interruption would be repeated. And so the passers-through might delay enlightenment through a whole period, but though the class was spoiled for teacher and pupils and it meant the whole struggle would have to be repeated the next day, Miss Jones was not ruffled nor provoked; or, if she was, it was not apparent to those whom she taught. She made up for the damage on sunny days.

After teaching for three years she attended the University of North Carolina in 1901–'02, and then returned to Saint Mary's for three more years. Besides mathematics she also taught astronomy; and of course during those early years she had various other duties, including such things as having charge of a dormitory and being directress of the St. Elizabeth Chapter of the missionary organization. She continued her studying in the summer at the University at Chapel Hill and at Teachers College, Columbia University. Not all of her summers were spent in studying, however, for in 1903 she was in California and another year in Maine; then there was a trip to Europe in 1907 and a second one in 1911, the year of her marriage.

The winter of 1905–'06 Miss Jones spent in New York studying mathematics and German at Columbia University and substituting in the Wadleigh High School and the Washington Irving High School in that city. That year was followed by further teaching at Saint Mary's, and then in 1911 she concluded her courses at Columbia, receiving a B.S. degree. The same year (1911) she was married to Mr. Ernest Cruikshank and in September returned with him to Saint Mary's. During the course of the next ten years their three children were born—Ernest, Mary Pride, and Olive. In 1921 they went to Columbia, Tennessee, where Mr. Cruikshank had accepted Bishop Beatty's call to the presidency of the Columbia Institute, an Episcopal school for girls. When Mr. Cruikshank died the following October, his wife took over the administration of Columbia Institute and continued as its head for ten years, working untiringly as executive and as teacher of mathematics, German, and Bible.

In 1932 Mrs. Cruikshank was called back to Saint Mary's to be Principal and Academic Head. Among the events of the past decade (a decade which has seen leaders in all fields publicized, spotlighted, and photographed for *Life*), she has moved, sidestepping the center of the stage as a person. But in spite of her personal, physical retreat from the limelight, her mind and spirit can be perceived clearly. Their essence can be recognized in the school's advance—academically, departmentally, physically, and spiritually—in the progress which on the surface might seem to have "just happened." And as swift changes have been made since 1932, so Mrs. Cruikshank will continue to move with the times. She is a great Lady, in the greatest meaning of that word, and she is also a liberal in her thinking and in her work as head of a school.

In student affairs and with her faculty she has refrained in small matters from forcing her opinions when she might have done so; for, above all, she respects the right of a group to govern itself democratically, to learn by making its own mistakes if necessary. Yet no detail is too unimportant for her attention. When the snow came, she announced simply in assembly, "Anyone who wishes may use my sled." (Many did!) Nor is any girl's need, no matter what it is, outside of her realm. Her mathematics coaching I have already mentioned. Many a morning behind her office doors special groups have met for spelling, geography, and current events classes. On the one occasion I remember when the infirmary was filled to capacity, she took the surplus of patients into her house and attended them personally. Once in a conversation with her, it came out that another senior and I had never seen Duke University, though we had lived within two hundred miles of it all our lives. She said she was appalled. The following Sunday she sent for us to come and ride over to Duke with her. Hers is the business of advising, planning, and making arrangements for each girl who wants to go on to college after graduation from Saint Mary's. Every girl's course—in fact, every girl—has Mrs. Cruikshank's individual attention. Her vision reaches far, and her sympathy is large. Her own daughters are excellent advertisement, if advertisement be needed, for her talent in educating young women.

Students and faculty enjoy the hospitality of her home—given with or without premeditation. Faculty coffees, Senior Buffet Supper, and after-the-dance spreads, her chicken salad, sandwiches, and cake are long to be remembered. Once in the early fall after Mary Pride Cruikshank had had a party, Mrs. Cruikshank found that there was a great deal of ice-cream left over. Though it was almost midnight, she sent a message to Holt Hall, describing briefly the situation and asking us to remedy it. Response was immediate and effective; however, a number of the new girls did not go because they thought the old girls must be fooling them. That was before they knew Mrs. Cruikshank.

Mrs. Cruikshank never fails to bring in to her faculty and student gatherings something helpful from educational meetings, something interesting from her reading and study. She loved her summer work and her winter commuting to Duke University where she obtained her Master's Degree in 1937 (on the side!). When a faculty meeting is fretted by a discussion of particular problems close at hand, it is she who in a few straight-to-the-point sentences makes the faculty members look beyond the petty issues; she, who relates their little problems to the larger issues embracing all schools, all life; and it is she who keeps them looking outward and forward when too much inward-looking and backward-looking threatens to cloud their perspective.

This outward and forward view has been the salient characteristic of the first decade of her regime. In connection with the beginning of the second decade of Mrs. Cruikshank's regime and the beginning of the second century in the history of Saint Mary's School, I have been thinking about what President Marion Edwards Park of Bryn Mawr College said in an address at St. Catherine's School, Richmond, on the occasion of that school's fiftieth anniversary:

"In a place where many girls have almost grown up, a place of intimacy and of habit, it is hard to give up the old measuring rod of recollection or even of the past in general. And yet at every college and every school in America we must lay aside these pleasant ways of comment and of estimate and take up strange and new ones. . . . We must turn the angle of our attention to the future and forget the dear, leisurely past; search the problem through to make sure that we, ourselves inexperienced, are in all we do giving this next generation tools that fit the fighting hand, virtues that the hour needs. Two fundamentals we must henceforth never set aside in the great spaces of education or postpone in the long years through which it extends: training in thinking and training in character."

Tools that fit the fighting hand, virtues that the hour needs—Training in thinking and training in character—Miss Park has put these side by side. The need today for the church school is more urgent than ever. The traditional heart of Saint Mary's remains unchanged. The "progress" of the school in the past decade signifies no change from the original end for which Saint Mary's was founded; it implies, rather, an increase in effectiveness of the means to that end. Greater are the potentialities for the development of Christian lives if young women can reach a greater understanding of the world they live in, its evil as well as its good.

> *"May the future unite all the good of thy past*
> *With the best that new knowledge can bring.*
> *Ever onward and upward thy course! To the last*
> *Be thou steadfast in every good thing.*
> *Generations to come may thy fair daughters still*
> *Fondly think on thy halls and thy grove*
> *And carry thy teachings—o'er woodland and hill—*
> *Of earnestness, wisdom, and love."*

THE REVEREND HENRY FELIX KLOMAN
CHAPLAIN, 1935–
"The hospitality of the Kloman household has become as characteristic of Saint Mary's as chapel and morning mail."

SMEDES HALL

"Main Building" was the scene of Saint Mary's opening in 1842, and though the years have brought it renovations and a change of name, it has ever been the center of the school's activities.

Ernest Cruikshank

A BIOGRAPHICAL SKETCH

By Katherine Batts Salley

ERNEST CRUIKSHANK was born August 19, 1879 in the family home at Elkton, Maryland. Elkton is in Cecil County on the "Eastern Shore," close to the Pennsylvania line. This country has in the past somehow blessed her children with a subtle native charm and placed upon them the mark of the gentle-born.

From his sister we know of his ancestry the following: The first Cruikshank (of that branch) to come to America was the younger son of an Irish earl, who, not having any patrimony, came to this country to make a living. He settled in Pennsylvania. Two of his three sons left that section, one going west, one south; the third settled in Cecil County, Maryland. This John Cruikshank was Ernest's great-grandfather. Two of his sons were Ernest's grandfathers; both lived in Cecil County and were born near the beginning of the nineteenth century; both were highly respected, prosperous citizens, planters and merchants. Ernest's mother was Sarah Elizabeth Cruikshank. His father, George Washington Cruikshank, was a lawyer, and for many years the editor of the *Cecil Democrat* in Elkton.

To the fact that his parents were first cousins, Ernest in later years attributed his delicate constitution. His weak heart was probably congenital, although it may have been developed by a severe attack of whooping cough while he was still an infant.

Ernest Cruikshank was one of three children, his two sisters being Gelert, 9 years older (Mrs. Julius W. Stuart of Baltimore) and Helen, 3 years younger (Mrs. Charles W. Riley), who died October 4, 1940.

Ernest's big blue eyes, fair hair and adorable smile gave him a very angelic appearance, but he was not always angelic by any means and had frequent tantrums in order to gain his own way, his weak heart lending to that spoiling. Naturally the child could not enter into very rough games, but he was a born leader. Their lawn was almost a public park. Ernest organized games and directed them even when not an active participant.

His uncle, Thomas Cruikshank, had married a "Saint Mary's girl," Lucy Walke, who had attended Saint Mary's in 1863–64. Ernest spent much time with her and her family on the plantation at Bloomingdale, Maryland. He was devoted to her, and we like to think that Saint Mary's touched his life even in those days. His cousin, Sara, particularly close for many years, is now the wife of the Bishop of Southern Brazil.

Of his younger sister we know that she was gay and active, "something of a rowdy and perfectly irrespressible"—quite different from himself. They were devotedly antagonistic; not happy together, but miserable when apart. It was probably her very rowdiness that most appealed to him and no doubt his desire to order her ways caused much of the friction.

In the Saint Mary's days later he talked more of his

older sister, a most charming person for whom he had the highest regard. To those of us who had any contact with Baltimore he paid her the highest compliment by wanting us to meet her. His father had died in 1902 and his mother in 1904.

As a child anything tiny or helpless appealed to him. He would go into ecstasies over a tiny kitten or a newly hatched chicken. His aversion was a "catter bugger" (caterpillar) or anything resembling one. A child had but to drop a pussy willow catkin or lay a feather in a doorway or on a porch step and Ernest was a prisoner; he would not pass.

His first schooling was with Miss Tabby Jones, a quaint little spinster, as her name indicates. She taught all the young hopefuls of Elkton, numbering among her pupils embryonic doctors, lawyers, and politicians. Ernest loved her dearly, and until the time of her death he always paid her a call on his infrequent visits to Elkton.

Ernest had always been much interested in statistics. As a small boy he would spend hours working out averages. His father thought he was destined to be a great statistician. In later years we could see this trait manifested in his love of detail and his endless attempts to get his "girls" to work out all problems and plans to the last particular. One evening a girl who sat at his table in the Saint Mary's dining room came in for dinner wearing a new string of beads. He asked her how many beads there were on the string. She, in amazement, said she had no idea. He estimated the number and later when they were counted she found that his estimation had been correct.

After leaving Miss Tabby, Ernest attended the Elkton Academy, "a High School with some private work paid for by parents." He began Latin there and must have had a splendid foundation for he was an excellent Latin scholar. So, too, he had the best of foundations for modern languages.

When Ernest was fourteen he was offered a scholarship at Washington College, Chestertown, Kent County, Maryland. Washington is a "Land Grant" college and each county in the State is entitled to a scholarship. The bestowal of the scholarships is in the hands of the Orphans Courts of Maryland counties. Mrs. Cruikshank's brother-in-law was an associate judge. He knew something was needed for Ernest, as he had nearly outgrown Elkton Academy, and there being a vacancy from Cecil County, he was instrumental in securing an appointment for Ernest.

Washington College is one of the oldest institutions of higher learning in the United States. Its earliest origins are lost in the past, for it began as a school established at Chestertown in 1707, or earlier. George Washington subscribed 50 guineas to an endowment when the school was to be raised to the status of college, and gave permission to call the college by his name. The State of Maryland granted the charter in 1782, but it was not until about 1890 that the legislature began to fulfill its promise of providing largely for its maintenance. By the time Ernest Cruikshank entered the Freshman Class in the fall of 1893 there were around one hundred students enrolled. It was co-educational.

His years at college must have been very full and very happy. He was unusually popular with both students and faculty; Dr. J. S. William Jones, his math professor, gives us this glimpse of him:

"I recall vividly his outstanding ability as a student and his excellent moral character. During the four years he was in college he was among those distinguished in scholarship, with an average for the four years of 94. During his Junior year he received the scholarship prize and shared this prize in the Senior Class with T. Howard Fowler."

We have been fortunate to locate three men who were his particular friends at Washington. All of them later entered the ministry, and his sister believes that they had hoped Mr. Cruikshank would do likewise. All of them wrote very intimately of their friendship; all paid him the highest tributes. We are indebted to them for a picture of this period of his life.*

One writes: "In college he soon became popular. People were naturally attracted to him and he kept his friends through life. He seemed to like one course as well as another and seemed to master his studies with the least possible effort. One rarely saw him study. The faculty, all of them, were always fond of him and he certainly never gave them trouble or anxiety."

"Ernest Cruikshank and I," writes another, "arrived at Washington College the same day, entered the same class, worked together for four years, during which we were roommates most of the time. He was one of the two most highly endowed men, intellectually, I have ever met. I have known many days in which he did not look at his work until after breakfast and then go into class within an hour. He could easily have graduated with one of the highest averages—if not the highest—ever attained at Washington College if he had chosen to study. I never knew him to be seriously sick but he was tall, slim and frail, with little physical strength. If he excelled in any particular line it was languages. He was often a 'pony' for the lower classmen in Latin and Greek. He was just as proficient in modern languages. He used the purest English in conversation and work. This was due to home influence for he told me he had never studied English grammar.

"He was as great a contradiction as I have ever seen. He was lovable to the full and yet could tantalize his intimate

---

* Reverend Messrs. George C. Graham, J. Wilson Sutton, and William F. Venables. Also of invaluable aid in the preparation of this sketch have been Bessie Poe Law Davis, Gelert Cruikshank Stuart, Mary Josey Page, and Hope Cobb Newell.

friends almost to distraction when he put his mind to it. He was one of the youngest in college, yet always commanding respect. Little influenced by popular opinion, he joined the Society to which the fewer were going, his friends thought to be different. Later he went to the Society where his friends belonged.

"He associated very little, if at all, with the young ladies either in college or in the town. Some of his friends teased him about two of the college girls but if he had any admiration for them, it was at a distance."

A congenial group of boys would often gather at the home of Professor and Mrs. Micou. He was vice-president and professor of Latin. She was a very attractive and interesting person, had a sincere interest in the students, and opened wide her home to them always. There they were happy and at ease without artificial restraint. It has been said that she, who was probably under forty, left the imprint of her influence on Ernest Cruikshank. Others say that he may have been influenced by his mother, cultured and forceful of character. But they agreed that he moved through life just about what he was as a youth, never speaking of religion but living a life above reproach in every way; faithful above the average in his religious duties; and always a gentleman.

From one who visited him in those days we know that his home life was very beautiful. The members of the family were genuinely fond of one another, and there was an atmosphere of peace and happiness. His father was a quiet man with a keen mind, and his mother was a woman of unusual sweetness.

In 1897 he received the B.A. degree. He stayed on a year and obtained the A.M. degree, at the same time doing some teaching. Next he went to teach in Sanford, Virginia, a little oystering village in Accomac County. He spent two very short school terms there, as the principal of what was then called a graded school, among the primitive oystermen's families, receiving very little by way of money, but enjoying the salt air, and we may be sure, the experience.

The Cruikshanks had moved to Baltimore in 1893, and in the fall of 1900, Ernest, feeling that his previous training was inadequate, matriculated at Johns Hopkins University. During the year, 1900–1901, he took the following courses: Early Anglo-Saxon Prose Literature, Old French Readings, French Literature, Gothic, German Seminary, Middle High German, and Contemporary German Literature. He also read two papers before the German Society; "The Unification of German Pronunciation," and "Das Altsächsische Taufgelöbnis."

Upon finishing this very full year he went to Shenandoah Collegiate Institute located at Dayton, Virginia, where, according to the Hopkins records, he taught Latin.

Whenever it has been possible to locate men or women who worked with Mr. Cruikshank in those early days of his teaching they have been wholehearted in their praise. J. H. Ruebush, of Dayton, writes:

"I cannot tell just how we did land Mr. C. for our small college, but it was a fortunate deal for us. He was one of the finest men as well as one of the finest teachers we ever had. We enrolled around 250 pupils at that time. S. C. I. was founded by the United Brethren Church, and has been carried on by them for 66 years."

In the fall of 1903 Ernest Cruikshank came to Saint Mary's. The Rector employed him without interviewing him, rare in those days and in these. How he got in touch with Doctor Bratton we do not know, although Mrs. Stuart thinks it was because of a notice in "The Churchman."

Never a more modest or forceful teacher came to Saint Mary's than Ernest Cruikshank. Not only was he a devoted, efficient and untiring teacher, he was a man unswerving in his honesty, conviction, courage and kindness, seeing life with both sympathy and humor. He possessed a shyness which had its origin in humility and a gentleness which belongs to the truly noble.

"Four qualifications: his intellectual acumen, his great simplicity, his wholesome sense of humor, and his religious faith were the bases of his personal influence. He was of course interested in people, but the particular nature of his interest was determined by these qualities. They made him quick to understand their difficulties, and capable of grasping what the essence of each difficulty was. They enabled him to put aside at once what had no direct bearing on the problems which were brought to him, to laugh kindly over whatever was humorous in a particular situation, and to rely on God for the strength and wisdom which were necessary for whatever needed to be faced."

He was very young to be the professor of classes for young ladies, but his earlier students attest to his capacity and capabilities. If you run across them now, or any of his later students, they not only revere his memory, but remember him with love and loyalty as well.

He taught Latin and Science until 1906–07, when he became Secretary of Saint Mary's as well as becoming Librarian and continuing with the teaching of Latin. It was always so; whatever was most needed of him, that he did. His duties accumulated with the years until when he left no one person was expected to do what he had done. Knowing his excellent foundation in languages we feel that the students missed much because he did not teach them. However, he made up to the girls in part by directing them in extra-curricular activities. He endeared himself to each succeeding class, some more than others, perhaps, but each in a genuine and unique way. The classes of 1909, 1911, 1915, and 1921 dedicated the Annual "Muse" to him. He was Librarian for only one year, becoming Business Manager (as well as Secretary) in 1909. He gave up teaching Latin after that year but continued teaching Science until 1914–15, when he took over Psychology and Current History which were then added to the curriculum. He also had become Registrar though he was never given that title.

From one of the few remaining teachers who was at Saint Mary's when he came and continued in that capacity even after he left we quote the following: "One cannot compliment him too much. He was a wonderful person to be associated with. He was the ideal gentleman always—always kind, considerate, helpful. A splendid teacher, he was glad to help any of the pupils who found her work hard, whether it was his subject or not. He was very retiring but a good fellow and ready to help out in every way and whenever called upon, be it for fun or for work. Everyone liked him and had every confidence in his knowledge of things, and not only asked but accepted his judgment. He was a fine companion on all occasions."

The chapters of this book dealing with that period of Saint Mary's history record the activities which he instituted and supervised. Many of the student occasions had their inspiration from him. 'In a Grove of Stately Oak Trees,' 'Alma Mater,' Alumnae Day celebration, Alumnae Day Luncheons, Christmas-tree celebrations, the Interclass Parties, the Junior-Senior Banquet, and the School Party, we think of now as old Saint Mary's traditions; these, with many other things, came into being during the years Mr. Cruikshank was at the school and each was inaugurated to further school spirit and to increase the student and the alumnae devotion to their Alma Mater.

Mary Traill Yellott (Mrs. George V. Denny, Jr.) in 1920 wrote the following, which because of its genuineness and its spontaneity, can express today what many paragraphs might not:

Never idle for a minute, but with always time to spare
  To arrange conflicting schedules or to chaperon to the Fair
Never in the least impatient, interrupted for his keys,
  And never known to miss an opportunity to tease;
Seeing teachers, pupils, drummers, and dictating mail between—
  Oh, there's no one at Saint Mary's who can wonder who I mean.

He's the first you think of asking for an "idea," old or new,
  And he never fails to tell you just exactly what to do.
Preparations for a party can't be started till he comes,
  You can't find the decorations and you hammer up your thumbs,
But you know when he's behind a thing it's surely going through,
  For judging by experience it will; they always do.

He's the one you tell your troubles to, about the exams you flunk,
  If your Easter hat or shoes don't come, or any sort of junk!
He's sure to tease, but no one minds; you know he sympathizes,
  And things will work out nicely, if you do as he advises.
But you're lucky if you find him in his office; that's the part
  That's hardest—he's so often "out," and finding him's an art!

He's the one who keeps the Muse Club up to what it ought to be,
  Or sometimes if it isn't, that's not his fault, you'll agree.
It's to him the Class of Twenty owes a debt we cannot pay

For his never-failing kindness from our Prepdom to today.
So now, about to graduate, and sadder, if not wiser,
We unite in loving tribute to our friend and Class Adviser.

Ernest Cruikshank was married June 17, 1911 to Margaret Jones of Hillsboro. In the chapters of this book you have read about her as a person, a teacher, and an executive. She had been studying at Columbia University in 1910–11, and the marriage took place in Saint Paul's Chapel there. The Reverend George W. Lay, at that time rector of Saint Mary's, performed the ceremony. The Cruikshanks had a wonderful summer honeymoon, sailing on the twentieth of June and remaining in Europe until the middle of August. They visited Germany, Holland, England and France, the trip being highlighted by a walking tour in the Rhine country. After his detailed study of Goethe and Schiller, and after considerable study of German literature on her part, the trip was a never-to-be-forgotten joy.

The Cruikshank home was always a haven, for them, for their friends—whether it was the apartment in Senior Hall or the cottage that was built for them in 1919. The Cruikshank children must have been models—they never disturbed us; apparently they were never sick. They were beautiful children, Ernest, born December 1, 1913, Mary Pride, March 17, 1916, and Olive Echols, April 4, 1919. They made outstanding records in college, Ernest attending Duke University and the girls Saint Mary's and the University of North Carolina, and have now taken their rightful places in society. Ernest was married on June 15, 1940, to Rose Louise Swindell of Baltimore, and Mary Pride on October 5, 1940, in the Saint Mary's Chapel, to Franklin St. Clair Clark of Greensboro, N. C. Mary Pride's daughter, Margaret St. Clair, was born August 6, 1941.

Mr. Cruikshank had remained at Saint Mary's eighteen years in spite of several rather flattering offers, but in the spring of 1921 Bishop Beatty, Coadjutor Bishop of Tennessee, persuaded him to accept the presidency of Columbia Institute at Columbia, Tenn.

His leaving was a distinct blow to the school, and it took not only the girls but the faculty and alumnae a long time to get used to Saint Mary's without "Mr. Cruik." Many resolutions of regret at his leaving were written and many were the tributes of love and affection paid him. The *Muse* that year (1921) voiced the sentiment of the entire school body in its loving praises of him, closing with: "That others may continue the work with as untiring zeal and wholehearted devotion and that he may meet with added success as he goes elsewhere is the earnest wish of the friends to whom he has meant so much at his and our 'beloved Saint Mary's.' "

And in the *Muse* that came out in 1922: "This page is reserved to express again the love and loyalty of each and every Saint Mary's girl to two friends who until this year have been for so long devoted and untiring workers in the interests of the School; and whose absence the Senior Class of Nineteen hundred and twenty-two has been first called on keenly to feel and regret

Mr. and Mrs. Ernest Cruikshank."

The Cruikshanks went to Columbia in June, 1921. They had a very nice home on the campus. Mary Josey, honor student and graduate of the Business Department at Saint Mary's, was Mr. Cruikshank's secretary and lived with the family that summer.

Columbia Institute was a very old Church school. It had been established in 1832 but had suffered a gradual decline in standing and influence prior to 1921. There were only approximately sixty boarding students, with a staff of about twelve. There was no college work offered. It was Bishop

Beatty's and the Cruikshanks' dream to build it up to the status of Saint Mary's.

When school opened in September the faculty was composed of two distinct groups: the ones who had been there before, most of them over sixty, and three Saint Mary's girls, not yet twenty. Mary Josey taught the Business Course, Tillie Lamb was one of the Primary teachers and Hope Cobb taught Algebra and History and coached Basketball. Mrs. Cruikshank taught Math but could do very little else as she had the three small children to look after. The Rector of the Episcopal church in town came three times a week for Chapel Services and Mr. Cruikshank served as Lay Reader the other days. On Sundays the student body attended church in town. The student life was carried on very much the same as at Saint Mary's, the three young teachers having charge of the activities such as the Hallowe'en party, etc.

Mr. Cruikshank was making his influence felt here as he had in times past. He was made a member of the Columbia Kiwanis Club and there was a gala affair the night he entertained the Club in the school dining room. Bishop Beatty's regard for both the Cruikshanks increased as the months passed, and they lost a real friend at his untimely death in the spring of 1922.

Even though the Institute was small Mr. Cruikshank had a large load to carry. He attended to the finances, planned the curriculum, made contact with the families and of course listened to the troubles of students and teachers. He had worked all day and a great deal at night during the preceding summer months trying to get the school buildings in shape for the coming year and complete the faculty as well as the enrollment. It must have been discouraging at times and it is felt that he impaired his health by working so hard that first summer and the following winter.

In the spring of 1922 Mr. Cruikshank had a very severe

case of influenza from which he would not take time to recover properly. He would stay in bed a while and then be back at work. He tried to carry on when he was too sick to be up but would not give in and go to bed until after school was out. Then he would dictate letters and directions to his secretary. He didn't want anyone to know how ill he was and tried to make everyone believe that he would soon be well. In July Mrs. Cruikshank took him to Dr. Ambler's Sanitorium in Asheville. When they realized there was no chance of his recovery they returned to Columbia where he died October 1, 1922.

Funeral services were held in the Chapel at Saint Mary's. They were conducted by the Reverend George W. Lay, former Rector of the School, assisted by the Reverend Warren W. Way, Rector at that time. Interment was at Oakwood cemetery where the services held at the grave were conducted by the William G. Hill Lodge of Masons of which he was a member.

As we stood there at the last, a single pine was etched against the clear October sky; serene, beautiful, lofty—above its fellows. Even so was Ernest Cruikshank.

INDEX

INDEX

Abbott, Ethel, on faculty, 155, 181
Aiken, Fannie Bryan, 199
Albertson, Bertha, 173
Albertson, Catherine, Dean of Students, 195; resignation of, 212; mentioned, 197, 204
Albertson, Minnie, 61
Alexander, Alice (Mrs. Charles Connor), Alumnae Sec., 233
Alexander, Elsie, 140
Alexander, Miss Annie, on faculty, 169, 170
Allen, Julia Washington, on faculty, 137, 138, 164
Allen, Virginia C., 160
Allen, Virginia P., 160
Allston, Carolina Frances, 87
Allston, Charlotte (Mrs. Maurice Moore), 89
Alumnae Association, organization of, 54; projects of, 232–233
Alumnae Secretary, 204, 233
Alumnae, gifts of, 195
Ambler, Dorothy, Alumnae Sec., 176
Amyette, Maude (Mrs. Stephen Bragaw), 86
Anderson, Lucy London, 177
Andrews, Mrs. Julia Johnson, gift of, 195
Andrews, Mary H. (Mrs. William Person), 98
Andrus, Helen, 201
Anniversary, Centennial of birth of Dr. Albert Smedes, 132–133; fiftieth of class of 1879, 55; seventy-fifth of school, 128
"Anniversary Year," 159–160
Areson, Helen, 133
Armistice. *See* War
Armstrong, Beulah, 107
Armstrong, Olive (Mrs. G. D. Crow), 95
Arthur, Bessie, 129
Ashe, Elizabeth (Mrs. George Flint), 92
Ashworth, Julia Winston, 188

Athletic Association, 98
Atkinson, Rt. Rev. Thomas, D.D., report on new Chapel by, 28; mentioned, 50

Badger, Kate, 5
Badger, Sallie, 5
Badham, Elizabeth, 75, 87
Badham, Emily, 160, 204
Bailey, Serena Cobia, 122
Bailey, Virginia, 120
Ballard, Elise, 191
Ballou, Betsey, 191
Ballou, Miss Natalie, on faculty, 181
Barbee, Adelyn, 140
Barnwell, Emily Hazzard (Mrs. Ravenel), 88
Barton, Agnes Hyde, 140; on faculty, 164
Bascom, Rev. C. H., 180
Battle, Elizabeth Dancy, as student, 52; as teacher, 65; Lady Principal, 78; memorial to, 83, 117, 219; mentioned, 85, 91
Battle, Helen, 173
Battle, Josephine, 201
Battle, Lucy P., 55
Battle, Madelon, 83
Battle, Hon. Richard H., addresses of, quoted, 7, 8–9, 93–94
Battle, Sallie Haywood, 125, 132
Batts, Katherine (Mrs. W. C. Salley), 177, 178
Beckwith, Evelina, 188
Bell, Rev. Thomas, 96
Belvin, Nannie, 98; memorial to, 117
Benedict, Anna Coates, 126
Best, Martha, 191, 192
Bierce, Miss Amaie, on faculty, 168
Bingham, Jane W. (Mrs. Walter D. Toy), student and teacher, 86, 195
Bishop, Mary Frances (Mrs. John C. Jacobs), reminiscences, 39–40
Blackmer, Annie Luke, 86
Blake, Blanch (Mrs. Manor), 89

INDEX

Blanchard, Virginia A., on faculty, 104
Blanton, Millicent, 177
Blessner, Mr. and Mrs. Gustave, music teachers, 29
Blume, Fraulein (Mrs. W. H. Sanborn), voice teacher, 55, 61, 62
Blykin, Meta C., 125
Bohannon, Mary Wilson, on faculty, 200
Bonner, Virginia Lucille, 139
Borden, Harriet, 5
Borden, Mildred, 132
Borden girls, 129
Bottum, Frances, on faculty, 173, 197
Bottum, Margaret Huntington, 139, 140
Bourne, Catherine, 139, 140, 149
Bowen, Ellen, student, 98; teacher, 106, 107
Boxley, Nancy, 206
Boylan, Florence, 80, 92
Boylan, Josephine, 120
Boylan, Margaret, 92
Boylan, Mrs. William, 54
Brandt, Mr. and Mrs., mentioned, 5
Bratton, Rt. Rev. Theodore DuBose, brief biography of, 97; some material improvements under, 103; consecrated bishop, 111; mentioned, 104
Bratton, Mrs. T. D., school mother, 104
Bridgers, Elizabeth H., 82, 88
Bridgers, Rebeccah Routhe, 97
Briggs, Loula H. (Mrs. John Brewer), 92
Brodie, Estelle, 89
Brown, Dorothy Valentine, dedication to, 167
Brown, Mrs. Harlan C., librarian, 218
Brown, Marjory, 126, 132
Browne, Elizabeth, 173
Brownlow, Ellen, quoted, 10, 22, 28; description of school by, 20–21
Brumley, Isabel Ashby, 113
Brune, Mr. and Mrs., teachers, 30
Brunson, Marie Bacot, 108

Bryan, Fannie (Mrs. Isaac M. Aiken), quoted in Muse, 10–11
Buildings, of the forties, described, 4, 21; minor changes in, 60; dormitories, 70, 119; enlargement of, 102; additions to, 130; repairs, 146, 155; remodelled 1919, 174–176; expansion of, 213–217; Art, 59, 80; Auditorium, 122; Chapel, 27–28; *see also* Chapel; Clement Hall, 102, 131; East Rock, 6, 77–78, 147, 148; East Wing, 102, 131; Holt Hall, 201; Infirmary, 38, 59, 75, 113; Library, 200, 218; Main Building, building of, 6–7; description, 68, 80, 146; remodelled, 174–175; Rectory, 103; Science, 67; Smedes Hall (Main Building), 174–175, 131; Swimming pool, 196; Senior Hall (North Dormitory), 103, 176, 214; West Rock, 76, 147; West Wing, 102, 131, 169
Bullitt, Margaret, 196
Busbee, Christiana, student, 96; teacher, 110
Busbee, Isabel B., 94
Busbee, Miss Louise T., on faculty, 95, 104
Bush, Charlotte Franklin, 88
Business School, started, 94
Burke, Nina, 173
Butler, Mary Brown, 135, 136, 137, 138
Buxton, Anna, on faculty, 106, 134
Bynum, Minna Curtis (Mrs. Archibald Henderson), 96, 116

Caldwell, Fanny, 79
Cameron, Annie Sutton, "To Saint Mary's Chapel," 153; quoted, 183–184; mentioned, 139, 140, 149
Cameron, Hon. Duncan, purchases school property, 7; and chapel, 28
Cameron, Frances (Mrs. Charles Burnett), 95
Cameron, Margaret, 204
Cameron, Pauline, 80
Cannady, Lucy Kate (Mrs. Harry Williams), 96
Carnegie Corporation, grant of, 219

INDEX 277

Carrison, Elizabeth, 140
Carson, Jean, 117
Carter, Laura, 82
Carter, Robena, 140
Carter, Sallie, 60
Carwile, Elise, 89
Cawthorn, Sue and Annie, students, 35
Chapel, first place of, 27; beginning of a building for, 27–28; described, 83; daily services in, 52, 99; and Commencement, 1884, 67; Easter Service in, 1880's, 63; Easter Service in, 1930, 211; choir of, 125; veils in choir, 194; chapel caps introduced for, 172; rebuilt and enlarged, 117; new organ for, and transept, 59, 197; marriages in, 84, 136–137; memorials in, 66, 83, 90, 117
Cheatham, Frances, 160
Checkley, Elleneen E., teacher, 104, 105, 106
Cheshire, Annie Webb (Mrs. Augustine S. Tucker), wedding of, 137; mentioned, 80
Cheshire, Rev. Joseph Blunt, at 86th opening service of St. Mary's, 200; celebrates 80th birthday, 209; death of, 211; mentioned, 95, 137, 199
Cheshire, Kate, 55
Cheshire, Sarah, 80
Class Day, first, 96
Clark, Anna Barrow, 112, 117
Clark, Annie Grist, 94
Clark, Olsie, 109
Clark, Rena Hoyt, 117
Cleaton, Carrie, 138
Clement, Madame, faculty, 5, 25, 28–29
Clement, Eleanor, life of, 28, 130; legacy of, 102, 130
Clement Hall. *See* Buildings.
Clements, Katharine Russell (Mrs. A. J. Ellis), recollections of, 40–42
Clench, Miss, music teacher, 73, 78, 92
Clifton, Lucy B., 96
Clubs, literary, 156, 157; College, 181, 194, 198; Letter, 198–199; departmental, 218. *See also* Societies.
Cobb, Lucy, 93
Coffin, Miss Jennie, nurse, 59
Cohen, Beatrice Hollman, 122
Cole, Nellie, 53
Coleman, Cornelia, 112, 113
Collier, Susan, 184
Colonial Dames of North Carolina, 59
Cone, Miss, on faculty, 181
Cooke, Miss, art teacher, 81
Cooke, Susan Reavis, 205
Cooper, Daisy, 191
Cooper, Julia Horner, 137, 139
Cooper, Nina, 177
Copeland, Hattie, 151
Cowper, Mamie Pulaski, 82
Cox, Mrs. W. R., 54
Craige, Nannie Branch, 80
Crawford, Sarah, 22, 23
Cribbs, Yanita (Mrs. Carol Lamb), on faculty, 106, 119, 131; marriage of, 132
Critz, Ruth, 134
Critz, Senah, 117
Crofut, Georgia, on faculty, 181
Crowder, Courtney, 139, 140
Crowder, Nannie, 204
Cruikshank, Ernest, biography of, 259; his coming to St. Mary's and influence, 111–112; advisor, 122, 178; marriage of, 135; resignation of, 182; tributes to, 182–184; death of, 191; mentioned, 128, 130, 131, 144, 145, 161, 173, 179
Cruikshank, Mrs. Ernest, life of, 252–257; made President, 210; work as President, 212–214; dances introduced by, 107; mentioned, 157. *See also* Jones, Margaret.
Cruikshank family, mentioned, 179, 187
Cummings, Margaret, on faculty, 181
Cunningham, Celeste Talley, 80
Cunningham, Maud, 60
Cunningham, Mildred L., 98
Cunningham, Sue (Mrs. Lewis Walker), 52
Curriculum, early days of, 13, 14, 51, 84, 85; Business School added, 94; Kindergarten added, 95; re-

278   INDEX

organized as college, 103; in the 1920's, 146; High School Department accredited, 191; consideration of four year college, 199–200; accredited as Junior College, 200; changes in, 210, 217–219

Czarnomska, Marie E. Josephine, life of, 44; as Lady Principal, 62; mentioned, 55, 59, 61, 64, 70, 75, 116

Dabney, Susan (Mrs. Lyell Smedes), author, 32
Daggett, Julia, 90
Daily schedule, in 1840's, 25–26; in 1863, 33; in 1880's, 71–72; in 1930's, 250
Dances, during thirties and forties, 241–243
Dancy, Charlotte, 81, 88
Dando, Genevieve, 199
Daniel, Mary Long, 5
Daniel, Olivia, mentioned, 5
Daniels, Nettie, 158
Davies, Helen, 110
Davis, Cathaline, on faculty, 135
Davis, Eliza Dickenson, 139, 140, 141
Davis, Florence, work in Dramatics, 225–227; mentioned, 144, 173, 191, 194, 239
Davis, Mrs. Jefferson, 40
Davis, Lizzie, 5
Davis, Mary Hill (Mrs. J. V. Higham), 89
Degan, Jessie, letter quoted, 85, 90–92
Dennis, Leah A., on faculty, 168
Denson, Kate (Mrs. Beverly Raney), 82
deRosset, Annie, 52, 79
deRosset, Catherine. See Meares, Catherine deRosset.
deRosset, Gabrielle de Gondin, on faculty, 50, 58, 61
Devereux, Nannie Lane, quoted in *Muse*, 11
Dickerson, Mary, 198
Diocesan ownership of St. Mary's, 93
Disosway, Fanny, student, 41
Dodd, Lily E., 97

Dormitories. See Buildings.
Dortch, Helen, 199
Dougherty, Dorothy, 196
Dowd, Martha Austin (Mittie), student, 61, 65; on faculty, 66; retirement of, 179; memorial to, 117; mentioned, 74, 76–77, 96, 104, 106, 129, 130, 143, 173
Drane, Eliza Harwood, 107
Drane, Jacqueline, 204
Drane, Katharine (Mrs. Bennett Perry), mentioned, 141, 158, 160, 167
Drane, Maria (Mrs. Gray Temple), 234
Drane, Marion, 173
DuBose, Janie, 131, 133
DuBose, Rev. McNeely, sketch of, 103; brief biography of, 111; resignation of, 123; death of, 135
DuBose, Margaret Rosalie, 117; teacher, 122
Dudley, Margaret, 5
Duff, Mary Katherine, 201
Dugger, Alice (Mrs. Walter H. Grimes), student, 84, 88; wedding of, 84
Dugger, Janet Wilson, 89
Dugghi, Annie (Mrs. J. D. Maag), 97
Duke, B. N., gift of, 195
Duncan, Clyde, 204
Dunlop, Anna, 82
Duvall, Ellen K., 126

East Rock. See Buildings.
East Wing. See Buildings.
Eaton, Roxanna, 205
Eggleston, Louise, poem of, quoted, 188–190
Eggleston, Sophie, quoted, 191–192
Eicholtz, Jacob, artist, 24
Eldredge, Margaret, 120
Ellis, Mittie (Mrs. Henley), 82
Endowment, campaign for, 155, 180; climax of campaign for, 191
Eppes, Alfreda, 71
Erwin, Bessie (Mrs. Hamilton Jones), 41
Erwin, Josephine, 173

INDEX

Erwin, Margaret (Mrs. Jack Glenn), 41
Erwin, Sarah (Mrs. Hargrove Bellamy), 41
Erwin, William A., mentioned, 41; wedding of, 84; gift of, 174; legacy of, 210
Everett, Lena Payne, 133
Everett, Mary Louise, 186, 188, 192
Evertson, Eliza, on faculty, 29, 41

Fairley, Jeanet, 160
Falkener, Sara, 201
Fallon, Margaret, 173
Farmer, Lillian Hauser, 120, 122
Fell, Betty, 194
Fenner, Clara, art teacher, 81, 108, 128, 143, 157, 173, 191; death of, 197
Fenner, Lillian, faculty, 138, 157, 164
Finley, Louise, 87
Fisher, Katherine, 194
Floyd, Mary, 139, 149
Fletcher, Rev. Joseph, chaplain, 251–252
Folk, Bessie, 167
Force, Miss M. D., on faculty, 181
Foster, Cecilia Dabney, "Sister Cecilia," 53
Foster, Ruth, 120
Foster, Georgia, 160
Fowle, Mary, 82
Freas, Mrs. Esther, 49
French, Miss, on faculty, 21
Frost, Mary Pringle, 88
Frost, Susan Pringle, 89

Galbraith, Selena, 149
Garrett, Ree, 201
Geitner, Frances, 149
George, Elmer, 112, 117
Genners, Miss, on faculty, 30
Gerber, Marie M., on faculty, 110
Gibson, Ellen, 117
Gibson, Jennie Marshall, 109
Giddens, Miss Kate, on faculty, 168
Gifford, Ann Kimberly, 109, 110, 113
Gifts, 180, 195
Gilkey, Jeannette, 204
Glass, Rainsford, 177

Glover, Sarah, 201
Goodyear, Evelyn, 75
Gordon, Rosa May, 107
Graves, Belle, 64, 65
Graves, Malvina, 87
Green, Miss, on faculty, 30
Green, Em, 205
Green, Jane Iredell, 120
Green, Mabel, 76, 90, 91
Green, Mary Owen, 133
Green, Nina Watson (Mrs. LeRoy Theim), 97
Gregg, Annie, 80, 89, 90
Gregg, Eleanor, 39
Gregg, Julia, 53
Gregg, Nellie, 80
Gregory, Betty Clarke (Mrs. E. O. Smith), 88
Gregory, Jessie, 87
Gregory, Kate Irene (Mrs. Roberts), 87
Griffin, Blanche (Mrs. Oscar Temple), 51
Grimsley, Lyman, 126
Guess, William C., on faculty, 205, 209
Guie, Madame, on faculty, 41
Guion, Mary, 5

Hagedorn, Mr., on faculty, 155
Hagood, Alice, 64, 65
Hale, Mabel, 87
Hales, Georgia Stanton, 125, 132
Hales, Lanie Stanton, 137, 139
Hall, Carrie Gilliam, 88
Hamilton, Lily, 79
Hancock, Matilda, 139, 140
Hanff, Blanche, 205
Hanff, Mary Merrill (Mrs. John Paylor), 94
Hanna, Isabel Atwell, 125
Hanrahan, Kate, 5
Hanson, Professor, music teacher, 36
Hardin, Fannie, 61
Harding, Phoebe, 201
Harding, Rena, 140, 149, 151
Harris, Carolina Estelle, on faculty, 219
Harris, Julia, 107
Harrison, Agnes Tinsley, 133, 134
Hart, William, painter, 22, 23

280 INDEX

Harvey, Annie, 69, 74
Harvey, Henrietta Rhea (Mrs. Bennett Smedes), 45
Havernick, Herr, music director, 77
Hawley, Kate McKimmon (Mrs. M. R. Bacon), 95
Haywood, Annie (Mrs. Samuel Ruffin), quoted, 23; mentioned, 5
Haywood, Dr. Edmund Burke, 41
Haywood, Eleanor, memorial to, 83; mentioned, 47
Haywood, Elizabeth G., 5
Haywood, Jane F., 5
Haywood, Martha Helen, 88
Hazard, Minnie Tamplet, 126
Hazard, Paula Elizabeth, 122
Heath, Rosa, 122
Henderson, Alice, 88
Henderson, Lucy, 36
Henderson, Mary, 109, 110
Hesse, Miss Marion, on faculty, 181
Hester, Lucy Gertrude, student, 88; Lady Principal, 165
Hicks, Lily Strong (Mrs. Bancker Smedes), 88
Hicks, Mary Lyde (Mrs. Marshall Williams), 60
Hicks, Pattie (Mrs. Buford), 53
Hickerson, Elizabeth, 191
Higgs, Jessamine May (Mrs. Henry C. Walter), 95
Hill, Louise, 122, 134
Hill, Margaret V. (Mrs. W. E. Schroeder), 92
Hines, Dr. Peter, school physician, 75
Hinton, Eugenia, 22, 23
Hinton, Jane, 94
Hinton, Martha, 5
Hodgson, Frances, 115
Hodgson, Herbert E., influence of, 115; mentioned, 131
Hohn, Miss Edith, on faculty, 200
Hoke, Mary, 177
Holden, Lula (Mrs. Frank Ward), 80
Holmes, Beatrice (Mrs. Robert Allston), 87
Holmes, Evelyn (Mrs. J. R. Brumley), 92
Holt, Claude (Mrs. Oates), 77

Holt, Erwin A., gift from, 180
Holt Hall. *See* Buildings.
Holt, Lawrence S., donor of Holt Hall, 203
Holt, Margaret Locke Erwin, memorial to, 201
Holt, Virginia Henry, Academic Head, 200; resignation of, 212
Holt, Whitney, 194
Homesley, Lillian (Mrs. Bott), 74, 79
Hood, Kalista, 194
Hoppe, Laura Margaret, 139
Horner, Daisy Louise (Mrs. Robert Strong), 88
Horner, Julia (Mrs. Henry Cooper), 86
Horsley, Mabel A., on faculty, 125
Houchen, Grace, on faculty, 181, 197
Houghson, Marjorie, 112
Huff, Susan Graham, 139
Huger, Fanny, 51
Hughes, Aline, quoted on Miss Thomas, 161–163; mentioned, 160, 167
Hughes, Elizabeth, 155
Hughes, Jennie and Nannie, 58
Hughes, Octavia Winder, 110
Hull, Charlotte Kendall, teacher, 106, 110
Huske, Addie Burr, 78, 191
Huske, May Katherine, 78
Hyde, Dora, art teacher, 59, 61, 62

Ihrie, Carrie, 51
Infirmary. *See* Buildings.
Ingle, Rev. Julian E., 95
Iredell, Mrs. Mary Johnson, on faculty, 45, 61, 69, 70, 77; memorial to, 117; death of, 173
Ives, Rt. Rev. Levi Silliman, in conversation with Dr. Smedes, 3; portrait of, 22, 23, 24, 69; mentioned, 5, 8

Jackson, Freida, 82
Jenkins, Elmyra, 160
Jenkins, Sadie, 117
Jeudwine, Mr. and Mrs. John Wynn, on faculty, 104–105, 106

INDEX   281

Johns, Laura (Mrs. Abbott), 79, 87
Johnson, Annie, 81
Johnson, Katherine, 194
Johnson, Mary, 76
Jones, Anna, on faculty, 95
Jones, Alice E., on faculty, 104; Lady Principal, 168, 170
Jones, Augusta Porcher, 110
Jones, Caroline, 138
Jones, Dora D., 80
Jones, Grace McHardy, 88
Jones, Hortense, 133
Jones, Lucy Alice (Mrs. Hancock), student, 80; on faculty, 104
Jones, Maggie, 57, 61
Jones, Margaret M. (Mrs. Ernest Cruikshank), student, 82; on faculty, 115, 130, 131; marriage of, 135
Jones, Martha Dabney, 196
Jones, Mary Pride (Mrs. Castleman), 92
Jones, Nannie Branch (Mrs. Thomas Ashe), 89
Jones, Sarah, 113
Jones, William H., Director of Music, 176; life of, 220–223; mentioned, 80, 206
Judd, Golda, 160
Jutkins, Velma, 151

Katzenstein, Selma, 80, 88
Kellogg, Georgina, on faculty, 130
Kerr, William C., State Geologist, 63
King, W. H., 80
Kinsey, Mary Anne, 5
Kirkland, Dorothy, 184
Kirtland, Mildred, 173
Kitchen, Elizabeth, 173
Kitchen, Kate, 204
Kloman, Rev. H. Felix, chaplain, 248
Kloman, Mrs. H. Felix, 248
Knox, Dr., physician, 170
Koonce, Lily Elizabeth, 94
Kursteiner, August, Head of Music Department, 62, 72, 77, 79
Kyle, Rebecca, 138

La Loge, Mlle. E. de Joubert, on faculty, 125
Lalor, Marjorie J., on faculty, 249
Lamb, Susan, 149
Lanier, Miriam, 92
Lassiter, Lettie (Mrs. Wilder), on History of May Day, 228–229
Lassiter, Mary T., 120
Latham, Alice, letter to Mrs. McAdoo, 158; mentioned, 140, 157, 160
Laughinghouse, Helen, 167
Lawrence, Ann, 196
Lawrence, Mrs. E. B., 196
Lawrence, Elizabeth, 188
Lawrence, Mary Theresa, *In Memory of William Enos Stone*, 201
Lay, Ellen, 173
Lay family, 124
Lay, Rev. George William, brief biography of, 123–125; sketch of, 102–103; Welcome to new students, quoted, 144–145; quoted, 158; tributes to, 128–129, 167–168; leaving of, 167; death of, 211; mentioned, 106, 138, 149, 158, 161, 191
Lay, Lucy, 191
Lay, Nancy, 177, 179
Lay, Virginia, 194
Leak, Shepherd, 134
Leary, Elizabeth Wood, 134, 135
Leary, Minnie, 132
Le Cron, Marguerite, 122
Lee, Lizzie, student, 47; sketch of, 141–142, 233; on faculty, 94, 104, 106, 128, 143, 173, 179
Lee, Marie D. (Mrs. H. H. Covington), 90
Lee, Marion, 196
Lee, Mildred, daughter of General Lee, 36
LeGal, Mlle., on faculty, 45, 61
Leggett, Genevieve, on faculty, 176
Lewis, Anna Hartwell, 86
Lewis, Nell Battle, 129, 132, 133, 134
Lewis, Pattie, 82
Library. *See* Buildings.

INDEX

Lineberry, Annie Ruth, on faculty, 200
Loaring-Clark, Ruth, 196
Lockhart, Caroline Ashe, 136
London, Camelia, 139
Long, Miss, on faculty, 5
Lord, Kate, 58
Love, Alice Leonora (Mrs. H. P. S. Keller), 98
Love, Annie S., 98
Luney, Bertha May, on faculty, 130
Lyell, Sarah Pearce (Mrs. Aldert Smedes), 8
Lyman, Rt. Rev. Theodore Benedict, 46, 50

Mack, Mr. Albert A., music director, 77
Mackay, Margaret, 120
MacRae, Frances (Mrs. John Lamb), 82
Main Building. *See* Buildings.
Mallett, Charles P., and painting of Bishop Ravenscroft, 25
Mallett, Marion A., 89
Manly, Cora, 5
Manning, Sally (Mrs. F. P. Venable), 51
Manuel of St. Mary's School, quoted, 14–20
Marriner, Frances, 199
Marriott, Mrs. Nannie H., housekeeper, 164
Marsden, Edith D., on faculty, 104
Marshall, Rev. Matthis M., 46, 52, 95
Marshall, Susan, 82, 92, 95, 219
Marshall, Theodora (Mrs. Duncan Cameron), 94
Martin, Sue, student, 35
Mason, Dr., on faculty, 25, 28
Mason, Helen, 167
Masonic Body of North Carolina, gift of, 195
Masten, Lillie (Mrs. DeBrutz Cutler), 89
Matheson, Carrie Lee, 86
Mathewson, Carrie, 64
Maxwell, Evelyn, 136, 138
May Day, history of, 186, 228–229

Mayhew, Frederica P. (Mrs. Troy Beatty), 87
McArthur, Helen, 133, 134
MacDonald, Laura, 199
McDowell, Katherine, housekeeper, 177
McIntyre, Julia Louise, 126, 131
McIver, Susie, 139
McKee, Eliza, 47
McKimmon, Miss Katie, sketch of, 47–48, 141; death of, 203; tributes to, 203–204; mentioned, 45, 54, 71, 77, 80, 83, 104, 106, 119, 143, 173
McLean, Elizabeth Wilson, 87
McNeil, Rosalie, 247
McVea, Emilie Watts, student, 57, 64; on faculty, 65–66; Lady Principal, 96; "To Miss Katie," quoted, 204; memorial to, 66, 219; death of, 204; mentioned, 85, 89, 116, 160, 195
McVea, Henrietta Smedes, 89
Means, Carolina, 98
Means, Esther Barnwell, student, 129; dedication to, 166
Meares, Mrs. Catherine deRosset, Lady Principal, 44; mentioned, 50, 53, 54, 61, 116
Meares, Kate deRosset, student, 109, 110, 129; on faculty, 168
Melick, Ellen, 194
Menzies, Catherine, 194
Merrill, Ardella, 94
Metcalf, Miss, on faculty, 155
Miller, Maude, 167
Mills, Eliza, 48
Moffatt, Mattie, 109, 181
Montgomery, Betsy, 219
Moore, Annie, on faculty, 85; student, 88
Moore, Carrie Helen, 113
Mordecai, Pattie, 35
Morgan, Bertha A., Lady Principal, 187, 192–193
Morgan, Henrietta, 167
Morgan, Mildred, on faculty, 181
Morgan, Rev. Rufus, 49
Morrell, Ellen, 82
Morris, Katherine, poem by, quoted, 193

INDEX 283

Moses, Susan W. (Mrs. Edward Kidder Graham), on faculty, 108
Moye, Novella, 167
Murchison, Jennie Atkinson, 117
Murray, Dixie Cooke (Mrs. Weldon Smith), 88
Muse, Mary Margaret, 199
Muse, Saint Mary's, started, 53; history of (annual and monthly), 116; monthly, 177; annual, 166–167; became *Stagecoach*, 194
Muse Club, first year of, 122; mentioned, 156; discontninued, 184
Myers, Josie, 55

Nash, Arabell, 107
Nash, Mrs. Frank, librarian, 200
Naylor, Mrs. Lola B., nurse, 247
Neale, Tempe, 245
Neave, Anne, office secretary, 176
Negro servants, Aunt Ellen, 73; Aunt Liza Cook, 46; Aunt Matilda, 37; Ellen, 62; Carrie, 74; Ducky, 123, 136, 190; Uncle Mose, 22, 37; Uncle Pim, 49; Uncle Shep, 37; Uriah, 124, 125; Uncle Wash, 22
Neville, Mary, 204
News and Observer, Raleigh, mentioned, 33, 89, 133; quoted on death of Dr. A. Smedes, 43
Newsom, Laura B. (Mrs. Maurice O'Neill), 90
Niles, Rev. Charles M., medal instituted by, 120
Niles Medal, instituted, 120
Nixon, Dorothy, 186
Noe, Rev. A. C. D., 180
Norris, Ethel, 80
North Carolina Churchman, quoted, 223–225
Norwood, Miss, art teacher, 62

Oertel, Rev. Johannes A., transept designed by, 59
Orchestra, organized, 110
Order of the Circle, founded, 231
Osborne, Rev. Francis, 155, 180
Osborne, Josephine, on faculty, 130
Osborne, Josephine Ashe, 97

Osborne, Mary, 60
Owen, Mary Hancock, 136
Owen, R. Blinn, on faculty, 132, 157, 160, 173, 176

Page, Mary, 90
Park, Hallie, 107
Park, Marion Edwards, address at St. Catherine's, quoted, 257
Payne, Farinda W. (Mrs. Cam MacRae), 92
Pearson, Alice, on faculty, 76, 81
Pearson, Laura, daughter of Chief Justice Pearson, 36
Pearson, Mary (Mrs. Davis), quoted in *Muse*, 27
Peele, Eva, 160
Pendleton, Sylbert, 196
Penick, Rt. Rev. Edwin A., chairman of board of trustees, 200; at Commencement, 1930, 208; mentioned, 251
Peoples, Helen, 140
Perkins, Mrs. Carolina V., Lady Principal, 176, 181
Perkins, Florence Eugenia (Mrs. R. S. Tucker), 54
Perry, Isabel H., 134
Pescud, Isabella Willis (Mrs. Walker Williams), 80, 94
Pescud, Jane Hinton (Mrs. W. A. Withers), 89, 95
Pettigrew, Alice, 51
Philips, Mary, 107
Phillips Annie, 64, 65
Phillips, Mary (Mrs. Hal Wood), 88
Phinizy, Marie, 108
Pickel, Virginia Randolph Bolling, 133
Pipes, David, 49
Pippen, Sallie, mentioned, 50
Pittinger, Anna Louise (Mrs. Leigh Skinner), 98
Pittinger, Rev. I. McK., 95
Pittinger, Louise, on faculty, 110
Pittman, Eliza Battle, memorial to, 122
Pittman, Mrs. Mary Eliza, gift of, 122
Pixley, Chelian, on faculty, 110

INDEX

Platt, Alicia, 196
Platt, Elizabeth, 201
Pleasants, Gertrude, 167
Polk, Lucia, daughter of General Leonidas Polk, 36
Pool, Eliza A., teacher, 122
Pool, Colonel S. D., 13
Pope, Colonel William, 5
Portraits, of Bishop Ives and confirmation, discussed, 22–24; of Bishop Ravenscroft, 24–25; mentioned, 68–69, 192; of Dr. and Mrs. Aldert Smedes, 69
Potwin, Gertrude M., on faculty, 104
Powell, Lenore, 188
Powell, Margaret, 205
Powell, Mary, 194
Pratt, Agnes, 167
Pratt, Annie Pearl (Mrs. J. J. Van Noppen), 98
Prettyman, Virginia, 133
Prince, Sue Brent, 122
Publications, first, 53; *Bulletin*, 218; *Grapevine*, 218; *Belles of Saint Mary's*, 218. See also *Muse*.
Purrington, Sara, 197

Quinby, Mrs. M. N., housekeeper, 104

Raegon, Lucy, 22
Ragland, Betty, 194
Raoul, Rosine, 206
Ravenel, Alice and Jennie, 56
Ravenel, Estelle, 158, 167
Ravenscroft, Rt. Rev. John Stark, portrait of, 23, 24–25, 68
Redwood, Lucy Taylor, 109, 113, 114
Reigart, Catherine, on faculty, 131
Relyea, Eleanor, 140, 160
Rembert, Esther, 126, 129, 132
Remenji, violinist, visit to St. Mary's, 64
Renn, Mary MacAlister (Mrs. Paul Taylor), 98
Reynolds, Miriam, 139
Riddick, Addie (Mrs. J. Alves Huske), student and chaperon, 78
Robards, Eliza and Sue, 36

Roberts, Chip, 52
Roberts, Lillian, 58
Robinson, Annie, 160
Robinson, Mary, 117
Rogerson, Ida Jean, 131
Rogerson girls, 129
Roosevelt, Theodore, President of U. S., visit in Raleigh, 119
Root, Dr. Aldert Smedes, 42
Root, Annie Gales (Mrs. William W. Vass), 42, 80, 92, 137
Root, Sadie Smedes (Mrs. W. W. Robards), 33, 42, 46, 82, 95
Rose, Nellie, 160
Rossell, Jean Graham Ellis, memorial to, 117
Rossell, Mary Ellis, 117
Roundtree, Isabel Davis, 107
Roux, Adele E., on faculty, 104
Royall, Mela, student, 199; Alumnae Sec., 204
Royster, Kate, 36
Rudnicka, Mlle., on faculty, 143
Ruef, Miss, teacher, 196
Ruffin, Annie (Mrs. Cameron), memorial given by, 117
Ruffin, Jane, 177
Ruffin, Mary, 236
Rules, 1857, 15, 16; "Dates," 243–245
Russell, Rosalie, on faculty, 106
Russell, Scharlie E., on faculty, 125

Saint Augustine's School for Colored People, 45, 62
Sanborn, Will H., music teacher, 44, 53, 55, 61–62, 110, 116
Sanders, Christine (Mrs. Edward Rembert), student, 76; wedding of, 84
Sargeant, Mollie, 72
Satterthwaite, Sallie, 199
Saunders, Anne, nurse, 75, 104, 108; memorial to, 117; death of, 119–120
Saunders, Madeline, 5
Saunders, Mittie (Mrs. M. M. L'Engle), quoted in *Muse*, 11, 22, 23, 26
Saunders, Sarah, 5
Schutt, Genevieve, A., on faculty, 104

INDEX 285

Seay, Leonore, 120
Settle, Mamie, 61
Shakespeare Tercentenary, celebration of, 128, 149, 151, 152
Shapcott, Mabel, on faculty, 197, 204
Sharp, Fanny (Mrs. Thomas Roberts Jernigan), voice student, 56, 61
Shaw, Esdale, student, 60; President Alumnae Association, 233
Shaw, Stella Virginia, story of, 12; memorial to, 117
Shearer, Elizabeth, on faculty, 176
Sheppard, Katherine, on faculty, 168
Shieb, Mrs. Leonora W., Lady Principal, 125
Shields, Rebe, 14
Shields, Rebecca Hill, 133
Shine, Mrs. Lee, 33
Shipp, Kate C., on faculty, 114
Shober, Mary Wheat, quoted in *Muse*, 12; mentioned, 21
Shore, Cleave, 196
Shuford, Mary Campbell, 126, 131, 132, 133
Shull, Zona May, on faculty, 145
Siler, Fanny, letters of, quoted, 49–50
Simbolotti, Madame Lora E., 197
Sister Eliza, deaconess, 59
Skinner, Lillie Piemont, on faculty, 135
Skinner, Nannie, 92
Slater, Florence, student, 57, 63; on faculty, 77, 81, 84, 219; death of, 66–67; legacy of, 67
Slaught, Helen Ann, on faculty, 197
Smallbones, Alice (Mrs. G. M. Brunson), 97
Smedes, Rev. Dr. Aldert, on founding of St. Mary's, 3–4; biographical sketch of, 7–9; tributes to, 8–12; account of St. Mary's written by, 13–14; exhortation by, 16–20; paintings bought by, 22; report on Chapel by, 28; reports on progress of school for 1856, '57, and '59 by, 30; and struggle at close of Confederate War, 40; death of, 43; scholarship as tribute to, 54; memorial to, 83; portrait of, 69; mentioned, 31, 35, 48
Smedes, Mrs. Aldert (Sarah Lyell), portrait of, 69; memorial to, 117
Smedes, Annie (Mrs. Charles Root), marriage and family of, 42; memorial scholarship to, 195; mentioned, 33
Smedes, Bancker, 45, 56
Smedes, Rev. Bennett, on succeeding his father, 43–44; at age of twenty-three, 32; marriage of, 45–46; glimpse of, 74; as teacher, 45, 81; and switchback accident, 90; death of, 95–96; memorial to, 197; mentioned, 22, 43, 48, 50, 52, 63, 71, 73, 78
Smedes, Mrs. Bennett (Henrietta Rhea Harvey), feasts given by, 73; marriage of, 45–46; mentioned, 75, 96
Smedes, Bessie, 46, 47
Smedes, Bessie (Mrs. Moreau Leak), 42; establishment of a scholarship, 195
Smedes, Charlie, 45
Smedes, Eliza (Mrs. Augustus Washington Knox), student, 55; on faculty, 58, 61, 62; wedding of, 84; mentioned, 45
Smedes, Emilie (Mrs. J. S. Holmes), student, 45, 57, 61, 65; mentioned, 219
Smedes, George, incident concerning, 37–38; mentioned, 42
Smedes, Helen, 46, 74, 80, 84, 96
Smedes, Henrietta Rhea, 45, 47, 86–87
Smedes, John E. C., sketch of, 45
Smedes, Margaret Harvey (Mrs. John I. Rose), 46, 64, 74, 95
Smedes, Mary, 46, 74, 80, 84, 92, 96
Smedes, Sarah Lyell (Mrs. William A. Erwin), 32, 41; wedding of, 84
Smedes family, Aldert, 22, 32, 41–42; gifts to school from, 25; Bennett, 46–47, 69, 74; John, 45
Smedes Hall. *See* Buildings.
Smith, Ada B., teacher, 122
Smith, Adelaide E., article by, 27, 28
Smith, Lena, student, 42

286 INDEX

Smith, Louisa Atkinson (Mrs. Warren W. Way), 168
Smith, Nannie, student, 42
Smith, Patsey Harry, 129, 134, 135, 136, 155
Smith, Pattie, 201
Smith, Rebe, 42, 50
Smith, Sally Hall (Mrs. Fab Busbee), 38
Sneed, Lucy, 36
Snow, Mrs. George, 54
Snow, Mary (Mrs. Charles Baskerville), 79
Societies, Literary, Epsilon Alpha Pi and Sigma Lambda formed, 105; third one organized, 122, 136; revision of, 165. *See also* Clubs.
Society, Philarmonic, 62
Somerville, Juliet and Johanna, 35
Sororities, history of at Saint Mary's, 105–106
Southwick, Sue Kyle, on faculty, 168, 169
Spann, Mary E., on faculty, 122
Spence, Clare, 194
Springer, Clara, 75
Spruill, Kate (Mrs. William Harrison), Alumnae Sec., 233
Spruill, Martha Byrd, 133
Sprunt, Mrs. Annie Gray Nash, gift from, 180
Spurlock, Sarah H., on faculty, 122
Stagecoach. See Muse.
Stallings, Fannie, 129, 149
Steadman, Kate, 75
Stedman, Margaret Gray, 109, 110, 113
Stein, Bertha, 92
Steinbrenner, Miss, teacher, 75
Stiles, Elise, 129
Stockard, Mary, 205
Stone, Florence, 179
Stone, Imogen, on faculty, 98, 104, 105
Stone, Nanette, voice teacher, 62, 78
Stone, Ophelia, Academic Head, 181
Stone, William Enos, on faculty, 112, 130, 143, 173, 196; poem to, 173–174; death of, 201
Strange, Helen, 122
Strange, Rt. Rev. Robert, 133

Strong, Frances, 140
Student government, beginnings of, 128; School Council established, 179; and Pan Archon Council, 188; established, 191; present organization, 229–231
Sturgeon, Amelia Pinkney, 134, 136
Sturgeon, Mary Bolling, 113
Styles in dress, 1842–1860, 16, 25, 39; 1865–1885, 41, 42, 49, 54; 1900–1915, 101, 109, 113, 118, 126, 132, 139; 1915–1930, 148, 172, 182, 195–196
Sublett, Eleanor, 177
Sullivan, Gertrude, memorial to, 117
Sullivan, Sarah Gertrude, 120
Sullivan, Lou, letters quoted, 33–36; mentioned, 39
Sutton, Juliet, life of, 223–225; on faculty, 94, 104, 119, 128, 130, 173; glimpse of, 141–142
Sutton, Kate, 61
Switchback Accident, 90–92; and thank offering, 83

albot, Florence W., housekeeper, 177
Tarry, Elizabeth, 139
Taylor, Virginia, 204
Terms, 1842, quoted, 4
Terrill, Miss Edith, on faculty, 200
Tew, Ella G. (Mrs. Lindsay), 48, 53, 55, 58
Tew, Emilie, 48
The Episcopal School (boys), established, 5, 6; break down of, 7
Thigpen, Martha, 199
Thomas, Arabelle, 129, 140
Thomas, Eleanor Walter, on faculty, 104, 106, 108; Lady Principal, 127, 143; quoted, 128–130; festival, quote, 151–152; tribute to and sketch of, 160–163; mentioned, 131, 145, 158
Thomas, Florence, 110, 129
Thomas, James, 80
Thomas, Marie, 129
Thomas, Martha, 205
Thomas, Sadie, 129
Thomas, Virginia Ellison, 88

INDEX

Thompson, Marguerite Vertner, 125
Thompson, Maria, 5
Thompson, Mary C. (Mrs. J. G. deRoulhac Hamilton), 98
Thompson, Miss, on faculty, 30
Thorn, Ruby, 140, 160
Thorne, Marcellite, 76
Thornton, Susan, on faculty, 168
Thurman, Mary, 199
Thurmond, Sophia Dabney, 86
Tilton, Mildred, 113
"To Our Living and Our Dead," pamphlet, quoted from, 13, 14
Toler, Louise, 173
Tompson, Miss, on faculty, 155
Tonnoffski, Josephine Pearl, 134
Tonnoffski, Mary, 95
Trapier, Jennie, 109
Trapier, Margaret (Mrs. Allan Rogers), 97
Trapier, Wyndham, 80
Trexler, Eugenia, 194
Trowbridge, Mildred, on faculty, 155, 176
Tucker, Adriana, 5
Tucker, Albert W., School Sec. and Business Manager, 187; office of, 240–241
Tucker, Rt. Rev. Beverley D., 137
Tucker, Carolina, 205
Tucker, Elizabeth, 186
Tucker, Lula, 60
Tucker, Mrs. R. S., 54
Tunstall, Frances (Mrs. Clem Dowd), 89
Turner, Nannie, 36
Turner, Sara, Academic Head, 181, 187, 188, 192, 200

Uniform, described, 16, 25; passing of, 39
Upchurch, Iva F., 95
Urquhart, Helen, on faculty, 134, 165

Vann, Sarah, Alumnae Sec., 233
Vass, Eleanor, 92
Vedder, Ida M., on faculty, 106
Venable, Frances, 184
Venable, Louise Manning, 108

Vincent, Almon W., on faculty, 122
Vincent, Mrs. Marie Agnes, on faculty, 122

Waddell, Elizabeth, 173
Waddell, Katherine, poem by, quoted, 184–186
Waddell, Mildred, 194
Waddell, Nellie (Mrs. Brenizer), 79
Waite, Daisy B., 89
Walker, Marie A. (Mrs. Hamilton Jones), 92
Wall, Mary Stuart, 80
Walton, Lola E., nurse, 108
War, Confederate, effect on school, 31–67
War, World, I, effect on school, 140, 155; relief work, 157; letters in support of President Wilson, 158–159; activities of girls for, 164; Armistice, 170–172
War, World, II, British War Relief, 218, 251
Ward, Miss R. V., music teacher, 80
Warren, Myrtle, 139
Warren, Pensie, 139
Washington, Laura, 5, 23
Watson, Edna, 80
Way, Rev. Dr. Warren W., sketch of life of, 168; and endowment fund, 180; changes in organization by, 181; and clearance of school debt, 191; resignation of, 211
Way family, 168
Weaver, Leize Holmes, 113
Webb, Elizabeth, 205
Weeks, Mary Spruill, 109
Wells, May, 79
Wesson, Laura Wirt, 89
West Rock. See Buildings.
West Wing. See Buildings.
Whitaker, Bessie L., 89
White, Bessie, 138
White, Bessie Hines, 95
Wickham, Louise Floyd, bequeaths library to St. Mary's, 219
Wilkes, Keevie, 172
Wilkins, Georgia, 82
Williams, Eleanor, 5
Williams, Erma, 201

Williams, Lucy, 5
Williams, Mary Webber, 139
Wilmerding, Mary A. (Mrs. F. W. Ambler), 90
Wilson, Eleanor (Nell) Randolph (Mrs. William G. McAdoo), student, 121, 126, 129; letter to, 158; letter from, 159
Wilson, Josephine, 140, 149
Wilson, Kate Connor, 97
Wilson, Lizzie (Mrs. Walter Montgomery), quoted, 12; reminiscences of, 35–38
Wilson, Loulie, on faculty, 176
Wilson, Mary C., 173
Wilson, Woodrow, President of U. S., 121, 158
Wingate, Claudia, and portrait of Bishop Ives, 23, 24
Winston, Alice (Mrs. F. S. Spruill), 57
Winston, Amabel Conyers, 136, 138
Winston, Amy, 129
Wolf, Frances E., 120
Woodell, Loula McK., 89; memorial to, 90
Woodruff, Jennie, 136, 138
Woolford, Nancy, 158
Worrell, Ethel, 95
Wright, Helen, 149

Yarborough, Eleanor, 194
Yarborough, Fannie Neal (Mrs. Thomas Walter Bickett), 86, 87; on Board of Trustees, 195
Yarborough, Mary Wiatt, 188
Yates, Ethel, 160
Yellott, Mary (Mrs. George V. Denny), poems by, quoted, 166, 173–174; mentioned, 177, 178
Young, Sally, 57, 61

www.ingramcontent.com/pod-product-compliance
Lightning Source LLC
Chambersburg PA
CBHW021118300426
44113CB00006B/204